# A SOAP OPERA
# FROM HELL

CLIVE SINCLAIR is the author of four novels and three collections of short stories, including *Hearts of Gold*, winner of the Somerset Maugham Award in 1981. In the same year he was awarded a Bicentennial Arts Fellowship, and in 1983 was chosen as one of the twenty Best of Young British Novelists. From 1983 to 1987 he was Literary Editor of the *Jewish Chronicle* and the following year he was the British Council Guest Writer in Residence at the University of Uppsala, Sweden. In 1996 he became the British Library Penguin Writer's Fellow. His most recent book, *The Lady with the Laptop*, won both the *Jewish Quarterly* Prize and the Macmillan Silver Pen Award for Fiction. He has a doctorate from the University of East Anglia, and is a fellow of the Royal Society of Literature. Clive Sinclair lives in St Albans with his son.

# CLIVE SINCLAIR

## A SOAP OPERA
## FROM HELL

ESSAYS ON THE FACTS OF LIFE AND THE FACTS OF DEATH

PICADOR

First published 1998 by Picador
an imprint of Macmillan Publishers Ltd
25 Eccleston Place, London SW1W 9NF
and Basingstoke

Associated companies throughout the world

ISBN 0 330 35523 6

1 3 5 7 9 8 6 4 2

A CIP catalogue record for this book is available from
the British Library.

Phototypeset by Intype London Ltd
Printed by Mackays of Chatham plc, Chatham, Kent

# ACKNOWLEDGEMENTS

·—·

Most of these essays first appeared in the *Independent*. They were commissioned and edited by Sarah Spankie, to whom I owe a special debt of gratitude. I should also like to acknowledge the editorial skills of the following: Isabel Fonseca, formerly of the *Times Literary Supplement*, Elena Lappin, formerly of the *Jewish Quarterly*, Karen White of *Modern Painters*, Ian Jack & Robert Winder of *Granta*, Ian Hamilton formerly of *The New Review*. Thanks are also due to Richard Price, of the British Library — say rather, Hawkeye of the stacks — for help when I was preparing 'Kidneys in the Mind'. I should also like to thank far-flung friends who have contributed to these pieces by offering shelter and more: Ivor and Evelyn Abrahams, Yosl and Audrey Bergner, Pamela and Jonathan Lubell, Roumen and Diane Mitkov. Finally I should like to thank my son, Seth, who has proved to be such an excellent travelling companion.

# CONTENTS

•––•

## Part One: Family Life

## Part Two: The Kidney Trilogy

## Part Three: Diary of a Single Father

## Part Four: Writers and Artists

## Part Five: Other Places

'Where wast thou when I laid the foundations of the earth?'
*Job 38:4*

'Why do I keep fuckin' up?'
Neil Young, from the album *Ragged Glory*

# PART ONE

—•—

# FAMILY LIFE

# 1. CABBAGE FACE

When I was a baby passers-by would peek into my pram with a 'coochie-coo' upon their lips, which was as far as it ever got. Instead, having caught sight of my prematurely prophetic little face, they said with one voice: 'Don't look so miserable, it might never happen.' In fact, as my friends will testify, I turned out to be a cheerful, happy-go-lucky sort of fellow, though you'd never know it to look at me. I am, in effect, a lousy advertisement for myself.

Needless to say, this poor presentation caused numerous problems as I progressed through the education system. Neither the teachers nor the pupils of Orange Hill Grammar School for Boys, an unwelcoming pile of red brick and prefab situated in Burnt Oak (not a meeting place for witches, but a seedy suburb of north-west London), were much concerned with the inner man. Mr Hunter, our Latin master, pained beyond endurance by my very presence, released this sibylline utterance: 'Sinclair, one day they will hang you.' This was not so far-fetched; the most famous alumnus of the secondary modern across the road was James Hanratty, who may or may not have been guilty of the A6 murder, but was strung up anyway.

Some of my peers, taking cognizance of my baggy eyes, called me Cabbage Face. This nickname was picked up by our kindly

chemistry master, Mr Harradine, whose sensitivity was equally
apparent as he chucked a lump of sodium into a glass bowl full
of water and sent three of my classmates to hospital. When he
called me Cabbage Face in front of the whole class it was the
psychological equivalent of that careless act; something fizzed
and exploded within. At that moment I separated into two
people: a caped crusader, a righter of wrongs, disguised as a
milksop who meekly swallowed his teacher's insult.

As Jules Feiffer put it in one of his cartoons: 'I know I would
be different if people only called me by my inside name "Spike".'
OK, I know I'm not really Spike, just as I'm aware that my
particular *kampf* is hardly unique; on the contrary, it's more of
an archetype.

The idea of the split personality is as old as Genesis. For a
start, Eve was manufactured from Adam's rib. Then there's Cain
and Abel, twins at war. They were followed by Esau and Jacob,
likewise divisible into hairy and smooth types. Moses and Aaron
are a more sophisticated variation. Moses the stutterer, the
wrestler with language, the disciple of an abstract and absent god,
whose clumsiness and self-doubt made him my ideal role model.
Set against this was Aaron's silver tongue. Indeed, Aaron may
well be the world's first entrepreneur.

In place of his brother's unimaginable ideal he offered a
concept, a god that could be seen and touched, a god that looked
good; the Golden Calf. What's more he sold stock in it, utilizing
an idea he'd picked up in ancient Egypt; pyramid selling. One
way or another he persuaded the sun-struck Israelites to part
with their jewellery and their precious bangles.

My natural inclination was to side with Moses but, for a few
years, I followed in Aaron's footsteps and became an advertising
man at Young & Rubicam. Of course copywriting was not my
first choice; the previous June (the year is 1973) I had published
my first novel, *Bibliosexuality*, for which I received an advance of
£150. There were hardly any reviews, and no royalties. When I
began dating the woman who was to become my wife, it quickly

became apparent that £150 was not sufficient foundation for a love life.

In order to get the job at Y & R I first had to take an aptitude test. I can recall some of the questions. How many uses can you find for a handkerchief? I wrote my answer on one. Invent an aftershave. I called it Hérotique; combining Frenchness, eroticism, and heroism, with just a dash of the heretical. I was apt.

Y & R was located on several floors of Greater London House, a nondescript shell constructed over the ruins of the Carerras cigarette factory, a neo-Egyptian temple which once dominated Mornington Crescent. I can still picture the building as it was, and can remember driving past the place with my father one Saturday while a crane smashed a ball into the bellies of the two enormous black cats that flanked the entrance. Nothing but ghosts now.

It turned out that my new colleagues were just as smart as any university faculty; they read the *TLS* and played chess during lunch breaks. Many dreamed of writing the Great English Novel. For example, one of the brightest writers there, the author of a famous campaign for Volvo, took a year off in which to fashion his masterpiece. Unfortunately he had finished it by the end of the first morning, and was back writing copy within the month.

This demonstrates the damage long-term abuse of language can inflict upon the soul. Copywriting cuts the communication cord between word and feeling. By offering instant gratification it atrophies more subtle emotions. It is all plot and no psychology. It depends for success upon buzzwords, upon fashion, upon sentimentality, upon kitsch. Try making a novel out of those ingredients.

We worked in teams – each copywriter had an art director – and we discussed our products with the same sagacity academics reserve for Shakespeare's late comedies, only we were brooding over cans of soup or bars of chocolate. Being a novice I was given small-budget accounts such as the United States Travel Service and Valderma – 'a spot's worst friend'. This was fine by me; the former allowed me to indulge my passion for America, for the arcane, for sentences without verbs, while the latter gave me scope to experiment with a series of unlikely narrators. I felt sorry for the spots, I identified with them, I wrote the commercials from their point of view.

'You've no idea how miserable it is being a spot,' said a lugubrious voice between records on Radio Luxembourg. 'I feel completely unloved, absolutely unwanted, no friends, no one to talk to, and when I do make one of my rare public appearances what happens? Is anyone pleased to see me? Oh no, not likely. I'll tell you what happens. I get hit with that awful Valderma stuff, and that's me done for. Don't people realize, I've got feelings too . . .'

Later Philip Madoc appeared as Count Spotski, driven to an early grave by garlic and Valderma, and Polly James read the tragic *Diary of a Spot*. Even sadder was the plea of the mad professor to save his beloved spots from extinction. Like all proper mad scientists he spoke with a pronounced German accent.

'I have been studying the love life of spots for thirty years now, and what I don't know about the little beggars ain't worth knowing. Now to begin with I must tell you that of course there are two kinds of spots: male spots and female spots. So when a male spot wants to attract a lady spot for a bit of canoodling, he glows a nice red colour, and the lady sidles over to him and says, "Hey, big boy, what's cooking?" And before you know it, there's a whole lot of little spots coming up. And believe me, this life cycle repeats itself again and again. But I have to tell you that there are crazy peoples around who are trying to prevent my research. They keep putting that dreadful Valderma cream onto my lovely spots, which puts them right off mating altogether, and means that there are no more little spots . . .'

Gradually I was entrusted with larger accounts and more daunting clients, such as Proctor & Gamble. I have never been to Salt Lake City, but I imagine its air is sanctified, much like the atmosphere at P & G's headquarters on the outskirts of

Newcastle. I certainly regarded it as no coincidence that the product I was working on – Crest – sounded not unlike the god of the Mormons.

We were ushered into the office of the product manager. He had close-cropped hair and wore a white short-sleeved shirt with a dark tie. He looked like Robert Duvall in mad-mode. He turned to me and said: 'Do you believe in Crest?'

I was tongue-tied. My face, as usual, registered misery. I remembered all the Jewish martyrs. I couldn't bring myself to say yes. Besides, I didn't think he would believe me. I lack credibility, even on those rare occasions when I am being sincere. I was rescued by my art director. 'I know I can speak for Clive,' he said, 'when I state that we would never work on a product we didn't believe in.' I regarded him as he spoke and observed no hint of mockery, no sign that he was pulling the guy's leg. This was the wonder of advertising; the complete absence of cynicism. It may have many mansions, but it has no room for Doubting Thomases.

My lack of faith became even more obvious when we were shown around the Hotpoint factory at Peterborough. Try as I might I couldn't counterfeit interest in the various washing machines we were shown, nor could I think of a single question to ask at the end of the tour. This failure did not go unnoticed, as I was to discover.

The summer of 1976 was so hot that bars of chocolate melted on the shelves before confectioners could sell them. Naturally this upset Cadbury's, one of Y & R's more important clients. They commissioned a commercial code named 'Ice Cold'. I was asked to write it. This is what I produced: various types are shown eating bars of Dairy Milk straight from the fridge or the ice bucket while a demented chorus chants: 'In the sweltering melting hot hot seventies isn't it nice to know there's still a dairy milk chocolate with the original Cadbury taste? In the keep it cool swimming-pool eighties ... nineties isn't it nice to know there's a great summertime treat ... ice cold Cadbury's ...' I don't think I'll include it in the *Collected Works*, nor do I imagine that the director – Tony Scott – regards it as essential to his filmography.

Unfortunately I missed the shoot, being on holiday at the time. I returned resolved to quit advertising in favour of academia. Accordingly, on 18 August I approached the hatchet man's secretary to request an appointment. 'That's a coincidence,' she said indifferently. 'He wants to see you.' Just my luck, I thought, the day I come in to resign I am offered a pay rise. I had good reason to suppose that this was why he had summoned me. On 5 July I had received a letter from the chief executive and managing director of Y & R. 'As a rather belated recognition of all the hard work and extra hours you have put in over the weekends on Heinz Soup,' he had written, 'I have arranged that you have to your credit £100 . . . Yet again, very many thanks for your very considerable contribution on this difficult project.' The letter concluded with a typical postscript. 'I am sure you will understand that this should not be discussed with any of your colleagues. A very limited number of people are entitled to this.'

My 'considerable contribution' consisted of dreaming up the idea that saved the account; an experiment in tele-telepathy. The screen is blank. A voice invites the viewers to concentrate on the thing they love the most. A can of tomato soup slowly appears . . .

So I went to see X feeling like ingratitude personified. 'There is no easy way to tell you this,' he began. That's a funny way to preface a pay rise, I thought. I attributed it to the fact that X was an acerbic Scot. I was still thinking of how to reject his offer without hurting his feelings when the sodium hit the water and I realized that I was being made redundant. I was too flabbergasted to ask why, not that I needed to.

'It's your face,' said X. 'Every morning I arrive at the office feeling chipper. Then I glimpse your gloomy mug at the end of the corridor. Bang goes my good mood. Believe me, my friend, it's a very depressing sight. It makes people feel miserable. Others have said the same. They also complain that you never show any enthusiasm.' He paused. 'I heard what happened when you went to Hotpoint,' he continued. 'You didn't say a single word, so I'm told. What impression do you think that made? No wonder we lost the account.'

I remembered when the account executive had come to my office to pass on the bad news. He looked like his mother had just died. I couldn't have cared less, but I tried to look suitably heartbroken out of politeness, an expression which – according to X – came naturally anyway.

Instead of calling X a bloody faceist, I turned around lamblike and left his room.

Then something happened. I discovered that my office mate had also been sacked. He was a friend. Ignoring office protocol I told him the size of my redundancy pay and learned that, notwithstanding the fact that we had joined the company at the same time, he was getting three times as much. I was infuriated, I was no longer Clive, I was Spike!

I stormed into X's sanctum and demanded an explanation for this injustice. I was aggressive, I was a bastard, and suddenly they loved me. I was offered my old job back. 'No thanks,' I said. Instead I was employed for a month at freelance rates to produce a new campaign for the United States Travel Service. One advertisement showed a smiling man beneath the headline: 'Free. With every holiday in California. A new you.' I even believed it myself, for a few days.

## 2. FIRST LOVE

•-•

'Ouch,' cried my wife.

'What's up?' I inquired.

'Nothing much,' she replied, 'I've just cut off the top of my finger.'

I rushed into the kitchen. There was blood on the walls, not to mention the ceiling.

Normally this would have been a disaster, but the timing made it almost tragic. It was June 1990, fifteen minutes before the kick-off of the vital Holland versus England match in the World Cup. What a dilemma!

Of course I had no choice. I rushed my wife to the accident and emergency department of our local hospital (an impossibility now, since the bastards shut it down last year) and offered to collect her at half-time. Sure enough I sped back as soon as the ref blew the whistle, but she was nowhere to be seen. I cruised the local streets in our topless 2CV until a shocked neighbour said he had just seen her wandering home with her arm in a sling. The rest is history. I was rewarded for my dedication with a Final from Hell; Argentina against West Germany. I watched it, of course, but only as a duty, out of loyalty to the game. Never before – or since – have I watched a match where I so desperately wanted both sides to lose.

Now it is four years later, and another World Cup is about to begin . . . in the United States, which is akin to holding the Winter Olympics in Kuwait. Don't get me wrong: I love America and Americans. I have to – my son is one.

Indeed, when he was but a few weeks old I took him over the Santa Cruz Mountains to see George Best play for the San Jose Quakes, just as my own father had taken me across the Watford Way in sleepy, suburban Hendon to watch Wingate Football Club. Ah, now we are talking Real Football (though not, alas, as in Real Madrid).

In those days, as I said, Hendon was a quiet place. The A41 was not a motorway *manqué*, not even a dual carriageway. Houses were protected from the traffic by lawns and rows of trees (when these were finally uprooted my brother made a bookmark from a leaf on the last tree). As winter approached I would sit beside the window in the front room on the lookout for lorries from the North, easily identified by their snowy cabin tops.

On Saturday afternoons my father would either take me to Hall Lane, if Wingate were at home, or to some distant outpost of the London League, such as Tilbury, Bletchley, Beckenham, Barkingside, West Thurrock, or Chingford, if they were playing away.

Hall Lane was a five-minute walk from our house. At its corner was a large Express Dairy depot and stables, whence our milkman would emerge every morning with his miniature stagecoach like some homogenized cowboy.

Anyway, everyone knew my father at the ground (he was, after all, chairman of the Supporters' Club). We bought our programmes (which always contained an advertisement for his factory, Simbros, manufacturers of kitchen furniture in distant Islington) and our raffle tickets (which we never won once, in all those years), and took our places along the touchline beside our fellow Jews.

The Arabs may have had Lawrence, but we had Orde Wingate, a rare philo-semite, who inspired Israel's armed forces and, more indirectly, the eponymous football club that captured my heart. Unfortunately Wingate did not win very much else, leading the editor of the programme to note one week: 'We know that our desire is to make friends on the field of sport, but not by presenting our opponents with two points!'

He was referring to the club's motto, *amicitia per ludis*. Being the 'only Jewish club in the country playing Senior League Football', Wingate was founded to demonstrate that Jews could be sportsmen as well as victims. Of course, no one believed that stuff about friendship through sport; respect is what we really wanted, the respect of others but, above all, self-respect as Jews. We knew that our opponents weren't Nazis or Amelekites, but the fact that they were goyim and we were Jews gave the games their edge. We identified, not with the rabbis in Rayleigh Close or Danescroft synagogues (I, for one, accompanied my father to his factory on Saturday mornings and sniffed sawdust and glue instead of snuff and ancient prayer books), but with those eleven men on the field.

Naturally we wanted victory, but we were prepared to settle for *style* or, failing that, wholehearted dedication to our cause.

And that, I fear, is what will be lacking in America; the players now worship Mammon, have sworn allegiance to froth rather than the fundament, to showbiz rather than real life. When the captain of the winning team raises his arms in triumph, he will not be Moses, but Aaron, and his prize will be the Golden Calf.

As the tension mounted on those long-ago afternoons men around me lit their Woodbines or their Players and the air became suffused with the smoky perfume of smouldering tobacco. To this day I only have to smell a cigarette in the great outdoors and I am transported, Proustlike, back to Hall Lane and the promised land of my childhood. As it happens, Hall Lane is still there, but all else has changed. The Watford Way is now uncross-able. Wingate Football Club, if it still exists, has moved. The ground has been turned into a housing estate. The owners do not know it, but their houses are built upon dreams.

# 3. IN PRAISE OF OPTIMISM

⚬

My mother's exhibition opened at the Sternberg Centre last month. The organizers, the Manor House Society, based at the Sternberg Centre in Finchley, North London, had chosen to call her show 'In Praise of Optimism'.

'They obviously don't know my mother,' I snorted. If asked to describe her character, 'optimistic' is not the first word I'd have chosen.

Most people hide their fears; not my mother. She wears hers on her sleeve. So why doesn't she paint like Francis Bacon? The truth is that she has managed to turn herself inside out, like a glove.

Her secret vice is not drug-taking or kinky sex, but optimism. Her back-to-front *Weltanschauung* may well be a consequence of her illness, which requires her to undergo dialysis three times a week. In effect her kidneys are outside her body. So why not her subconscious too? What else do you need to fear if, every other day, you can watch your blood circulate through the wiry intestines of a machine?

Perhaps this explains why her interior landscape has remained so unclouded. It is this image, above all, that dominates her paintings (which are, fittingly, entirely untutored). Nor did the joyful colours fade when her condition was first diagnosed, a decade or more ago. The shadow did not fall within. She continued to paint her abundant landscapes regardless.

There were exhibitions, including a remarkably successful one at the Manor House three years ago. And now there is 'In Praise of Optimism'.

Unfortunately my mother did not make it to the opening. At midday on the day before the opening, my father telephoned and said: 'We've got a problem.' This was a typical understatement. A mere two hours after a driver from the Sternberg Centre had collected her paintings, my mother had become seriously ill. It was uncanny, as if there were some causal connection between the two events.

By the time I reached the house, my mother was barely conscious. Between us, my father and I somehow got her to the Royal Free in Hampstead. On Tuesday, ten minutes into the opening party (already somewhat muted), there was a call from the hospital summoning my father. I accompanied him. We arrived, not anticipating good news.

A doctor led us to an office and told us, in a calm voice, that my mother had septicaemia and was, in effect, mortally ill. He did not say so precisely, but it was clear to both of us that he did not expect her to live. We were faced with a decision; did we want her transferred to intensive care, where so-called life-support machines would be available?

In fact, my mother had already been asked the same question twice; the first time she had declined, but now the doctor was no longer sure if she grasped the implications of her choice. Hence our dilemma. And so it came to pass that my father and I calmly and lucidly discussed with a doctor we had only just met whether to prolong my mother's life by artificial means.

In one sense, the question was a tautology, since she was already dependent upon a machine. My mother (tubes and all) was transferred (by mutual agreement) not to intensive care, but to the renal transplant unit (which, incidentally, our mean-spirited government would like to close).

Meanwhile, back at the exhibition, Fran (my wife) and other members of the family were trying to sustain some interest in the pictures. But all eyes were really on the door. When I eventually opened it, the remaining guests looked at me as weary gladiators must once have appealed to Augustus. But life and death weren't my prerogative, I was in no position to give the thumbs-up or the thumbs-down. All I could do was organize the transfer of the immediate family from the Sternberg Centre to the Royal Free.

Once there, we paraded past my mother's bed – husband, sons, daughters-in-law, grandsons. Just as my mother had once been able to read me at a glance, so now I could see, displayed on various monitors, her heartbeat, her blood pressure, and her pulse rate, even the percentage of oxygen her blood was absorbing.

I tried to tell her that the opening had been a great success, and tried to impress the memory of her multicoloured daydreams upon the present nightmare of gloom and blood. It was difficult to make out her response, muffled as it was by the oxygen mask, but it went something like this: 'It doesn't matter about my paintings, did you tell them about your book?'

For the next day or so, my mother hovered between life and death. She must have known how ill she was because she ordered my father to omit her age from the death notice in the *Jewish Chronicle*.

Later, when she was on the mend, she told me what she had been thinking about as she tottered on the cusp between this world and the next. I prepared myself for a revelation. 'I was going through my wardrobe,' she said, 'and wondering which of my dresses would fit Fran.'

This confirmed what I had already begun to suspect: that the true study of my mother is through her paintings. Her landscapes do not represent England or Israel or anywhere else in the known world, but are lyrical manifestations of her inner eye.

Her world is luxuriant with brightly coloured flora, with

placid waters and evergreen trees. All the inhabitants, be they children or lovers, always hold hands.

The style is naïve. However, my mother is not. She has read the book, knows well enough how the story will end; that even the brightest of flowers must wither and die.

Her optimism may bubble up from the subconscious, but it is not unconscious. It is, in short, a willed force. There are no precisely placed lines beneath the paint, no firm foundations, as there are none beneath us. But while my mother paints this knowledge is wilfully suppressed. Her deceptively simple pictures are hard-earned. They are truly moments of happiness.

## 4. 'I FEEL GOOD'

·•·

There are times, as I stand beside Fran's bed, willing her to complete yet another unfinished sentence, that I feel like Hercule Poirot urging a dying victim to reveal the identity of her murderer.

Except in Fran's case there is no mystery; the culprit is cancer. In the beginning, I used to joke that Aids was beneficial in one respect: it made cancer seem less scary. I was an innocent. I did not know.

I am talking now about the last few days of Fran's life, when she was immobilized and supine, a featherweight on a bed of air.

By then, the pain was unbearable and the doctors at Mount Vernon, in their desperation, could do nothing but prescribe massive doses of morphine and other, related narcotics. Peace came eventually, but at an outrageous price.

As it happens, Fran was able to describe the side effects to one of her doctors. It was as though there had been a revolution in her senses. All sensations were suddenly equal, making it impossible for her to sort out what sights or sounds were important or even relevant. Midway through one conversation she would tune into another, inconsequential dialogue between strangers (the morphine dulled all her senses, save hearing; I

think she could hear till the very end) and, utterly confused, her
wires crossed, she would lapse into silence.

Whereupon she would panic because she wasn't sure what
the silence signified. Was her interlocutor – sometimes a visitor,
sometimes a doctor – awaiting an answer to a long-forgotten
question? Hence those unfinished sentences.

To make matters worse, she frequently used the wrong word.
Sometimes the misunderstandings were easy to repair. One day,
having trimmed my moustache, I kissed her on the lips. 'Ooh,'
she giggled, 'that's technological.'

'You mean ticklish,' I said.

'That's right,' she replied.

Another time she suddenly started to talk about Italy. For a
moment, I thought that she was rambling; that her mind, unable
to bear the present reality, had transported her to Amalfi or Sicily.

Then I heard a cleaner whistling '*O sole mio*'.

'Are you Italian?' I enquired.

'Ah yes,' he replied. 'I was talking to your poor wife the other
day. She was telling me all about her many visits to my country.'

There was, I am convinced, a rational explanation for all Fran's
apparent digressions. Alas, more often than not, the key could
not be found. The meaning, whatever it was, vanished like
smoke.

Nor was Fran's hand steady enough to write. When she was
transferred to Mount Vernon, she requested a notebook because
she intended to keep a journal. However, all she managed to
transcribe was a shopping list at the back and a few enigmatic
words at the front which – try as I might – I still cannot decipher.

Last night, I saw Fran as she was, before the disease and its
putative cure stripped her to the bone. We were in a field. A
blanket was spread out, upon which were items of underwear
and a few jumbled letters from a Scrabble set. Ahead of us was
a large house with many rooms. Fran entered and I followed,
begging her to be careful. You can work out the meaning of the
house et cetera for yourself, but only I – Fran's writer-husband

– am foolish or arrogant enough to try to make some sense of those scrambled letters, to be my late wife's mouthpiece.

That's why I am telling you all this. Not to dwell upon Fran's dying, but to record the final fleeting triumphs of a compassionate and graceful woman.

No, it is not wrong to count them as victories. You must first of all understand that time passes differently in a cancer ward.

So intense is a visit to the dying that each moment expands to encompass you both, while expelling all else so that nothing else exists, neither past nor future. You are embedded in the moment, and feel capable of miracles.

Your wife is unconscious? Ah yes, but her consciousness is still there, drifting like a wreck on the seabed. And you feel strong enough to raise it. Afterwards, you know full well that this is a delusion, that your willpower is insufficient, that you are really no miracle worker.

But, just occasionally, your wife, by reason of her inner strength, does break surface. Whereupon she says: 'I don't understand what's happening to me. I want my body back.' Subsequent comments make it clear that she does understand, only too well.

'Am I dying?' she asks, already knowing the answer. 'They mustn't let me die,' she cries. Still later she says: 'I am dying . . . I am dying . . . Does Seth know?'

Seth is our son, aged thirteen. He is one of the reasons why Fran is determined to live. 'Fuck the disease,' she says, with gusto.

On Monday 27 June, a hot day, we turn up to find Fran cooking in the sun. We obtain a fan, close the blinds, and she calms down. For a few moments, she is her former self. She demands to speak to Seth alone. 'There is a bond between us that can never be broken . . .' she begins. The rest is his secret.

Seth plays the saxophone. On 28 June he is performing in the school concert, a song by James Brown. At the same time, I visit Fran and remind her what is going on elsewhere. As I leave, she has her arms outstretched. Her head, bald, skull-like, is rocking from side to side. There is a smile on her face.

She is singing: 'I feel good . . . da da da da da . . . just like I knew that I would.' Over and over again.

'My wife has not gone mad,' I explain to the sister. 'She is merely adding the vocal to our son's distant solo.'

Fran was a great teacher and an incorrigible optimist. Even now, when I look at photographs of her, I can see no shadow of what was to come. I thought she would live to be ninety, like her beloved grandmother. Instead she died at forty-six.

A few days before the end she suddenly became excited, as if we were about to embark upon a journey.

'Let's get going,' she said. 'What are we waiting for? Where's Seth? Where is everyone?' Then she shut her eyes and kept repeating: 'I love you all. I love you all. I love you all.'

I can still hear the echo.

# 5. 16 JULY 1996

◦•◦

I am looking at a photograph taken in Lynn's house on Bonair Street, La Jolla. Sunday morning, early Sunday morning, 2 August 1992. It is a group portrait: Lynn, Fran (my wife), and Seth (our son). Thanks to the delayed action mechanism on my camera I am present too, kneeling breathlessly between Lynn and Fran as the shutter clicks. They are both wearing mauve T-shirts, sporting similar cascades of dark hair, and possess the same slim figures. They could easily pass as sisters. Later Lynn was to write: 'I liked Fran so much – and always felt that if our geographies had been different we would have become close friends.' We met her in 1981, when we were living in Santa Cruz (Seth's birthplace), but our real home was 6,000 miles away in England. Lynn added: 'She had a presence that composed everything around it, she created a conduciveness, a lost art.' Lynn could equally have been describing her own personality, she too created a conduciveness. I look at the photograph in more detail. Lynn has prepared us breakfast; *pain au chocolat*, orange juice, fruit. All around are found objects: fossils and rocks from Ano Nuevo, a State Reserve to the north of Santa Cruz, where the elephant seals rest in the winter; turquoise beads, sand, and a bird's skull, all glued to the skin of a tom-tom; Navajo wall hangings. Although relocated, these ornaments remain undomesticated, retain their

migratory spirit, the untamable wildness of desert and ocean, of
fire and water. Lynn too is a transient; a sceptical and sexy child
of the East, bringing flesh to the fire and water; a sensuous,
smart, mystic. After breakfast she poses beside her 1968 Dodge
Dart (another photograph), and we drive off in our borrowed
Volvo, heading for the Ancient Bristlecone Pine Forest, high in
the White Mountains. Hardly any Californians have heard of
the White Mountains, let alone the Bristlecone Pines. Except
Lynn. She, needless to say, has actually seen them. 'They're
magical,' she promises, 'you'll see.' She leans beside her car,
waving, as we turn left on Draper Street, and disappear. The
Ancient Bristlecone Pine Forest stands directly beneath the
heavens at a height of 11,000 feet. The stunted trees have been
burnished by the wind, snow, and sun, until they resemble gold-
plated driftwood. Some are 5,000 years old. They are the oldest
living things on earth. The forest is a Garden of Eden with
altitude. 'Dear Lynn,' I write on the back of a postcard, 'this is
indeed an awe-full place. Pity I couldn't become a permanent
resident. Alas the elevation affects my sinuses and gives me
nosebleeds. Still it affords a comforting sense of beauty and
longevity . . .'

A false sense, as it turned out. Our going down was a descent
toward Death Valley. When Fran's cancer was diagnosed in
December 1993 Lynn wrote: 'What I am doing is holding in my
mind's eye an image of Fran well – healed, having fun at the
ocean, and in the mountains, and once again feeling the sweetness
of a normal routine. And you too, feeling that sweetness. I hope
that you can get to your desk now and again – the anchor.' If
only the imagination could work such miracles. Lynn was in
hospital herself when she heard of Fran's death the following July.
Now she too is unearthed, unanchored, adrift in the universe. I
return the framed photograph to the shelf, where it sits beside
Lynn's books. I think about the delayed action mechanism that
enabled me to enter the picture, and the premature malignancy

that erased my wife, and my friend, from the visible world. If I had the power I would reincarnate both at the summit of the White Mountains; green saplings, with 5,000 years ahead of them.

# 6. THE *NOUVEAU ANGLAIS*

•—•

Although not a believer my late father liked to attend the Liberal Jewish Synagogue on the sabbath. Situated in St John's Wood, one of the capital's more salubrious districts, it is (as its name implies) a broad-minded and tolerant institution. So tolerant that it has even accepted our Home Secretary, Michael Howard, as a member. My father (né Smolinsky) was the son of refugees, as is Mr Howard (formerly Hecht). Nevertheless, the latter (a right-winger even among right-wingers) has vowed to restrict immigration. A new act of parliament categorizes asylum seekers as either 'genuine' or 'bogus'. Only the former, a minority, are now admitted. In making this distinction Michael Howard has betrayed both his Jewish heritage (which privileges the stranger), and the local tradition of sheltering the dissident. August Strindberg once wrote an essay entitled 'My Anti-Semitism', in which he satirized the exaggerated Swedishness of some assimilated Jews. It would be easy to apply these remarks to Michael Howard, and portray him as a 'bogus' Englishman, but it would not be accurate. For Mr Howard is the archetypal *nouveau anglais*, a self-made man whose interior passions are entirely subjected to political (or material) ends.

My father detested the Tories, a prejudice I am proud to have inherited. He was counting the days to the election, and their predicted defeat. Alas, he will not see it; he died in December, and was buried on Friday the thirteenth. It seemed appropriate to visit his synagogue on the following day, in order to say *kaddish*, the mourner's prayer, as our tradition demands. More a paean of praise than a howl of lamentation, its climax is hope rather than despair. 'May the Almighty, source of perfect peace, grant peace to us, to all Israel, and to all mankind, and let us say, Amen.' It will, I fear, be a long wait. My father, a modest man, had never expected perfect peace; a glimpse of social justice would have sufficed. He came of age in the 1930s, when there were plenty of causes to champion: the Negroes of Alabama, the Republicans of Spain, the unemployed, and the Jews just about everywhere. The indigenous threat to his co-religionists came in the shape of Sir Oswald Mosley and the blackshirts. On 4 October 1936 the dark knight led his racist acolytes to the gates of London's East End (then, as now, a repository of immigrants). My father and his comrades (by no means all Jews) placed themselves at the confluence of Cable and Leman Streets, at a place called Gardiners Corner, and began to chant, '*No pasaran*,' a war cry pinched from their Spanish heroes. Mounted police tried to break the line with numerous charges. Heads were cracked, but to no avail. On that famous day the Fascists did not pass.

Unfortunately many other mendacious philosophies have emerged and flourished since then. And so, as the prayers continued, I was inclined to echo a famous Jeremiad: 'Wherefore doth the way of the wicked prosper? wherefore are all they happy that deal very treacherously?' At the time of writing Jeremiah's observation remains valid; the meek have yet to inherit the earth. On the contrary, corporate raiders, asset strippers, and privateers who plunder the world's stock markets as pirates once ravished the Spanish Main are offered as role models. Their abundance, we are assured, will eventually benefit all society. Not by means of progressive taxation (God forbid!), but by a form of osmosis, too vague for any statute books, and called the 'trickle down effect'. In other words, all the rich need do is piss *goldwasser* upon the poor, simultaneously easing their bladders and their consciences. Thanks to their efforts Britain is now universally recognized as the Lion of Europe. Or so Mr Major, Mr Howard, and their cabinet cronies boast. Recognized by whom? Not by me. I picture instead the melancholy features and moth-eaten pelt of the cowardly lion, as played by Bert Lahr in *The Wizard of Oz*. This is the true face of the British worker; imperial fancy dress merely making a mockery of the sad reality. The fact is that the working class is obsolete, redundant, surplus to national requirements. Once upon a time it was needed by local capitalists, who had factories to run, or by the army, which had an empire to conquer and subdue. But now the old satanic mills are shut, and the colonies free, leaving the lumpenproletariat without a *raison d'être*. The roles available to a home-grown prole are neither numerous nor attractive; assuming that they are already unemployed, they can become beggars, single mothers, soccer hooligans, muggers, drunks, or drug addicts. The government, having washed its hands of most other social responsibilities, has elected to privatize poverty, to rid itself of this burden, this embarrassment, this eyesore. And so, instead of forcing the *nouveau riche* to use their profits for the common good, they have relied upon inward investment, and sent the poor into internal exile, to slave away in micro-Koreas or mini-Japans.

There is, I suppose, some poetic justice in the fact that our workers – unskilled, but house-trained – are now regarded as cheap labour by the tigerish economies of south-east Asia. But this is justice on a cosmic scale, and has little to do with quotidian fairness, the idea that the weak need protecting from the unbridled appetites of the strong. It is a philosophy eschewed by latter-day Tories, who have put their faith in the disinterested mechanics of market forces. As a result (surprise, surprise!) the poor get poorer, and the rich get richer. During their four administrations (1979–1997) the wealthiest 10% of the population have increased their incomes by 65%, while the poorest 10% earn 13% less. Furthermore, as many as 2,000,000 children

now live below the poverty line; meaning that they are malnour-
ished, underweight, and subject to all the ailments of deprivation,
such as rickets, anaemia, and tuberculosis. You would expect such
divergent fortunes to offend the English credo of fair play, a
cherished component of the national self-image. The forth-
coming election will tell whether anything remains of the ancient
preference to play fairly rather than win.

Now it so happens that the Liberal Jewish Synagogue, with
its neoclassical portico, stands opposite another quasi-religious
building; viz., the main entrance to Lord's Cricket Ground,
headquarters of the game that is (or perhaps was) synonymous
with old-fashioned English virtues. These are writ in stone
(literally so), carved into the wall that encloses the stadium;
which is to say that on the corner of St John's Wood Road there
is a large and revealing relief, not unlike those that once adorned
the palaces of Assyria. In this instance a variety of sportsmen and
women parade from left to right like a beautiful sentence. First
come a couple in tennis togs, tagging after a pair of golfers (the
gentleman sporting plus fours), who are in turn trailing crick-
eters, footballers, oarsmen, and swimmers. All are in profile, and
dressed for play. However, at the centre of the composition, full-
face to the viewer, is an athletic fellow, wearing nothing but a
loincloth. Kneeling at his feet is another cricketer, his bat laid
horizontal in a form of obeisance, as though wishing to acknowledge the classical origins of his ideals. These are spelt out across
the top of the frieze: 'Play up! play up! and play the game!' The
words are taken from 'Vitai Lampada', a stirring poem by patriotic Sir Henry Newbolt (a Victorian relic, who died just before
the outbreak of the Second World War). Although the ostensible
subject is a cricket match, its true matter (needless to say) is the
Englishman, and his behaviour in extremis.

> There's a breathless hush in the Close tonight –
>   Ten to make and the match to win –
> A bumping pitch and a blinding light,

*An hour to play and the last man in.*
*And it's not for the sake of a ribboned coat,*
*Or the selfish hope of a season's fame,*
*But his captain's hand on his shoulder smote —*
*'Play up! play up! and play the game!'*

The relief was designed by Gilbert Bayes. It is signed, and dated 1934. Those were the days when the phrase 'It's not cricket' (meaning, 'You are cheating, old boy') was just about the most damning rebuke one gentleman could offer another. It is a world as safe as pasteurized milk, the whiteness of the worked stone offering a stark contrast to Mosley's blackshirts, whose contemporary activities (needless to say) are not part of the landscape. Equally the working classes (more useful than today, but still culturally insignificant) are excluded from the narrative, from the island story. This is not to disparage Bayes, who was actually well aware of the huddled masses. As an architectural sculptor he had a long association with Royal Doulton (manufacturers of tiles and other polychromatic stoneware), and used their materials to add gratuitous *joie de vivre* to the housing estates of the poor. One hopes they were duly grateful. In short, the illusion of a pacific nation 'at ease with itself' (to borrow one of Mr Major's clichés) could only be maintained by the time-honoured method of turning a blind eye, and (when unable to ignore the truth) offering a little patronage.

More recently, when our Prime Minister described England as a land of warm beer and village cricket he was evoking the same demi-paradise, already lost in 1934. It is lost, but the memory lingers. Which is why you still hear Mr Major demanding 'a level playing field' on which to fight his political wars. Note, incidentally, the use of 'playing field' (as in 'the Battle of Waterloo was won on the playing fields of Eton') rather than the more plebeian 'pitch'. He frequently complains that only Britain obeys the rules of the European Union, whereas wily foreigners (who do not understand cricket) bend them at will. In other words, all his opponents are cheats, prepared to tilt the playing field, to take advantage of an innocent abroad. 'It's not fair!' wails our abused Prime Minister, echoing the eternal complaint of the wronged child. This, needless to say, is disingenuous tosh. The Tories (Mr Major no less than Mr Howard) have long since ditched the rule book, are mouthing old platitudes to disguise the machinations of mini-Machiavellis. The game is realpolitik, and it is dirty.

Nor has sport retained its innocence. When Pakistan thrashed the English cricket team, not so long ago, their bowlers were accused of bamboozling our batsmen with the use of doctored balls. In retaliation Pakistan's former captain, Imran Khan, accused several English players of cheating, among them Ian Botham, who sued for libel. The case filled the newspapers for several days, revealing unexpected allegiances. Although Khan hailed from Pakistan he was pale-skinned, aristocratic, public school and Oxbridge educated; in a word, a gentleman. Whereas Botham was a working-class hero, poorly schooled and vulgarly dressed. His nickname was Beefy. In *The Turn of the Screw*, a creepy tale by Henry James, the heroine attempts to describe a mysterious apparition: 'He's tall, active, erect . . . but never – no, never! – a gentleman.' The same was said of Botham. In the event the Anglo-Saxon establishment sided with the well-spoken and discreetly attired Khan. It seemed that their prejudice against *hoi polloi* was greater than their dislike of off-white foreigners. In England class always trumps race. Botham, incidentally, lost the case. As a matter of fact the courtroom drama made clear that the original fault-line in the game of cricket, that between Gentlemen (who, being independently wealthy, played for love) and Players (who were rewarded for their efforts), had been covered up rather than abandoned. In reality it is a division that continues to dominate life in England. The meta-money class, denizens of Lords and the London clubs, continue to lead lives apart from the lower orders. England remains the spiritual home of social apartheid.

It is true that Margaret Thatcher, the Boudicca of the *nouveau anglais*, despised the toffs, the chinless wonders, who had done nothing to earn their advantages, save being born to the right parents. But the revolution she initiated did nothing to alter the structure of society. The bastions of privilege remain. Instead of tearing down the walls, her disciples merely sought entrance for themselves. Everything was done in the name of the individual, nothing in the name of the common good. As a consequence private schools and private hospitals have multiplied, along with the belief that state services – especially those concerning education and health – are irredeemably second rate. Whereas the upper classes were content to thank their lucky stars for their inheritance, the *nouveau anglais* are inclined to ascribe their rise to moral superiority. As far as they are concerned poverty is simply the visible sign of spiritual bankruptcy. Besides, most of the poor (like nearly all refugees) are 'bogus', worthy of contempt rather than sympathy. They are best left to rot in their own crime-infested estates, comprehensive schools, and National Health hospitals. They have earned their hell on earth. This is instant gratification elevated to religious status; the afterlife, with all its rewards and punishments, is available now, here in England's green and pleasant land. The hypocritical pretence at fair play was bad enough, but it is even harder to endure the emetic sound of self-righteousness that emanates from our government and its beneficiaries.

I cross St John's Wood Road and reenter the sanctuary of the synagogue. I have but one question: 'How long, O Lord, how long?'

# 7. A SOAP OPERA FROM HELL

∙◗∙

**EPISODE ONE**
The facts of life. He learns them at Bournemouth, in the following order. (1) The body is a fragile thing. His brother, not yet four, trips over a beach ball and snaps his leg. He is in hospital for three months, while the fractured limb heals. (2) Life can be short. A pair of fledgling blue tits hop around the hotel swimming pool. All the bathers laugh. It is like watching a Disney cartoon. Until a tom cat appears. He is not worried. In cartoons the predator always goes hungry. But this is a real cat, which eats the birds, one after the other. (3) Appearances can be deceptive. Sometimes the family visits the south coast in winter. He has a photograph of his brother, dressed as a pirate, shaking hands with a man disguised as Father Christmas. The former has just won first prize in the fancy dress competition. He comes nowhere, is zippered from head to toe in ersatz ursine fur. Not a very convincing bear. Not a very convincing boy either. 'You have a very pretty daughter,' say a couple to his parents. Had he really been a bear he would have devoured them on the spot, leaving only the bones. After the competition there is a tea party. He dips his spoon in a bowl, and delivers the contents to his mouth, only to experience temporary revulsion, rather than the anticipated delight. The stuff looks like chocolate ice cream, but isn't

cold. On the contrary, it is warm and spongy; a shocking and horrid impostor. (4) Mind and body are not indivisible. Visiting Corfe Castle for the first time he sprints up the hill towards the picturesque ruins. Reaching the shattered portal he turns around and, confronted by the Isle of Purbeck far below, freezes on the spot. His head is not swimming. It is not vertigo. He has simply ceased to believe in gravity, does not trust his feet to stay earthed. Or perhaps it is the ground beneath that he doubts. Either way, he is stranded.

## EPISODE TWO

University. His parents deliver him in the Jag. On the return journey his father suffers a panic attack and is unable to drive in excess of twenty miles per hour. No explanation is ever offered for this uncharacteristic lapse. At the Freshers' Ball, that same night, he dances with the girl who is destined to be his wife. It is an unlikely destiny. She finds her partner physically repulsive, and accepts his invitation only because she is too kind to do otherwise. He asks her because he fancies her friend (already snapped up). The campus is equally ignorant of its future, being little more than a building site. Students are accommodated elsewhere; on a redundant airfield. The former dormitories have been partitioned with plywood, granting individual privacy, though the bathrooms remain communal. The tiled floors are stone cold throughout the winter. In spring the pollen count breaks all records. He never stops sneezing. At the end of his first academic year he is informed that he has been lucky, has been assigned a room on the campus, always assuming that Denys Lasdun's famous ziggurats will be habitable at the commencement of the winter term. He greets the news with indifference, since he does not expect to survive the summer.

**EPISODE THREE**
War and Peace. 'You realize the dangers,' says the recruiting officer when he volunteers to fly out to Israel on the eve of hostilities, 'it is possible that you will come under fire.' He shrugs his shoulders stoically. *Que sera sera.* Although his parents are passionate supporters of their endangered co-religionists they aren't too keen on donating their first-born to the cause.

'What's the problem?' he grumbles, looking at his father. 'You were prepared to sacrifice your life for the Spanish republic.'

'Up to a point,' he replies, 'the point being Waterloo Station.'

Unfortunately they are arguing in his erstwhile bedroom, with its Lascaux-style wallpaper, and picture windows. These afford fine views of the mirror-image house across the garden. His mind wanders. He wonders if the buxom au pair is still as careless with her curtains. He acknowledges his disadvantage; this is hardly the place in which to feel a wholly autonomous unit, a grown-up. Nevertheless, he persists. He is determined to be a hero; heroic at least. The dispute is terminated by the arrival of Yves Montand, visible only to the eager young warrior. 'Let it be,' advises Yves, '*la guerre est finie.*' As it is, in six days.


**EPISODE FOUR**
The big question. He arrives, not as a volunteer, but as an ordinary tourist. Though the atmosphere is anything but ordinary. People watch newsreels in the cinema, and cheer whenever Moshe Dayan or Yitzhak Rabin appear. He stays on the coast, and shares his room with a convalescent soldier. After a few days he ascends to Jerusalem. Most pilgrims arrive with a hard question. Where do we come from? Why are we here? Where are we going? Does God exist? He is no exception. What he wants to know is this: Where is his friend Pamela? She has left London and enrolled at the Hebrew University. This is the limit of his knowledge. He has no address. What can he do? He

searches the campus. But she is one among ten thousand, a needle in a haystack. It is hopeless. He admits defeat, and joins the other passengers-in-waiting outside the university gates. That's when he sees her, sitting in the back of a departing bus. She sees him too, waves, and disembarks at the next stop, where their friendship begins anew. Was their meeting simply a coincidence? Or was it another twist of fate in the city of crossed destinies?

## EPISODE FIVE

Make love not war. After graduation our hero flies to America. Another university; the University of California at Santa Cruz. Alas, he misses the summer of love by a whisker. But is in time to demonstrate against the war in Vietnam. Joan Baez comes to the campus; not to sing, but to encourage new conscripts to tear up their draft cards. He meets Linda R in Los Angeles. A friend of a friend, described by the latter as the most experienced virgin west of the Mississippi. She looks the part; Doris Day sans bleach. The must-see movie is Z. When Yves Montand is struck down by Fascists in the first reel Linda R grabs her date's hand. She continues to grip it throughout the movie. So he has great expectations when she agrees to return his visit the following weekend. Nixon, unfortunately, prefers armour to *amour*. He orders his Air Force to bomb Cambodia. More demonstrations. 'Apologies,' says Linda R, calling from UCLA, 'I'll have to take a rain check. We're organizing a big protest, and I need to be part of it.' She writes him a few passionate notes, but he never sees her again. He also receives letters from his future wife, doing voluntary service in St Vincent, and an invitation to Pamela's more imminent marriage in Jerusalem.

## EPISODE SIX

Two weddings. The first takes place at the King David Hotel, on a terrace overlooking the walls of the Old City. A few days after the ceremony he accompanies Pamela and her new husband to see *L'Aveu*. Yves Montand stars. He plays a character based upon Rudolf Slansky, sometime vice-premier of Czechoslovakia, who is falsely accused of being a traitor and – this awakens a flicker of interest in the restless cineasts – a Zionist. *L'Aveu* means 'the confession', and Montand's torturers do their best to extract one. Still trusting the party, the prisoner persuades himself that an error has occurred, but finally is forced to accept the dismal truth. He refuses to sign, thereby saving his soul, if not his neck. The struggle bores the audience, which emits a collective yawn. Individuals fidget in their iron-framed chairs. They place their empties on the cement floor, and watch the bottles roll down the slope towards the screen. They talk. They laugh. Unluckily two of the worst offenders are beside the happy couple and their friend from overseas. They treat Pamela's strictures with contempt. Their lack of respect – not for her, but for the tragedy re-enacted on the screen – drives her to distraction. And so, as they leave, she spits in their faces. The reaction is violent, and directed at her two male escorts (who retreat, *con brio*, and thereby preserve their skins). The wedding guest departs. His weapon is the biro, the poison pen. He writes a novel, and eventually marries Fran, the girl he asked to dance thirteen years before. The ceremony is performed at the register office in Bury St Edmunds. It takes seven minutes.

## EPISODE SEVEN

A normal life. He shouldn't complain; against all expectation it lasts for nineteen years. They live in Blackheath, Malmesbury, Bury St Edmunds, Santa Cruz (where their son is born), Uppsala (briefly), and St Albans. His wife teaches children with

behavioural and learning difficulties. He writes books. At night
he locks the doors, looks in on his sleeping son, slips into bed
with his naked wife. He cannot believe his luck. Others begin
their day with a jog around the block, in the confident expectation of averting the evil decree. He is not so ambitious. He
merely hopes that his nerves will be sufficiently strong when the
blow falls. To prepare them he fits in a daily session of light
worrying. The first test comes on 12 July 1993, when his father
makes the understatement of the year: 'We've got a problem.'
His mother survives septicaemia, only to succumb to peritonitis
(when her bowel is accidentally perforated in an attempt to
uncover the source of the infection). She doesn't die at once. In
fact she endures emergency surgery and several days in intensive
care, where one of the drugs makes her crazy. She imagines she
is in a hotel. She thinks it is breakfast, and the sheet a slice of
bread. She holds the cotton between her fingers and nibbles an
edge. Her son finds a doctor and explains that this behaviour is
out of character. The drug is withdrawn, and his mother restored.
She is also returned to a general ward, where another doctor
assures the family: 'Mrs S is not only stable, but recovering.' How
little he knows her. When a nurse reveals the stoma bag for the
first time she says, 'The operation was a mistake.' The following
day, 24 August, she is feverish. A fan is placed beside the bed.
In the afternoon she requests toast. A nurse brings a plate; two
slices, cut diagonally, with pots of Marmite and pats of butter.
His mother takes a few bites, then announces: 'I've had enough.'
'But you enjoyed it,' says his optimistic wife. Does his mother
smile? Either way she dies three hours later. 'I've had enough,'
are her last words. His wife outlives her mother-in-law by less
than a year. He remembers her last day of consciousness. How
can he forget? The unassuageable terror apparent in her eyes.
The fact that she too plucks at the sheet and puts it in her
mouth.

## EPISODE EIGHT

To the beach. He wants to get away. But he has inherited polycystic kidney disease from his mother, and is in end-stage renal failure himself.

'Can I risk a trip to Israel?' he asks his doctor.

'Go,' he is told, 'but be prepared for dialysis on your return.'

In Tel Aviv he informs his thirteen-year-old son of his condition, and that he has a fifty per cent chance of passing it on. The boy absorbs the information. 'OK,' he says, 'now let's go to the beach.'

They also fly to Egypt, hoping that the perfumes of Arabia will sweeten the bitter season. Pamela accompanies them, to protect the boy lest his father sickens. From Cairo they take the night train to Luxor, arriving before dawn. A guide leads them to the banks of the Nile, where they board the boat that will ferry them to the West Bank, the dominion of the dead. The full moon is descending, the sun warming up. As moonlight falls upon the still waters he unexpectedly recalls a sentence from a famous story by Anton Chekhov. Later, while parading in slow motion along the corniche at the blaze of noon, he feels that he has been transported to Yalta, and half expects to encounter the spectral presence of Anna Sergeyevna, the lady with the little dog. Instead he meets his new reality instructor; Lucy, the dialysis nurse. She teaches him how to inject himself with erythropoietin, to counteract his anaemia. He is on dialysis for eleven months, at which point he receives a transplant.

## EPISODE NINE

Viva Zapata. The new modus vivendi lasts until 11 December 1996. That morning he awakes convinced that he has been very ill during the night, but can recall no nightmare, nor find any other evidence. He prepares breakfast. The telephone rings. It is still only 7.30. Will he accept a reverse-charges call from Mr S?

'You'll never guess where I am,' says his father. It has to be one of two places; prison or hospital. He guesses correctly. He finds his father is sitting up in bed. His father has a good colour, but is in the coronary care unit. He explains that he had been playing bridge and was denouncing Netanyahu and his government, when he began to feel more and more unwell. He returned home and telephoned his doctor, who wouldn't come out. She told him to summon an ambulance if he was worried. He was. He did. But he didn't call either of his sons, lest they should worry too. By the afternoon he doesn't look so well. By the evening he is wearing an oxygen mask. 'Sleep well,' say son and grandson, as they depart. The following morning the former receives the 'come quickly' phone call all children dread. He collects his own son from school. They are greeted by a nurse at the reception desk. She smiles. Her teeth are tiny and exceptionally white. Could it have been a false alarm?

She says, 'Let me show you to a family room, where a doctor will come to see you.'

'Are you telling me he's dead?' he asks.

'I'm afraid so,' she replies.

His father has been placed in a side ward. They take their leave, watched by another nurse. Then they have lunch in a Mexican cantina across the road. After the meal he makes the funeral arrangements. His father is buried the following day, alongside his mother. In 1991 he cooked an alfresco meal to celebrate their golden wedding anniversary. Later he took some panoramic photographs of the family in the back garden. The scenery remains the same – the fig tree, the oak, and the spruce – but the figures in the foreground are sparse; his son, his brother, his two nephews. Gone are his mother (peritonitis, aged seventy-three), his father (heart attack, aged eighty-one), his wife (osteosarcoma, aged forty-six), his sister-in-law (breast cancer, aged forty-two). The house is on the market for less than a week. Relatives and friends are invited to see his mother's paintings *in situ* before the new owners take possession. Most hang in his old bedroom, long since redecorated. However, the well-remembered wallpaper remains inside the fitted wardrobes, the troglodytic testament of his ancestral self. The Last Picture Show is over. Now he must remove the paintings from the hooks; luxuriant flowers and trees vanish in the blink of an eye, leaving a vacant space, a suburban desert. It reminds him of something. Of course! *The Cherry Orchard*, act four. Instead of a concluding 'twang', there's the owlish howl of the burglar alarm as he closes the front door. Shalom, finito, the end. Within days newcomers will change the code, turning him into a stranger, exiling him from his past.

## EPISODE TEN

Dead is every word. He finds he can readily describe the externals, but lacks a vocabulary to explain his feelings. No. The vocabulary exists. What is missing is an internal dictionary to provide individual meanings. He is familiar with the word 'grief', but cannot be sure he has experienced it. How can he make such an assumption, if he has not shed a single tear? He has forgotten how to cry, which facial muscles to use. Therefore it comes as no surprise when an ophthalmologist informs him the tears he does produce – the consequence of various allergies – are deficient, poor quality facsimiles of the real thing. The ophthalmologist writes him a prescription, which he exchanges for a pot of artificial tears. Later he reads that genuine tears are life preservers. It seems they rid the body of harmful chemicals. The death rate among widowers who do not weep is alarmingly high. Serves me right, he thinks. When he was a student at the University of California he wrote a long paper entitled 'Towards a Definition of Jewish-American Literature'. One of its major themes was contained in these lines from a Yiddish poem by Alter Esselin,

> 'Dead is every word.
> Would you say to a woman you really love,
> "I love you"?
> Unless with tears or a violin
> The words no longer ring true.'

He remains fascinated by the curse of self-consciousness, the impossibility of spontaneously translating feeling into language. The sad truth is that what the heart knows cannot be uttered; it emerges banal, inarticulate. Art is required to enable the hearer – or reader – to share the feeling. But by resorting to artifice the speaker – or writer – compromises the original impulse, subjects it to manipulation, works it up for the benefit of an audience. The writer finally has no choice; literature must always come before life. He writes a book called *The Lady With the Laptop*. It includes a description of his wife's death. His wife had an aunt who drowned herself. She left her niece a fur coat. A friend, seeing it for the first time, asked: 'What poor creature sacrificed itself to provide you with such a coat?' He couldn't help himself. 'Her aunt,' he said. His wife, not knowing whether to laugh or cry, did both. Now, if someone were to ask a similar question about his book, he would have to reply: 'My wife.' The book wins a literary prize. As a result its author is invited to the Jerusalem Book Fair.

## EPISODE ELEVEN

Jorge Semprun. The highlight of the fair is the presentation of the Jerusalem Prize to Jorge Semprun. 'Have you heard of him?' he asks Pamela. She shakes her head. 'Me neither,' he replies. The ceremony is preceded by music. Mario Vargas Llosa supplies a passionate appreciation of the life and works. Semprun studied philosophy in Paris. But abandoned his studies when the Nazis occupied France. He joined the resistance, was betrayed, tortured, sent to Buchenwald. A finishing school, of sorts. Liberation arrived, but Semprun's struggles continued. He subdued the impulse to write. Instead he became a Communist and dedicated his life to the defeat of Franco. The radical therapy failed. He was expelled from the party. In the end he had no choice, he had to write; novels, memoirs, film scripts. Mario Vargas Llosa names the movies. 'Ah,' thinks a listener, 'I know this man better than I thought.' He purchases a copy of Semprun's new book, *Literature or Life*. The title reminds him of his own abandoned thesis. The coincidence pleases him, as does the fact that he begins reading it on 11 April, the same day that Buchenwald was liberated. The book is a meditation upon Semprun's capture and incarceration there. It begins at the end, so to speak, with the liberation of the camp fifty-two years ago to the day. The coincidences multiply: ten years previously – 11 April 1987 – Semprun was working on a novel when he felt an unaccountable compulsion to compose something other. So he recreated a strange encounter with three Allied officers – two Britons and a Frenchman – which occurred on the day after liberation. Having recorded the scene to his satisfaction Semprun collected the accumulated pages and placed them in a file which he unhesitatingly marked, 'Literature or Death'. Only then did he learn that Primo Levi had taken his own life that very day. Semprun ascribes such curious linkages to 'a strategy of the unconscious mind'. It pleases his reader to believe that some similar force caused him to open the book exactly ten years later. There is the pathetic fallacy, in which an indifferent universe is supposed to reflect the prevailing emotional atmosphere, providing storms for troubled souls and sunshine for the contented. And there is biblio-fallacy, in which the reader believes that the author is speaking exclusively to him, or even – in more severe cases – for him. Both are a subspecies of paranoia.

## EPISODE TWELVE

Literature or life. He believes that he has found his internal dictionary, the book that can define his feelings. True, he is merely acquainted with a cancerous force independent of human will, while Semprun had to contend with 'absolute evil'. Nevertheless, when he reads the following, he dares nod his head in agreement. 'I want only to forget, nothing else. I find it unjust, almost indecent, to have made it through eighteen months of Buchenwald without a single minute of anguish, without a single nightmare, carried along by constantly renewed curiosity, sustained by an insatiable appetite for life . . . having survived all that – only to find myself from then on the occasional prey of the most naked, the most intense despair, a despair nourished as much by life itself, by its serenity and joys, as by the memory of death.' Semprun now lives – or tries to live – 'with the carefree immortality of the revenant'. He has experienced death, and feels that – unlike the rest of humanity – he is moving away from it, rather than towards it. A trajectory that is not reversed until he begins *Literature or Life* on the day that Primo Levi dies. His reader also rides the roller coaster of exhilaration and misery, with senses heightened, as if by a drug; all the while attended by an uncanny sense of untouchability (vanished since the death of his father – someone said it was an 'inevitable event' – the word 'inevitable' did it). He too has been spared insomnia or nightmares – at least until he dreamed his father's death. Like Semprun he remains curious, as well as stricken. 'It helps you to hang on in a way that is impossible to evaluate, of course,' he reads, 'but is surely decisive.' Semprun quotes Primo Levi: 'I felt a deep desire to understand, I was constantly filled with a curiosity that someone later described, in fact, as nothing less than cynical.' Suddenly his own cynicism seems more forgivable.

## EPISODE THIRTEEN

The material of fiction. While still in the camp Semprun and
other survivors initiated a discussion; how should they tell their
stories, so that people would listen, and understand? We must
tell the truth, insists one, with no fancy stuff. Semprun disagrees:
'Telling a story well, that means: so as to be understood. You
can't manage it without a bit of artifice. Enough artifice to make
it art!' Yes, says another; the essential truth of the experience can
be imparted only through literature. Later Semprun describes
the effect newsreel footage of Buchenwald had upon him. 'The
grey, sometimes hazy images, filmed with the jerky motions of
a handheld camera, acquired an inordinate and overwhelming
dimension of reality that my memories themselves could not
attain.' It really happened; Buchenwald was no singular nightmare. Even so, says Semprun, the film, silent and unannotated,
could do little more than turn the spectator into a sickened
voyeur. In order to convey the reality of the experience itself, a
writer would have 'to treat the documentary reality . . . like the
material of fiction'. His reader breathes a little easier; perhaps he
is not such a cold-hearted monster after all. Except . . . Semprun
has a responsibility to history, and to the memory of the unnum-
bered dead, while he, on the other hand, has no imprimatur but
his own loss. Just as an unknown woman donated her kidney to
revitalize his body, so the beloved dead have revived his career.
He recalls sitting on a log with Dr R outside the cancer ward,
discussing the disposal of his dying wife's organs. In the event –
given the systemic nature of cancer – only her corneas are taken.
And her death, which he reserves for himself.

## EPISODE FOURTEEN

The story of his life. Semprun may have favoured life, but literature was his *raison d'être*. When he finally returns to Ettersberg,
which accommodated both Goethe and Buchenwald, the best

and the worst, he is forced to acknowledge his dual inheritance. Like the Ancient Mariner he must tell and retell his story. His earlier visit to the museum where Goethe once lived took place in the first anarchistic days of liberty. He was accompanied by an American officer. They found the house in the charge of a curator with Nazi sympathies. So they locked him in a closet. This is the story that Semprun has to tell; of a civilization *sans pareil*, whose serenity is for ever shaken by a Nazi hammering on the cupboard door. Let the beast out at your peril. Pamela, who has helped Semprun's new admirer keep hold of life, is driving the two of them – father and son – to the airport at Lod. All week he has been determined to utter the word love, preferably as the component of a comprehensible sentence. Now he has about thirty kilometres to say something. He counts the kilometres; twenty, ten, five. Still nothing. Finally, as they unload their bags, he manages: 'Take care of yourself, there are not many people in the world that I love.' Fuck, he thinks, as they wait to board their plane, that was nowhere near what I wanted to say. The story of his life.


## EPISODE FIFTEEN

The answer. About a week before he flew to Israel for the Jerusalem Book Fair he stood in his attic contemplating the heavens. Hale-Bopp was unmissable, a spume of silver in the north-western quadrant. A picture-book comet, a fantasy from childhood made real. He could have happily watched it all night. No aliens contacted him, nor did he hear divine voices. Instead he was transported to the shores of the mighty Pacific, to the cliffs near Santa Cruz, from where he scanned the ocean for the salty exhalations of the grey whales. Whales are miraculous in their own right, fishy myths made flesh, but there is something equally marvellous about their presence in the sea, a secret life-force concealed beneath a blank sheet of water. Equivalents are the sculpture hidden in the stone, the words that wait to fill an empty book, the ancient treasure baked beneath a crust of earth, the secret bubbling up from the subconscious, the comet in the heavens – a celestial leviathan, snorting silver sequins. It gave him some comfort to observe that there was indeed something new under the sun. On the last afternoon of his wife's earthly existence – when she seemed entirely insensate – he suddenly became aware that she was expecting him to say something. 'Don't worry,' he said, without forethought, 'I'll keep in touch with your family.' His wife did not stir. Even so he was struck by a palpable wave of relief. So much so that he was moved to exclaim: 'It seems I've said the right thing.' He sought the comet night after night as it drifted by. The last people to witness it were the ancient Egyptians. Now it was his turn. What was humanity to Hale-Bopp? Nothing but plankton, sentient plankton.

PART TWO

•—•

# THE KIDNEY TRILOGY

# 1. MY LIFE AS A PIG

.•.

It is the end of the afternoon. The new arrival, a little boy clutching Captain Scarlet, takes one look at me and turns to the nurse. 'Mummy,' he says, 'is that man dead?' I perk up immediately. 'Of course I'm bloody not!' I cry. Nor am I Captain Scarlet, though my blood is having an out-of-body experience. It is being pumped out by my heart and drawn into a machine via a soft plastic tube. This is where most people with no kidneys end up. There is a variety of ailments that can get you here. I have polycystic kidney disease, formerly a killer. In fact, if it weren't for my mechanical organ, that little boy would have been dead right. Welcome to my secret life.

Other men sneak off to the apartments of their paramours to enjoy old-fashioned infidelity. I am more futuristic; on Mondays and Fridays I get intimate with a machine. Don't be fooled by the sign which says Renal Dialysis Unit, this is no medical facility. It is a bloody chamber whose woozy inhabitants recline like the denizens of an opium den, the better to indulge their most outrageous whims. It is a decadent brothel, an emporium of *fin de siècle* vices, a pit of sadomasochistic iniquity. No, my innocent friend, I am not dead, nor even sick. I am simply possessed by a depravity which, if it is not indulged at least twice a week, will surely kill me.

It is in the genes. Polycystic kidney disease was imported from Stashev, Poland, by my maternal grandfather. Three of his four children inherited the condition. Two, denied dialysis, died in the 1970s. The third, my mother, was luckier. She commenced dialysis in the mid-80s and continued with it until her death in 1993. And so, when a grim-faced specialist broke the news that I was following the family tradition, it wasn't exactly a shock. That was some years ago. The information made surprisingly little difference; at least it didn't until last summer, when my normal life came to an end.

In September, having been informed that my kidneys had finally collected their P45s, I was sent to see Mr T, a surgeon at the Lister Hospital in S—. The waiting room was full of fellow sufferers. There was an old couple I recognized from last week's clinic calmly browsing through the *Reader's Digest* while some younger counterparts seemed more distraught. The woman, an attractive blonde, clutched her husband's hand; her face was white and she was trembling. 'Are you here for treatment?' asked a nurse. The woman nodded. 'My wife is very nervous,' added her husband, whereupon the woman began to weep.

A doctor approached me. He wore thick glasses, and he had a very loud voice. 'Ah, Mr Sinclair,' he said, so that the whole neighbourhood could hear, 'you are in end-stage kidney failure, and you have been thinking about what form of dialysis you prefer. Is that right?' As it happened, he was wrong. For the past week I'd been trying to evade the subject altogether, assisted, it must be said, by the hospital's inefficiency. 'Hasn't anyone from the unit contacted you?' he enquired. I shook my head. He summoned a nurse. 'Right,' she said, 'follow me.'

There are two types of dialysis available: the familiar, vampiristic haemodialysis and the more mysterious CAPD (an acronym for continuous ambulatory peritoneal dialysis). The latter sounds much less fearful, less traumatic, and can be done at home; but it does require the dialysand to infuse a special fluid, which absorbs excess waste and water, into the peritoneal cavity four times every day. Alas, this isn't done via the bellybutton.

The nurse led me to a large room. In its centre, hanging like a grotesque fashion accessory, was something that resembled a flak jacket with a six-inch plastic umbilical cord. The nurse tweaked it. 'This is the catheter through which the fluid is admitted and expelled,' she explained. 'It's Mr T's job to insert it in your abdomen.' I tried on the jacket and peered in the mirror. It did not suit me. I definitely did not like the idea of sprouting a second omphalos in my mid-forties. Presumably I'd also sound like the kitchen sink, with two litres of that special fluid continually on the move in my belly. The nurse handed me a booklet entitled *Peritoneal Dialysis*. It had a rainbow on the cover. Inside were drawings of a man with various bags attached to the catheter. He was naked, but had no genitals. Were the anonymous authors sending me a subliminal message?

We were talking big issues here, so I decided not to be shy. 'How about my sex life?' I asked.

'There's usually some embarrassment at first,' admitted the nurse, 'but if your partner is willing there's no reason why you shouldn't continue to enjoy normal sexual relations.' My late wife would have been game, I am sure, but what is a complete stranger going to think when I start to look shifty on our first night and whisper, 'Before I take off my clothes there's something that you ought to know about me . . .' I remembered that the sight of David Bowie sans *pupik* in *The Man Who Fell to Earth* made me want to throw up. How could I expect a girl not to faint if she witnessed something even more grotesque?

Of course there were other considerations beside getting laid, but this isn't *War and Peace*, so we'll stick to the point. I was asking the nurse if there was any evidence that the alternative method – haemodialysis – caused impotence, when Mr T's secretary appeared and beckoned me to follow her to the surgeon's lair.

Mr T was invisible, being flanked by two opaque flunkies,

one of whom I had already met. All I could hear was a plummy voice that sounded on the point of demanding a Pimms No. 1. No one looked at me, let alone offered a word of greeting. The secretary and the nurse, who had tagged along, stood in front of the door, as if to prevent my escape. I sat down and tried to convert my apprehension into aggression. Eventually, after ten minutes or so, the bit-players parted like the Red Sea and the newly revealed Mr T said, as if to no one in particular: 'All right, roll up your sleeves and lie on the couch.'

'Are you talking to me?' I said, trying to pitch the sound somewhere between naivety and fury.

'Come to the couch, *please*,' said Mr T.

At first things went swimmingly. 'No problems here,' said Mr T as he pumped up my left arm and examined the veins. If I plumped for haemodialysis he would have to effect a subcutaneous connection between an artery and one of those unproblematic veins. The resulting confluence being called a 'fistula' or a 'Cimino' (after the clinician who developed the procedure, rather than the bloodthirsty film director). Incidentally, Mr T's comment was not directed at me, but at his sidekicks (neither was introduced, so I'll call them 'Glasses' and 'Moustache').

The latter, Moustache, then ordered me to unbutton my shirt and loosen my trousers. I undid the belt. It didn't suffice. 'We need to feel around your groin,' said Moustache, as he exposed his cousin, Pubic Hair. 'A big cough, please,' said Mr T, as he began to palpate Tierra del Fuego. 'Cough again,' he continued. Before long it sounded like Franz Kafka was in the room. 'What do you make of this?' he asked Glasses. 'A bit facel-vega, don't you think?'

Facel-vega? Had I heard right? Isn't that a make of car?

'Definitely,' agreed Glasses.

I was asked to stand up. 'Lower your trousers a bit more,' said Moustache. I dropped them a couple of inches. 'No,' said Moustache, 'let go of them altogether.' I was particularly reluctant to release them, although they were covering nothing. But I had no choice. My penultimate line of defence crumpled to the floor. I thanked God that I was wearing my Greenpeace boxers with their discreet dolphin motif, rather than my brazen Popeye shorts with the cartoon characters and the hearts. Not for long. With a single tug, Moustache removed them and Mr T grabbed my naked balls and ordered me to cough yet again. 'Yes,' he said, 'definitely facel-vega.'

I was thinking three things. 1) That I didn't like this Sloane Ranger fondling my balls as if they were kiwi fruit in a supermarket. 2) That he had discovered some further, dread disease in the body politic, such that my polycystic kidneys will be looked upon as old and trusted friends. 3) That the nurse, with whom I was discussing my sex life a few minutes before, would now be of the opinion that I actually had nothing to lose.

'No doubt about it,' echoed Moustache, 'it's facel-vega.' I can take no more.

'Would you mind translating?' I said.

'In good time,' replied Mr T, still holding my balls. Eventually he permitted me to pull up my trousers, informing me that I had the beginnings of an inguinal hernia, which would have to be repaired with extra surgery if I opted for CAPD. That settled it. 'In that case I'll go for the haemodialysis,' I said.

'I'm beginning to feel like a waiter taking orders,' complained Mr T, wittily, 'with patients saying they'll take this, or don't feel like that.'

'Better a waiter than the main course,' I replied.

And so the fistula was made. There were three of us in the ward who had all survived the operation. We shuffled around, our wounded arms forming right angles, outstretched and wrapped in white mufflers. We resembled a trio of trainee falconers awaiting the return of our absconding birds.

The doctor at the next renal clinic confirmed that Mr T had done an excellent job. The fistula was working well. When touched it buzzed like a live wire. In the trade this was known as a thrill. I had never seen this doctor before. He was wearing a black tie. Dr V (a name tag was attached to his stethoscope) was obviously not big on tact. None the less, I attempted to make contact. He had a pronounced Spanish accent. 'Where are you from?' I enquired.

'Colombia,' he replied, 'in South America.'

'I know where Colombia is,' I said.

'Oh,' he said, 'most people don't.'

I began to wonder if this man could be an ersatz doctor, an impostor, an out-of-work actor who had wandered in off the streets. Especially when he made the dread pronouncement: 'You must commence dialysis as soon as possible.'

The first time is like losing your virginity. 'You will feel a little prick,' said the nurse as she drove in the needle.

'Don't worry,' I replied, 'I feel one already.' Needless to say, the nurses don't regard themselves as sex objects. To them the dialysis unit is utterly devoid of erotica, merely a place of work. They obviously want me to stay well, but aren't particularly interested in the characteristics that usually attach themselves to that condition. In their eyes I am not a man, I am a patient. As such I am required to be good humoured, stoical, dependent, and sexless; *Homus dunkerqus*.

And so it happens, on occasion, when I am having the needles removed at the end of my trial, I feel soft flesh nesting in my cupped hand and realize that I am holding the left breast of my saviour. I don't blame the nurses for regarding me as an *it* rather than a *thou*, I recognize that they require strategies to retain their equilibrium, just as I do. I understand why they prefer to keep their real lives under wraps, but must advise them that their uniforms are much more charitable with their underwear. Like Andre Agassi's shorts at Wimbledon these tend to transparency. You can find out a lot of things about a person by studying their knickers, which I often do as the hours drag by. Forgive me, my sisters of mercy, forgive my voyeuristic impulses, forgive my petty attempt to reassert my masculinity, to convince myself – if not the little boy with Captain Scarlet – that there's life in the old dog.

There is just one escape from my predicament (excluding death): a transplant. At present the only available donors are the brain-dead, a much smaller proportion of the population than you'd expect. So I'm investing my hopes in Astrid. Astrid is a pig. Hitherto any xenotransplantations would have been negated by a protein called 'complement'. This is the immigration official from hell, the body's own Dirty Harry, conditioned to track down every scrap of foreign tissue and blow it away with the equivalent of a .45 magnum. Astrid, however, has been genetically engineered to develop hearts and kidneys that will sweet-talk and switch off this rejection process. She is already the matriarch of three generations, hundreds of descendants, all running around with what are, in effect, human organs. I'd be proud to call her Mum.

I am well aware that some have ethical problems with this use of animals. Supposing I decide to remarry (about as likely as a transplant). I can't quite picture my bride-to-be, but I can see my prospective mother-in-law with frightening clarity.

'Well,' she'll ask, 'is he Jewish?'

To which her daughter will reply, 'Most of him.'

Whereupon she'll want to know which bit isn't. So I'll tell her. The vision of grandchildren with trotters and curly tails will surely prove too much for the poor woman. 'Oy!' she'll wail. 'Fetch the rabbi!' Actually she need not torture herself; the former chief rabbi has already given his blessing to such transgenic procedures, as has a senior Muslim cleric. So long as the unkosher flesh is not ingested, the animal isn't forbidden; anyway, both religions regard the preservation of life as the most pressing and sacred of duties.

A more radical alternative is offered by David Cronenberg – an aficionado of metamorphosis – in his horror flick, *Shivers*. 'What we were trying to find was an alternative to organ transplant,' explains a scientist while chewing on a gerkin. ' . . . To you organ transplant is just yesterday's kishkas, right? Look, you got man, right? And you got parasites that live in, on, or around man, right? So. Why not, why not breed a parasite that can do something useful, huh? A parasite that can take over the function of a human organ. For example; you breed a parasite that you implant in the human body cavity. It locks into the circulatory system, and it filters the blood just like a kidney does. So it takes a little blood for itself once in a while, what do you care? I mean, you've got enough, you can afford to be generous, huh? . . . Look, you got a guy with a bad kidney, right, and you put the bug in. The bug goes to work on the kidney – dissolves it – the body assimilates it. Now, what have you got? You've got a perfectly good parasite where you used to have a rotten kidney, right?' Needless to say, the project goes horribly wrong; is sabotaged at the outset by the explicator's partner, who has an entirely different agenda. His aim is to free the body from the mind, the id from the ego. Instead of new kidneys or new hearts his victims end up with uncontrollable urges to fornicate.

Lest you begin to believe that I have been thus doctored, I shall forget about sex, and reveal my serious side. For instance, when the nurse runs tubes around my left arm, as she connects me to the machine, I recall the days before my bar mitzvah, when I was compelled to wrap phylacteries around that same limb, thereby dedicating my heart to God. What I didn't know then was that God was equally keen on kidneys. Recently a well-educated friend pointed out that in biblical times the kidney was regarded as the seat of guilt and, as such, was often the subject of divine scrutiny. I consulted the Good Book, and saw that he was right. 'O let the wickedness of the wicked come to an end; but establish the just,' saith David the psalmist. 'For the righteous God trieth the hearts and kidneys.' Later he adds, for good measure, 'The darkness and the light are both alike to thee. Thou has possessed my kidneys.' Jeremiah is even blunter: 'But, O Lord of hosts, that judgest righteously, that triest the kidneys and the heart, let me see thy vengeance.'

Most would regard this as an abstract concept, certainly nothing to worry about in this life. Not me. My heart is tried periodically with an ECG, my kidneys tested week in week out. I may pretend that the hospital is a whorehouse devoted to the pleasure principle, but I know that it is really a place of severe judgements. I go there because of my guilt. If modern philosophers are correct and there is no distinction between mind and body, then this guilt is a material thing, nameable and quantifiable. There is my creatinine, five times higher than normal, and my urea, a mere three times over the top. What has led to this guilty state I really do not know. Perhaps I am being punished for an unpardonable iniquity committed by a distant ancestor. Anyway, there is irony in an atheist (albeit a Jewish one) who has always regarded God as immaterial suddenly finding himself subject to a machine with divine attributes. Surely our nonverbal communication is a form of prayer.

The machine is my shepherd. It leads me through the valley of the shadow of death. It judges my kidneys and finds them wanting. Even though I am full of guilt, it forgives me. It effortlessly draws the poisons from my body, it cleanses me of sin. At the end of my three hours I am ready to return to the world, shriven, my soul like a newly laundered sheet. 'I'm done!' I cry. One of the vestal virgins approaches. She releases me, then unhooks a transparent bag, bulging with my filtered venom, and drops it in the bin.

Suddenly, as if in a vision, I recognize my crime. I am here because I am a writer. The entire process is but a metaphor for my craft. For creatinine read creativity. It builds up within, like poison, until I can do nothing but discharge it. Out it flows, lava from Mt Ego, streaming across the page. And where do these outpourings end up? Like my other toxins, in the bin. Poetic justice, you might say.

## 2. A MAN OF A DIFFERENT KIDNEY

•◦•

The telephone is ringing. I look at the alarm clock. It is 5.50 on a Saturday morning, hardly a propitious time to be getting a call. I pick up the receiver, hoping against hope that it will be a wrong number. 'Is that Clive Sinclair?' says a strange voice at the end of the line. I reluctantly agree that it is, and prepare for the worst. 'This is St Mary's,' continues the stranger (as I feared, a next of kin call), 'we have a kidney for you.' I can hardly believe my ears. Exactly a week after publishing an article in *The Independent Magazine* about dialysis and the possibility of receiving an organ from a pig in the indeterminate future, I am being offered a cadaveric kidney here and now. *Inter alia* I also boasted of my atheism. Is this God's response? If so I feel like St Augustine. Of course I want a transplant, but not just yet. Sensing hesitation the doctor points out that the kidney is a perfect match, a rare opportunity, not likely to occur again.

'So I would be a fool to turn it down?' I ask.

'Yes,' replies the doctor. I am no fool.

By 8 a.m., my affairs in order, I am at St Mary's in Paddington, West London. Or at least that is what the signs say. To tell the truth, I feel more like I have been abducted by aliens. In fact, the ward, on the ninth floor, bears an uncanny resemblance to the Starship *Enterprise*. The aliens, who man it, are obviously

a thoughtful race; not wishing to scare me with their true appearance they have chosen to represent themselves as heroes from
popular culture – my own heroes. So the Captain has the premature grey hair and humane gravitas of Jean-Luc Picard. His
Number One, by his side, is none other than Tintin come to
maturity (having found a better outlet for his skills than
journalism). Another reminds me of Gary Cooper, as he was in
*High Noon*. The remainder of the officers (whose insignia of rank
seems to be the stethoscope) resemble the good guys from
Bunter's Greyfriars. Head of communications is a dead ringer for
Uhuru.

I turn away from the bridge and explore the rest of the cabin.
It is packed with cots, all of them filled with Earthlings, most of
whom are supine and attached to a variety of bottles and illuminated machines. At the far end is a wall of glass, which I identify
as the viewing deck. The ship is apparently in stationary orbit,
high above London, below is a panorama that stretches from
Hampstead Heath to the Houses of Parliament and beyond.

Having allowed me time to acquaint myself with my surroundings the Captain rises. 'Welcome,' he says. 'Now, before we go
any further, we need to be sure that your plasma contains no
antibodies that will do in the donor kidney.' At once fellow
officers weigh me, take my temperature, measure my diastolic
and systolic pressure, draw blood from my arm, and generally –
like the God of Jeremiah – triest my heart and my kidneys.
Finally, I am assigned to a bed in the acute area. It is clear to me
that I am helpless in the hands of these strangers from outer
space. My neighbours are asleep or, more likely, unconscious.

Before I can manage either merciful state, I am handed a Bic
disposable razor and a canister of foam, and ordered to shave
from my chest to my groin. This gives me pause for thought;
how come such an advanced civilization hasn't come up with a
better way of removing unwanted body hair? I find a bathroom,
unbutton my shirt, and spray foam all over my upper body and
abdomen, until I look like a horse that has just won the Grand

National. I try to scrape it off with the razor, but only succeed in dispersing the foam more widely and flattening the hairs. I return to my bed to wait . . . and watch.

However sophisticated these aliens are on the home planet they seem to have retained a definite class system on board their flying saucer, something resembling a master–slave relationship. While the officers sit at the bridge, processing reports or whatever, hyper-kinetic factotums, most of them female, rush from bed to bed performing protean duties; I observe that they are chambermaids, handmaidens, comforters, as well as being proficient medical orderlies. Whence comes this overabundant energy? I can only guess. Perhaps it has something to do with that golden box on the bridge, from which they occasionally draw brown lozenges, which are carefully examined before being popped in the mouth.

One of them is even now approaching my berth, accompanied by John Lee Hooker. I look at the clock; it is exactly twelve hours since I first set foot in this place. The factotum holds my hand while the great bluesman begins to wheel my bed off the main deck and out into the long corridor. We enter a lift and descend to a lower level, where a woman in green overalls and a baker's hat awaits. She resembles the publicist from my first publishing house. I begin to wonder if my whole life is going to pass before my eyes in the next few moments. But there is no time. Before I know it, I am in the femme fatale's cabin and a mask has been placed over my nose and mouth. I am advised to breathe deeply. Without warning the doors of perception slam shut, and it's as black as a film noir. Everything has vanished, including consciousness and memory.

•◦•

I seem to be back on the main deck, in my former berth, giving a fair impersonation of Frankenstein's monster. Instead of the famous bolt, I have a triple line protruding from my neck. Two polythene bags hanging from my side collect the blood that is draining from the wounds. A larger bag is draped over the side of the bed. It is full of urine, the colour of red wine, and is connected to my bladder via the catheter. One of the factotums places some pillows at the head of the bed and says, 'Right, Clive, you've been on your back long enough, time to sit up.' As I raise myself with my elbows I realize these outlandish women possess hitherto unsuspected powers. They are also shape-stealers, obviously with open access to my memory, for now I can see walking towards me across the deck the living image of my only son, whom I lovest.

'Hi, dad,' he says, 'how are you feeling?'

'Better than I look,' I reply.

'You must go now,' says a factotum to my son, 'the Captain is making his rounds.'

We kiss. 'Best boy,' I say.

'Best dad,' he replies. And he vanishes.

Within moments the Captain is moving from bed to bed, like a priest leading his acolytes in some sort of religious procession. Only on these occasions do the aliens converse in their own tongue, as they probe the abductee and browse through the case notes at the end of the cot. If you are lucky, one of the officers – perhaps Tintin – will look down upon you and say, 'You are comfortable, yes?' However, when the examination is over, the officers relax and are even prepared to engage in conversation. After all, every abductee is also a learning experience.

But I too have a need to know; in particular, what happened to me after the lights went out. It seems that an especially skilled officer, whom I shall call Christian, effected the transplant. When he shows up to inspect his handiwork, I ask him if he would mind describing exactly how he did it. 'With pleasure,' replies Christian, sitting at the end of my bed. As he speaks I begin to feel like one of the credulous souls whose memory of alien abduction is retrieved by a hypnotherapist.

•◆•

I see my body, as through a glass darkly. It is on a trolley under spotlights. It is indubitably my body but I see it as if it belonged to a third party. My gown has been removed and padding laid the length of both flanks, strategically placed to absorb any spills. A pipe has been forced down my throat to assist my breathing; a line implanted in my neck to facilitate the entry of drugs; a catheter inserted through my penis to drain off the urine. Someone then does a proper job of shaving my body, subsequently painting me with what looks like iodine.

A masked man draws near. He is holding a scalpel. Only his eyes are visible. He proceeds to the first incision, a lateral cut, which exposes my abdominal cavity, though the peritoneum within is spared. Instead of being punctured or penetrated, it is gently pushed aside, like an unnecessary ingredient at a banquet. All the major vessels are now exposed. Those running down the leg are carefully dissected. That accomplished, the masked man, like an Aztec priest running backwards, picks up the foreign kidney and places it in its new site, leaving my redundant kidneys undisturbed. The two renal arteries are connected to the iliac arteries that descend to the leg, and the renal vein to one of my veins. Whereupon the kidney pinks up and does what kidneys were made to do. It begins to pee. The thing is alive! Urine spurts from the ureter at its latter end. At once the room fills with spontaneous cheers, and I realize that my performance is being witnessed by the entire crew. By way of an encore the transplanted ureter is connected to my bladder, all other arteries reconnected, and my belly stapled together with a surgical gun.

'So I really am a man of a different kidney, whatever that may mean,' I say to Christian.

'It would seem so,' he replies, patting me on the leg.

Later I feel well enough to read and unadvisedly choose *Flaubert in Egypt* from the flying saucer's infinite library. 'The best was the second copulation with Kuchuk,' boasts the Frenchman, before offering a vivid description, which ends with the words, 'I felt like a tiger.' Learn from my error. Do not read such stuff while attached to a catheter. The consequent erection nearly makes me levitate with pain. I look down and see that I have done better than Flaubert; I have come blood. If there is a hell, this will be the punishment reserved for fornicators; eternal attachment to a catheter. The damned souls will wander aimlessly, clutching their little yellow attaché cases, dreading memory and its consequences. I don't know if there is any causal connection, but within hours my testicles have expanded to the size of watermelons, and there is a hump on my penis worthy of a dromedary.

I reveal my affliction to Captain Picard. He has obviously learned the vernacular well. 'You've got a swollen plonker,' he observes. 'It's almost certainly excess fluid, but there's an outside chance that urine is leaking somewhere in the system. We'd better have a look, just to be on the safe side.' Shortly thereafter, John Lee Hooker turns up with a wheelchair and takes me to a distant chamber where I am laid flat, and injected with a radioactive isotope, which is swept down to my new kidney. This is followed by a diuretic, which causes me to pee copiously. A strange predator-like machine records the progress of the luminous dye, as well as my involuntary micturition. The procedure (which uncovers no internal malfunction) takes about forty minutes, giving me plenty of time to reflect upon my strange predicament.

I recall how, a couple of days previously, in an adjacent room, I had seen the kidney for myself on an ultrasound screen. There it was pulsating in the depths of my abdomen, for all the world like one of those exotic jellyfish on display in a fashionable aquarium. The swishing of my blood sounded like the deepest of deep sea currents. The point is, it didn't look human. To be honest, I've never really considered my organs to be an integral part of the Sinclair body politic. On the contrary, I've always thought of them as bolshie agitators bent on overthrowing it.

Consequently my own kidneys are as much strangers to me as the one I have just received from my unknown doppelgänger.

Not that I am an ingrate, for I have some understanding of the feelings involved. It so happens there is someone walking about at this moment with my late wife's corneas. I regard that donation as Fran's last good deed, and certainly do not think of the recipient as part spouse. I am an old-fashioned Cartesian; *cogito ergo sum* has always been my motto, I think therefore I am. Now I have to consider the possibility that I feared my body because I was ill, even though I didn't recognize the fact until my forties. Who knows, if the transplant is a success I may have to recast my credo; alter it to something like, I pee therefore I am.

Nine days after the early morning phone call, on 23 October, I am discharged and returned to *terra firma*. That evening I dine upon asparagus. Later, when I pee, the bathroom is suffused with a half-forgotten perfume. I sniff the air greedily. The next few months are uncertain, a lengthy game of snakes and ladders, as the doctors labour to outwit my body's natural desire to oust the alien organ, but tonight I am happy just to relish the unfamiliar aroma of asparagus arising from the toilet bowl.

# 3. KIDNEYS IN THE MIND

•—•

## 1. KIDNEYS IN THE MIND

Marcello Malpighi, the founder of microscopic anatomy, injected a kidney with a mixture of black ink and wine, and discovered within the cortex, 'numerous glands between the bundles of the urinary ducts . . . in the form of an ornamental tree, or just as apples hang on their stem'. Accordingly he called them *pomula*. And so we have our Tree of Knowledge. Now consider the metaphors used in spare-part surgery – 'harvest', 'transplant' – with their echoes of good husbandry, and we can picture the Garden of Eden itself. Yes, the so-called 'gift of life' has a long pedigree.

As a matter of fact, the world's first organ harvests took place in the land of the pharaohs. Like operating theatres today, a rigid hierarchy prevailed in the embalming room. 'Another stiff,' says the lowest of the priests, really a porter. 'A female, by the smell of it,' notes the one called the 'Scribe'. In those days husbands of women struck down in their prime preferred to let their wives become a little gamy, to stifle any necrophiliac tendencies among the mummifiers. Holding his nose the 'Scribe' marks the cadaver from the pubis to the hip bone (a line which, incidentally, mirrors the trajectory of my own more recent scar), whereupon a 'Slicer' or 'Ripper Up' makes the actual incision with a flint knife. Having completed his task the transgressor is verbally abused and chased from the scene with stones; a ritual that has, alas, lapsed.

Each organ had its own canopic jar, not unlike the thermos flasks used for storage these days, though not quite so anonymous. Thus the lungs were placed in an alabaster pot with Hepi, a baboon, on the lid. The stomach was topped with a jackal, the intestines with a falcon. Imseti, a human, headed the liver. The heart, however, by virtue of its importance, was left *in situ*. It would be required by the deceased in the hall of judgement, where it would be placed on a pair of scales and weighed against a feather. If the heart was too heavy, too full of human passions, the unfortunate supplicant was fed to the 'Devourer'.

The kidneys were not removed either, though for a different reason; no one knew they were there. Situated outside the abdominal cavity, and hiding their light beneath perinephric fat, they were invisible to the anatomical novices of the Nile. It is doubtful whether they even had a name, though some scholars suggest *ggt*. Either way, they certainly did not figure in the lists of organs placed under divine protection. Perhaps that is why Jehovah, always contrary, valued them so highly.

Here is the menu for a typical sacrifice (Exodus 29: 22):

Also thou shalt take of the ram the fat and the rump, and the fat that covereth the inwards, and the caul above the liver, and the two kidneys, and the fat that is upon them . . .

Grotius, the boy wonder of Delft, proposed that the kidney offering represented the abnegation of sensual appetites, an acknowledgement of impotence to the omnipotent, hence its importance. Some Aborigine societies in Australia likewise attributed great virtues to the kidney fat of their enemies; so much so that, when possible, they ate it.

As it happens, the carnivorous quotation from Exodus recalls another famous Jewish meat-eater, the hero of James Joyce's *Ulysses*. Chapter 3 opens with him padding softly around his kitchen with kidneys in his mind.

> Mr Leopold Bloom ate with relish the inner organs of beasts and fowls. He liked thick giblet soup, nutty gizzards, a stuffed roast heart, liver slices fried with crustcrumbs, fried hen-cod's roes. Most of all he liked grilled mutton kidneys which gave to his palate a fine tang of faintly scented urine.

Like Leopold Bloom, like the God of Abraham, Isaac, and Jacob, I too have kidneys in the mind. Not on account of their bodily services, but because of their other metaphorical life, which turns out to be a rich one indeed.

It is probable that the Children of Israel gained their knowledge of anatomy from preparing the sacrificial animals. However, the interior of the human body was not regarded as a soft machine, but as a place of 'psychico-spiritual experiences and activities', to borrow a phrase from Professor Franz Julius Delitzsch. A guide of sorts is provided in the Midrash (that is, the expositions of the sages). Here is their commentary on Leviticus 4: 4:

> Ten things serve the soul: The gullet for food, the wind pipe for the voice, the liver for anger, the lungs for drinking, the first stomach to grind [the food], the spleen for laughter, the maw for sleep, the gall for jealousy, the reins think out and the heart decides; and the soul is above them all. The Holy One, blessed be He, says (to the soul): 'I have made thee superior to all of them, and yet thou goest forth and committest robbery and violence, and sinnest!'

How does God know the soul's guilty secrets? The answer may be found in Psalm 26 verse 2. 'Examine me, O Lord, and prove me;' says King David, 'Try my reins and my heart.' The Authorized Version always favours 'reins' when referring to human kidneys. Deriving from the Latin *renes*, it is now more or less obsolete in English, though echoes can still be heard in the medical world, with its renal wards. The French, *au contraire*, stay loyal to their roots. Indeed *reins* remains an evocative if not provocative *mot*, as we shall discover in due course.

In the Tanach (commonly called the Old Testament) the heart is assigned attributes now associated with the brain; it contemplates, it decides, it wills. Even so, it often plays second fiddle to the kidneys, which, retaining their status as Jehovah's favourite titbit, are the intestines *sans pareil*. Scripture, maintains Professor Delitzsch, 'brings the tenderest and the most inward experience of a manifold kind into association with them'.

> When man is suffering most deeply within, he is pricked in his kidneys. When fretting affliction overcomes him, his kidneys are cloven asunder; when he rejoices profoundly, they exult; when he feels himself very penetratingly warned, they chasten him. When he very earnestly longs, they are consumed away within his body; when he rages inwardly, they shake . . . Of the ungodly it is said, that God withdraws from their reins.

They are, in short, the repository of the emotions.

Presumably King David, at least when composing Psalm 26, was confident that his heart and reins were in good order, would stand up to divine scrutiny. This is the song of a man with twenty-two-carat organs. Even in the Authorized Version the terms *examine me, prove me, try me*, sound like invitations to the Great Refiner to assay his innards for purity. In the original, however, the association is explicit; the Hebrew – *tzoref* – not only describes an ultrasound, but also the smelting of metal, generally gold. Thus the process, whereby the ore is released from the dross, is linked to a moral valuation, in which the heart or kidney is assessed for signs of corruption. In God's eye a healthy kidney is one from which virtue shines; literally, a rein of gold. A tarnished kidney, however, would betray a sorry state within, an organ overwhelmed by supernumerary sins. Not that the kidney is entirely passive; like a sieve it may purge the penitent soul of vice. It is doubtful whether King David realized that he was, in composing his paean of praise, making some advanced anatomical observations. How could he have known that a major function of the kidney was to filter urea from protein, creating another sort of golden rain? We often say more than we realize, leaving the truth of the matter lodged in the text's subconscious. Perhaps language itself is blessed with the gift of prophecy.

According to Professor Delitzsch the kidneys, in addition to their other qualities, also possess prophetic powers. He quotes from Job: 'Who hath placed in the reins wisdom, and given the cock insight?' From which he deduces that, just as the cock predicts the coming day, so the kidneys foresee the future. The Midrash itself is more circumspect. Taking his cue from Psalm 16 verse 7 ('I will bless the Lord, who hath given me counsel: My reins also instruct me in the night seasons'), Rabbi Simeon ben Yohai endeavours to solve the problem of how Abraham became acquainted with the Torah, despite the lack of an enlightened parent. *Instruct* is the key. 'The fact is, however,' explains the rabbi, 'that the Holy One, blessed be He, made his two kidneys serve like two teachers for him, and these welled forth and taught him wisdom.' This Mr Chips-like persona is, incidentally, very similar to that adopted by the narrator of a 1970 *Reader's Digest* article entitled 'I Am John's Kidney'. In the opinion of this self-styled 'master chemist' with the Quasimodo Complex ('I am quite unappealing in appearance,' he confesses), John would do well to 'listen attentively' to his promptings.

Jeremiah, a rather more aggressive pedagogue and prophet – in other words, the hyperactive kidney personified – is quite prepared to lecture the Teacher of Teachers:

Righteous art thou, O Lord, when I plead with thee: yet let me
talk with thee of thy judgments: Wherefore doth the way of the
wicked prosper? wherefore are all they happy that deal very
treacherously? Thou hast planted them, yea, they have taken root:
they grow, yea, they bring forth fruit: thou art near in their
mouth, and far from their reins. (12: 2)

Which is to say; the wicked may honour the Lord with their
lips, but their utterances are hollow; language and feeling being
dislocated. What, then, will Jehovah discover when he tries the
kidneys of these dissemblers? Poison, of course, nothing but
poison; poison and tarnished gold. The kidney's spiritual role
again parallels its biological vocation.

The oft-quoted Professor Delitzsch was a nineteenth-century
German theologian, touched by the new sciences of the mind,
but still uncomfortable about reconciling the 'actions of the
kidneys in secreting urine, with the psychical importance
attributed to them in scripture'. Worse, a 'mutual relation of the
function of the kidneys and the sexual function' had been
observed. The Professor doesn't name a source, but I'll hazard a
guess that he is referring to the seminal book on the subject, *A
Treatise of the Use of Flogging in Venereal Affairs also of the Office of
the Loins and Reins*, by John Henry Meibom, printed in Germany
in 1639. Although the original publisher specialized in medical
texts the English edition – dated 1718 – is clearly designed to
appeal to devotees of *le vice anglais*. The translator, a 'physician',
defends his decision to render the treatise from a scholarly tongue
– Latin – into a vulgar one – English. Black, he says – by which
I assume he means the garb of the priest – is no defence against
'the devil of the flesh'. Besides (he maintains) men who require
flagellation to achieve an erection are less likely to come to harm
than those he terms 'hanging-lechers'. *Plus ça change*.

However, the true purpose of Meibom's investigation – which
began as a letter to Christianus Cassius, Bishop of Lübeck, no
less – was to prove the connection between flogging and sexual

excitement, and to propose it as a cure for impotence. Drawing upon a vast knowledge of biblical, ancient, and contemporary history, he cites numerous examples of forcible resurrection. Poor Encolpius, afflicted hero of *The Satyricon*, offers the following description of his privates: 'The part of my body, in which I was formerly a very Achilles, was quite languid and dead, it retired, cold as it was, colder than winter, into my belly; and covered with a thousand wrinkles, and all looked more like a bag of leather in water, than a man.' Taking pity, the priestess of Priapus promises to make him stiff as a horn. First she mixes up the juice of watercress with southernwood, and besprinkles his thighs; then she takes a rod of young nettles and thrashes his nether regions. *Hoi polloi*, similarly afflicted, are compelled to seek less respectable practitioners. As a consequence an unfortunate cheesemaker of Lübeck, who dwelt in the Miller's Street, found himself having to answer for his sins to the local magistrates. He admitted that he could only perform the duty of a man when flogged with rods by his mistress. This wanton – called 'the Lübeck Strumpet' by Meibom – confirmed his account, adding that the blows were always delivered to the back.

Meibom is convinced that this phenomenon is physiological rather than psychological, and so begins his case with an anatomy lesson. Echoing Isaiah, he proceeds:

Now the loins compose the chief part of the back . . . Within are the reins, left and right, and take up the space of about four vertebrae, and are annexed to the vena cava and the large artery: But the reins receive as well from the vena cava as the arteria magna, large and notable vessels which are called emulgents, each receives of each side one vessel, a vein and an artery, which by many ramifications are variously dispelled into the substance of the reins themselves. On the right of the vena cava, just under the emulgent, arises the right seminal vein; and in the same place, from the arteria magna, arises the seminal artery, both descending into the right testicle. On the left, the seminal artery arising from the trunk of the arteria magna, and the seminal vein from the left vein of the emulgent are both inserted into the left testicle. Besides these, there are nerves coming from part of the spinal marrow, contained in the vertebrae, that reach to the reins, and not only pierce their coats, but penetrate their very substance. Lastly the ureters, produced from the cavity of the reins themselves, are inserted into the bladder.

What Meibom is describing is a soft machine whose end product is 'elaborating the seed . . . performing the work of generation'. He reinforces this claim with quotations from the scriptures and their saintly commentators. 'Kings shall proceed from thy loins.' (Genesis 35: 12). 'The son who comes out of thy reins.' (I Kings 8: 19). In his homily on Psalm 38 the castrato Origen understands 'My loins are filled with a loathsome disease,' to mean 'The loins are said to be the receptacle of the human seed, from whence that kind of sin is here insinuated, which is the effect of lust.' Likewise St Augustine maintains, 'That the pleasures of venery are signified by the word reins', which (if true) would give a welcome spin to the words 'renal unit'. Meibom interprets grumpy Jeremiah's request to be purified in heart and reins as a plea to be freed from concupiscence. St Peter demands no less when he commands his readers to 'gird up the loins of your mind' (I Peter 1: 13). Ghostly kidneys appeared in Leopold Bloom's mind when he felt peckish, whereas St Peter's mental loins obviously excite appetites not fit for the godly. A man with a reputation for venery was anatomized and found to have reins of progidious size. Certain authorities contend (no surprise to Meibom) that the reins were dedicated to Venus by the ancients. Hence the jest (now obsolete, I assume), that those who sacrifice to Venus purge their reins. According to the Roman polymath Varro the reins were also called the canals of the obscene humours.

Having established that flogging causes blood to engorge the member, and that the reins or loins are where the spermatick vessels rise, Meibom is obliged to establish a connection between the two points. Heat is the answer. Flogging the loins heats the blood, which increases the warmth of the reins, and thereby quickens the seed. This explains why lustful dreams and nocturnal emissions occur when men slumber in a supine position. Moreover, as the veins which descend to the testicles pass through the reins they 'imbibe a salt humour and an irritating faculty . . .' whose 'salt pungency raises a furious desire of emitting the seed'. Flogging is therefore to be recommended as medically beneficial, since 'the refrigerated parts grow warm by such stripes'. As far as I know flogging is not available on the National Health. Nor, alas, does the word 'kidney' excite lustful thoughts. In modern Hebrew (a language with a long memory) to say *musar kelayot* – literally, 'I have pangs in my kidneys' – means, 'I'm full of remorse' or 'I feel guilty'. Only in French is the legacy of Meibom still apparent; *elle est chaude des reins* is no medical diagnosis, but street slang for 'she's hot stuff'. It therefore came as no real surprise when a book entitled *Coups de Reins*, by the coquettishly named Marléne, turned out to have nothing to do with diseases of the kidneys.

It was at the top table of the British Library's venerable North Library – the omphalos of the scholarly world – that I opened the precious book and was immediately seduced by Marléne and her hot kidneys. Her likeness was on the jacket. I cannot better her own description. 'My dress was taut over my reins,' she whispered, with that delicious French accent, 'my bust bursting out.' No wonder she is subject to constant and violent spasms in the lumbar region. The cause usually being a foreign body, a transplanted organ of sorts, known affectionately as the 'magic rapier' or the 'dagger of vice'. 'Suddenly I had the impression that my entire body was jolted by a high-voltage current,' she records. 'My legs arched, my haunches surrendered to the urgings of my muscles, my reins shuddered ferociously, and a shiver shook me to the fundament.' This was not dialysis as I knew it. Having found their voice, Marléne's reins are prepared to express themselves anywhere:

> One evening, having just left the insurance company where, during the day, I miserably improvised on an Underwood, I found myself on the crowded deck of a bus. Suddenly, it became apparent that one of my neighbours, profiting from the crush, was taking a special interest in my outstanding charms. Indeed, an audacious hand was gliding across my reins, and sliding beneath the flimsy fabric of my summer skirt . . .

*Et voila . . . encore un coup de reins!*

Actually it is the juxtaposition of the typewriter, the Underwood, with the kidney that interests me. As in Jeremiah the link between language and feeling, the word and the kidney, is fractured. In Jeremiah the wicked laud Jehovah with false praise. Marléne too pours forth words that leave her cold. How to effect a reconnection? Jeremiah counsels piety and good deeds; Marléne, being more hot-blooded, favours sexual activity. It may not be strictly kosher, but it works for her. The fingers that manipulate the reins bring forth joyous sounds, unlike the hand that plays the unsympathetic Underwood. Marléne ends up with tingling reins, impaled upon a 'triumphant phallus', ever true to herself. The image reminds me, irresistibly, of a line in Ezekiel (9: 2): 'O man . . . clothid with lynnen, and an ynkhorn of a wryter in his reynes.' Would that I were that man, with such direct access to my feelings!

Wait a minute! In 1985 I published *Blood Libels*, an apocalyptic novel narrated by Jacob Silkstone, whose body is the locus of a civil conflict between an embattled mind and bolshie organs. He lives in constant fear of an internal putsch, a *coup de reins*. 'I see my devilish kidneys distributing the *Protocols of the Elders of Zion*,' he wails. I now know that the *I Ching* contains a similar vision of a body at war with itself. In those days (only a few centuries after King David is supposed to have composed his Psalms) a rebellious spleen was compared to an insubordinate servant, and a lazy intestine likened to an indolent son. By contrast a healthy body reflected a well-governed state; both being ordered and harmonious, with yin and yang in dynamic equilibrium. In which case my unbalanced hero, with his self-hating kidneys, was heading straight for purgatory. But maybe, just maybe, the anti-Semitic organs were trying to tell me something en route, were offering fair warning of a pogrom in the belly – mine as well as his. As King David knew about renal function (without actually being conscious of the fact), perhaps I was also dimly aware that encoded in my DNA were the dread words, polycystic kidney disease. If so I did my best to keep my kidneys out of mind.

Perhaps I should have consulted Annie Armitage, a character in Muriel Spark's *The Hothouse by the East River*. 'My new method is strictly bio-psychological,' she explains to a prospective client.

> I locate in the various organs of the body the psychological disorder and I treat the patient strictly on the basis of the defective organ. Right now I'm treating a patient who suffers from schizophrenia of the pancreas. I have a gentleman with a hyper-introspective bladder complicated by euphoria of the liver. I have under my care a manic-depressive kidney . . .

A genuine (or possibly genuine) case of the last named is detailed in a strange little book entitled *Kidney Breakdown*. This is either the accidentally revealing memoir of a dim woman who is more disturbed than she realizes, or a brilliantly executed postmodern counterfeit with the usual unreliable narrator. The author (called Rosie Bee on the jacket, and Rosalinde Innes on the title page) ascribes a lifetime of frailty due to defective kidneys. The reader quickly recognizes, however, that the fault is located elsewhere. Just as the ultrasound screen eventually revealed that my malaise was anything but psychosomatic.

In a volume entitled *Psychonephrology* one of the contributors, a real psychiatrist named Atara Kaplan De-Nour, describes the mental state of a typical renal failure. 'On a number of psychological tests,' she writes, 'patients came out as normal, which was understood to be caused by denial.' *Denial* is a telling word. It makes us all sound like red-handed prisoners hopelessly protesting our innocence. But Dr Atara Kaplan De-Nour can see through us. She has examined our reins. 'It's no use denying it,' I can imagine her saying, as though auditioning for *NYPD Blue*, 'you're all as guilty as sin.' Alas, there is no cheating destiny; eventually I had to own up, to accept the diagnosis. I had always felt like Joseph K. Now I know that, in my case, K stood not for Kafka but for Kidney.

## 2. KIDNEYS IN THE BODY

It seems that the Greeks were the first to give the kidneys their due. Galen, commenting on the doctrines of Hippocrates, wrote: 'It is agreed that the action of the kidneys and of the gall-bladder purifies the blood.' The Greeks (and the Romans, for that matter) believed that blood consisted of nutrients and *serum*, the latter being its watery lubricant. They further believed that the kidneys cleansed the blood by drawing out the *serum* via the vena cava and various other veins and arteries. Galen proposed four questions to explain this phenomenon. 'First, Does the secretion flow into the kidneys by its own power or motion? Or, secondly, Does it fill up a vacuum there? Or, thirdly, Is it propelled by an explosive power of the veins? Or, fourthly, Is it drawn thither by the attracting power of the kidneys?' The kidneys, he concluded, were like a tree, which sucks moisture from the soil through its roots. In short, they worked unconsciously, completely independent of their possessor's will.

Sometimes the attraction could be too violent, causing the kidneys to become instantly overfilled. The overflow was discharged, in its turn, to the bladder, whence it was expelled as urine. 'Urines offer signs of the parts from which they are excreted;' notes Galen, 'thus the urine tells us about the kidneys and ureters, the bladder, and the penis (especially in the case of bad sedimentary urines, those that are acrid, fetid, and bilious).'

> The best urine [Galen continues] is the most natural, of a colour verging on yellow or red, and, if it has a sediment, it should be white, smooth, and even . . . Of the sediments there are three bad types, which suggest the flesh is unequally melted. The first is when it is thick like lumps of flour, when there is great liquefaction and feverish heat. The second is when it looks like metal leaves . . . The third is scaly and bran-like . . . These are all excretions of semi-concocted humours . . . The worst case, the blackened urine, is a urine no one survives.

In all but the last instance Galen recommends diuretic drugs. 'And I really succeeded,' he adds.

Thus the system was purged of poison, but of poetry too; the once gilded kidneys, of which kings sang, were now nothing more than *sulci aquarii*, sluices or water drains. Reading the manifesto penned by John's kidney (the one with the inferiority complex) it is clear that this image has hardly changed in two thousand years. Listen to the lovelorn moan of the sulky organ: 'He thinks of me simply as the producer of an unglamorous fluid – urine – and as a kind of secondary waste-disposal unit.' This pisses off John's kidney. 'John's intestinal tract is not his main waste-disposal system—' he says with some petulance, 'I am.' Had he been wittier, or more poetic, he might have added, '*Après moi, le deluge.*' But these are prosaic times, when the 'master chemist' counts for more than the man with 'an ynkhorn of a wryter in his reynes'. Lawrence J. Kirmayer, a medical anthropologist, demonstrates what happens when these disparate conventions collide over the issue of a life-saving transfusion.

Part of what makes the patient's self-description unintelligible to the biomedical physician is the practitioner's tendency to take the metaphoric constructions of illness experience for literal statements within the empirical realm of biomedicine. Language is treated not as personal expression but as a transparent universal code. But 'blood' for the patient [who regards it as a carrier of possible character contaminants] is not 'blood' for the physician [who regards it as a neutral chemical cocktail]. The inability to see the metaphoric and contextual basis of discourse limits the physician's comprehension of the patient's life-world.

At the same time it must be said that I, for one, would look a little off-colour sans the discoveries of science and the ministrations of the medical professions. When necessary I speak their language; try to translate my bodily sensations into the aforementioned 'universal code', rather than the metaphorical constructions I usually favour. Even so, this may be a false distinction, as Kirmayer himself acknowledges. 'There is an inescapable circularity between the order of the body and the order of the text,' he writes.

Past infancy, bodily experience is most conspicuously elaborated and communicated through language. Language, in turn, is grounded in bodily experiences that provide common referents for a lexicon . . . How can we say the body is 'so and so', when that knowledge is worked out through language that imposes its own structure on experience and thought? On the other hand, how can we claim to encompass all possible worlds of meaning in the permutation of language, when bodily pain and suffering up-end our orderly lives and drive us to the most desperate gestures of faith?

Thus far modern medicine has enabled me to keep my lack of faith intact, though it has been a narrow squeak, for many of its advances are very recent. Our old friend, Galen, remained the voice of authority until well into the seventeenth century. For example, *The Method of Physick, containing the causes, signes, and cures of inward diseases in man's body, from the head to the foot*, by Philip Barrough, published in London in 1639, contains little that was not known to surgeons of the classical world. Here is Barrough on 'reines that send forth bloudie urine', clearly taking his cue from the Greek. 'It is caused through weakness of the reines,' he avers, 'which be not therefore able to divide the urine: or it is caused through amplitude of the reines, which straine out the urine from *vena cava* unto the reines.'

Let's imagine Dr Barrough attending a man – we'll call him Sir John Falstaff – who shows up complaining of a stabbing ache a little above the 'bastard ribs'. Nor does the pain stop there, avows the sufferer, but instead descends into the bladder and privy members. The doctor further observes that Falstaff's extremities are cold, and learns that the patient must piss continually and painfully. Dr Barrough promptly diagnoses 'inflammation of the reines'. 'Both corrupt humours, and stripes, and rubbings together, and drinking of medicines, do ingender inflammation of the reines, and specially continual and vehement ridings,' he remarks, suggesting a possible cause. This is bad news, but it could get worse.

> And if the inflammation increase still . . . commeth disposition to vomit, the gnawing of the stomacke, and vomiting of choler. Many of them are vexed and sweat until their hearts fail them. Their belly is stopped, so that they are puffed up with wind, and send out belchings continually.

'Think of that, a man of my Kidney . . .' cries Falstaff, 'that am as subject to heat as butter.' The *Thesaurus of Traditional English Metaphors* informs us that contemporary wisdom held, 'probably via augury', that 'the shape of the kidneys determined a person's type and temperament'. In other words, poor Falstaff's kidneys first compelled him to fornicate, and then conspired to made it impossible. Although Barrough is a medical man he remains familiar (unlike his counterparts today) with the language of metaphor. He therefore feels required to deliver a homily on Falstaff's lifestyle. 'Carnall copulation is marvellous evill, not only for ulcers, but also for all other diseases of the reines,' says Barrough primly, 'specially in old men, and in them that be weak of nature.'

As well as chastity he prescribes diuretics. 'What if they do not work?' demands Falstaff. 'Ah,' replies Barrough, 'sometimes (as Galen saith) you must let bloud of the arme [that is] when the inflammation is new, and aboundance of bloud is present . . . And if the pain be not eased by those things . . . apply a cupping glass to the loins and the guts, and searification being made you must draw out much bloud.'

In an appreciation of Montaigne, the French essayist (and contemporary of Falstaff's creator), Guy Davenport notes how the pain of his kidney stones was counted an integral part of his personality, as was the heroic search for a panacea. Thereafter, as humanism and science began to go their separate ways, the innards became an inconvenient secret, an invisible Siamese twin. 'Dickens' characters,' observes Davenport, 'have no kidney stones because they have no kidneys. From Smollett to *Ulysses*, there is not a kidney in English literature.' With Joyce, as we have seen, the organ makes a triumphant reappearance. Until then, however, our inner self, our secret sharer, was addressed only by scientists and eccentrics.

*A Popular Treatise on the Kidney*, published in 1839, appears to be a veritable encyclopaedia, packed with every known fact concerning the most 'wonderful and curiously constructed organ of the human economy'. Despite the overtones of Victorian materialism in this phrase, the old poetry keeps breaking surface, as the scientific discourse is interrupted by wilder and wilder paroxysms of religious fervour. It would be no exaggeration to call the book's author, one George Corfe, the kidney's John the Baptist. He is obsessed with perinephric fat, which he calls

'the log of oil' after the language used by God 'the Holy Ghost
in His word describing the various offerings of the Jewish
people'. Experiments have shown, he maintains, that a portion
from 'the bosom of the kidney burns silently, rapidly, and is truly
pure oil'. Thus anointed the kidney sits sovereign in the body,
hotter and holier than the heart, the very source of life, our
back-pocket saviour. This is the New Testament; the kidney no
longer a Jeremiah, but a portable Jesus Christ. I may be jaundiced,
but I cannot share this evangelical fervour; as far as I am
concerned my kidneys are back-stabbers, conspirators, would-be
assassins.

'No man is an *Iland* intire of it selfe;' preached John Donne,
'every man is a peece of the *Continent*, a part of the *maine*.' It is
impossible to ignore the truth of this observation when you
are connected to a dialysis machine every Monday and Friday.
Formerly closed and invisible your circulatory system, your life-
blood, quits its usual confines, and shamelessly makes a show of
its attachment to an ersatz kidney. How can you continue to
maintain that you are an autonomous unit, now that the hitherto
inviolable borderline between self and nonself has been so pub-
licly breached? Nor is the machine a passive partner; on the
contrary, it noisily assesses the quality of the product it dialyses,
and has the power to veto the procedure if alarmed by its findings.
It is no longer Jehovah who tries our hearts and reins, but
mechanical judges; one for the kidneys, and an ECG for the
heart. In addition to our dependence on the dialysis machine,
there is also our debt to the nurses, who effect the connection
and, when necessary, persuade the machine to continue cleansing
our unworthy gore.

A would-be wit, obviously under the impression that chairs
in a dialysis unit are on a par with those in Oxbridge, made the
following wisecrack: 'If someone didn't qualify for a kidney
machine, he wouldn't qualify to be a character in a Stoppard
play.' Actually Antonin Artaud's Theatre of Cruelty might be
a more apt comparison, 'a theatre which upsets all our

preconceptions'. Even Artaud himself was not entirely certain what he meant by the word 'cruelty' but, according to Martin Bright, it is connected with his determination to by-pass the intellect, and reach a stage where artistic expression could emerge unmediated from the body. Its prototype was the actor's cry which, Artaud believed, originated in a void of silence deep within the belly. Where else but the kidneys, the seat of the emotions?

Then I recalled the late Rosencrantz and Guildenstern. Like them I felt vulnerable, insecure, no longer in control of my future (as if I ever had been!). Not wanting to share their fate I invented strategies to retain my self-respect. This was, in fact, a common response. As Jon Streltzer observes in *Psychonephrology*, dialysis 'has a culture of its own, with unique traditions, customs, rituals, beliefs and expectations'. It's almost a cult, perhaps even a religion. I had joined because I had *musar kelayot*, pangs in the kidneys. The machine was my rabbi, my father confessor, who knew all my sins and forgave them. Others sought a more permanent relationship, a union in the 'till death do us part' league. Thus John Newmann (a doctor who is also a dialysand) viewed his initial encounters with the same 'importance as many give to the first year of marriage'.

At the end of my initial session I felt light-headed. 'Cold turkey,' explained Lucy the nurse, 'your body is not used to being free of toxins.' She was right. I hardly knew myself; a Sinclair minus sin. OK, I had lost my corporeal integrity, but I had also found a way of unloading my guilt. A fair exchange; I had no complaints.

I was on dialysis for eleven months; from November 1994 until October 1995. On Saturday 14 October, at 5.50 a.m., I received an unexpected call. By 8.00 a.m. I was at St Mary's, Paddington. Twelve hours later I was wheeled into the operating theatre where Christian Koo, the 'Slicer', was waiting. I awoke on the Sunday, scarred like an Egyptian mummy, but with a new kidney for my pains.

In the United States (and elsewhere, for all I know) it is common to celebrate such new dawns as 'rebirth-days', and mark their subsequent anniversaries with an appropriate cake. Perhaps it was because I had not been resurrected, was only a 'kidney wimp' (to use a dismissive phrase coined by *nouveau* lion-hearts), but I did not feel like throwing a party. I have no taste for kidney-shaped sponges. Besides, there seems something communionlike or even cannibalistic about such ceremonies; as though the celebrants were absorbing the organ's essential qualities to rejuvenate the guest within. Certainly many involved in transplantation see these characteristics as real and transferable. 'In our culture,' writes Lesley A. Sharp, 'each organ has an assortment of metaphors associated with it that leads to various patterned responses among transplant staff, recipients, and the latter's wide array of kin, friends, and acquaintances.' I hardly need tell you that hearts are associated with love, with courage, with inner truth, et cetera, while lungs exhale the very breath of life. Thus a middle-aged impotent can fancy himself a Don Juan, or a wheezy slow-coach imagine that he's now a whizz. I was spared any such association by the kidney's fall from fashion, its current cultural obscurity, its negligible symbolic weight.

Some recipients are convinced that in addition to the generic properties of the organ, they will also inherit personality traits particular to the donor. This is not without precedent. The hero of Li Yu's seventeenth-century fantasy, *Jou Pu Tuan* or *The Prayer Mat of Flesh*, receives a canine implant where it matters and becomes a priapic wonder. In James Whale's 1931 movie we know Boris Karloff is doomed from the moment Baron Frankenstein inserts a lunatic's brain in his skull. I have learned little about my kidney's provenance, save that it came from a woman in her forties. Is this a threat to my masculinity? Does it make me bisexual? 'If you see me sitting down to pee, you'll know I've changed,' I said to my friends (only to read that exactly the same joke had been made by a transplanted fireman in Indianapolis). Of course I continue to pee standing up; an affirmation of self, to be sure, if slightly less than heroic. In fact it is relatively easy to remain unthreatened by the incorporation of another's body part when you already consider your own innards to be strangers, if not mortal enemies. The doctors, however, insisted upon referring to them as my 'native organs', as in Native Americans.

Although I considered myself fundamentally unaltered by the events of that momentous weekend in October there had in fact been a revolution in the body politic; overnight the old constitution had been replaced by the new. The Chinese, as you know, thought of the body as the state in microcosm. The *Nei Ching (or The Yellow Emperor's Classic of Internal Medicine)*, contains a remark by a long-dead prime minister to the effect that, 'the human body is an imitation of heaven and earth in all its details'. We continue to see the body as society writ small, the only difference being that our century has provided a bloodier role model. The title of Claude Lefort's *The Image of the Body & Totalitarianism* makes the comparison sufficiently explicit. Dialysis had forced me to concede that the external boundary between self and nonself was elastic, but even so the *ancien régime* with its merciless securitat had remained unchallenged within. Lennart Nilsson, in *The Body Victorious*, describes the atmosphere behind the flesh curtain:

> Every body cell is equipped with 'proof of identity' – a special arrangement of protein molecules on the exterior . . . these constitute a cell's identity papers, protecting it against the body's own police force, the immune system . . . The human body's police corps is programmed to distinguish between bona fide residents and illegal aliens – an ability fundamental to the body's powers of self-defence.

When an illegal is detected alarms sound and the securitat alerted. The hit men – that is, the T-cells and the phagocytes – mobilize. T-cells are the macho crew, who destroy foreign organisms by

shooting holes in them. The phagocytes, a lower form of cell
life, are more feminine. They operate by producing *pseudopodia*,
or 'false feet', with which they embrace their victims, not unlike
the murderous Ms Onatopp in the most recent James Bond
movie. Meanwhile a pouch forms between these fresh limbs, a
process called (tellingly enough) 'invagination'. The result is truly
a *vagina dentata*, being a death cell in which the strangulated
stranger is horribly devoured. The problem the transplant team
has is to prevent such an attack upon my new kidney, to somehow
stop my native organs and their death squads expressing their
natural xenophobia – hence the need for an October Revolution.

As it happens I am addicted to Westerns. A few weeks ago I
took the afternoon off and watched Raoul Walsh's *They Died
With Their Boots On*, starring Errol Flynn as George Armstrong
Custer. In one scene Custer's 7th Cavalry are to be inspected by
top brass from Washington. But wicked Arthur Kennedy, an
unscrupulous businessman (are there any other kind?), has a
vested interest in destroying Custer's reputation, so he ensures
that the soldiers are supplied with unlimited liquor. Cut to parade
ground, following day. The visiting General is about to take the
salute. The troop approaches. Now I have seen the sequence a
dozen times, but on this occasion I viewed it with new eyes.
Instead of well-disciplined horse-soldiers turned woozy novices
by whiskey, I saw my squiffy T-cells – Fort Sinclair's main
defenders – and impersonating shifty Arthur Kennedy I beheld
the head of the renal unit at St Mary's (not a natural Trotskyite)
clutching a box of FK 506s, the immunosuppressant of choice.

In reality it was the Native Americans were quelled by a near
genocidal version of immunosuppression (they, rather than the
cavalry, being the continent's T-cells), but not before they had
their pyrrhic victory beside the Little Big Horn. You all know
how the film ends. Custer, the last Anglo left alive, is surrounded
by the Sioux, and seemingly swallowed whole by them. I identified with the fallen hero on behalf of my new kidney, which
will be for ever vulnerable.

The crucial clinical point about rejection for transplantation [writes Donald Joralemon in 'Organ Wars: The Battle for Body Parts'] is that the body never accommodates the presence of foreign tissue. The moment the immune system is released from its pharmacologically induced stupor, it immediately initiates an all-out attack on the transplanted organ(s). The boundary between 'self' and 'nonself' is, from an organic view, non-negotiable and indelible. Although the dosage and mix of antirejection drugs initiated after surgery may be fine-tuned over the months and years that follow, survival for the transplant recipient is contingent upon the continued suppression of the immune response.

One of the few immunologists to attempt to find a more pacific metaphor for the body's defence mechanisms was Ludwik Fleck. His circumstance – a Jew in interwar Europe – presumably made him reluctant to provide a biological justification for the Master Race and their Purity Laws. Another survivor, the writer-cum-chemist Primo Levi, likewise penned the following hymn to impurity: 'In order for the wheel to turn, for life to be lived, impurities are needed . . . Dissension, diversity, the grain of salt and mustard are needed: Fascism does not want them, forbids them, and that's why you're not a Fascist; it wants everybody to be the same, and you are not.'

I too have reason to praise and admire the alien in my abdomen. Forced from its birthplace, it ends up as a stranger in a strange land, a land populated by hostile natives. Despite the fact that it brings only benefits to the body politic it is not welcomed, and is only tolerated because indigenous prejudices are suppressed by new laws and policed by red guards. Nevertheless it can never be fully assimilated, and must live with the constant threat of sudden rejection. It is the history of my grandparents, the biography of every immigrant. If you want a metaphor for my kidney, for every transplanted organ, look no further than the twentieth-century Jew.

Having completed my research in the British Library for this lecture I went downstairs for a farewell pee. There, in the lumbar region of the Museum, where the air was heavy with the scent of urine, I saw the writing on the wall, transcribed by an unknown hand. It said: 'The Jewish holocaust was wrong in only one respect; the Nazis didn't finish the fucking job.' A few more lines from a different Theatre of Cruelty. I'm not fluent in Kiddish – the language of the kidneys – but I offer the following translation of the rumbled response in my belly, 'Now you know what it's like in here.'

Finally, I should like to assure you, ladies and gentlemen, that you understand far more Kiddish than you think. For are we not all transplantees, ripped untimely from our mother's wombs, and left to wander this unholy planet until one unfriendly element or another ushers us out? And are we not all children of Eve, the first transplantee, manufactured from Adam's rib? She ate of the Tree of Knowledge, which made spare-part surgery possible, and expulsion from Eden inevitable. Transplantation is thus the story of all our lives; here today, and gone tomorrow – or the day after, if our immunosuppressants do their work.

—•—

## BIBLIOGRAPHY

### 1. BOOKS

All biblical quotations are taken from the Authorized Version, save for Ezekiel 9:2, which is quoted from John Wyclif's edition of 1382.

Delitzsch, Franz Julius, *A System of Biblical Psychology*, T. & T. Clark, Edinburgh, 1867.

Epstein, Rabbi I., *The Babylonian Talmud*, The Soncino Press, London, 1935.

Freedman, Rabbi H., & Simon Maurice, eds & trans, *The Midrash*, The Soncino Press, London, 1939.

Kirkpatrick, A. F., gen. ed, *Cambridge Bible for Schools & Colleges*, Cambridge University Press, Cambridge, 1906.

Oehler, Gustav, *Theology of the Old Testament*, T. & T. Clark, Edinburgh, 1874.

Roth, Cecil, ed, *Encyclopaedia Judaica*, Keter, Jerusalem, 1972.

El Mahdy, Christine, *Mummies, Myth & Magic in Ancient Egypt*, Thames & Hudson, London, 1989.

Lamy, Lucy, *Egyptian Mysteries*, Thames & Hudson, London, 1981.

Reeves, Carole, *Egyptian Medicine*, Shire Egyptology, 1992.

Nunn, John, *Ancient Egyptian Medicine*, British Museum Press, London, 1996.

Barton, Tamsyn, *Power and Knowledge, Astrology, Physiognomies, and Medicine under the Roman Empire*, University of Michigan Press, Michigan, 1994.

De Lacy, Philip, ed, *Galen on Semen*, Akademie Verlag, Berlin, 1992.

Siegel, Rudolph, ed, *Galen on the Affected Parts*, Karger, Basel, 1976.

Barrough, Philip, *The Method of Physick*, London, 1639.

Cogan, Thomas, *The Haven of Health*, London, 1636.

Corfe, George, *A Popular Treatise on the Kidney*, Baisler & Renshaw, London, 1839.

Davenport, Guy, *Every Force Evolves a Form*, North Point Press, San Francisco, 1987.

Floyer, John, *The Physician's Pulse-Watch*, London, 1707.

Frazer, J. G., *The Golden Bough*, Macmillan, London, 1922.

Helman, Cecil, *Body Myths*, Chatto & Windus, London, 1991.

Levy, Norman, ed, *Psychonephrology*, Plenum, New York, 1983.

Meibom, J. H., *A Treatise of the use of Flogging in Venereal Affairs*, E Curll, London, 1718.

Grossman, David, *The Yellow Wind*, Jonathan Cape, London, 1988.

Innes, Rosalinde, *Kidney Breakdown*, Adelphi, London, 1993.

Joyce, James, *Ulysses*, Picador, London, 1997.

Marléne, *Coups de Reins*, Collection 'Citer', Mont Saint-Aignan, 1962. Translation by Anthony Rudolf and Clive Sinclair.

Sinclair, Clive, *Blood Libels*, Allison & Busby, London, 1985.

Spark, Muriel, *The Hothouse by the East River*, Macmillan, London, 1973.

Wilkinson, P. R., *Thesaurus of Traditional English Metaphors*, Routledge, London, 1993.

## 2. ARTICLES

Joralemon, Donald, 'Organ Wars: The Battle for Body Parts', *Medical Anthropology Quarterly*, vol. 9 no. 3, September 1995.

Kirmayer, Lawrence, 'The Body's Insistence on Meaning: Metaphor as Presentation and Representation in Illness Experience', *Medical Anthropology Quarterly*, vol. 4 no. 4, December 1992.

Martin, Emily, 'Toward an Anthropology of Immunology: The Body as Nation State', *Medical Anthropology Quarterly*, vol. 4 no. 4, December 1990.

Ratcliff, J. D., 'I am John's Kidney', *Reader's Digest*, June 1970.

Scheper-Hughes, Nancy, & Margaret M. Lock, 'The Mindful Body; A Prolegomenon to Future Work in Medical Anthropology', *Medical Anthropology Quarterly*, vol. 1 no. 1, March 1987.

Sharp, Lesley A., 'Organ Transplantation as a Transformative Experience: Anthropological Insights into the Restructuring of the Self', *Medical Anthropology Quarterly*, vol. 9 no. 3, September 1995.

Sinclair, Clive, 'My Life as a Pig', *The Independent Magazine*, 7 October 1995.

Sinclair, Clive, 'A Man of a Different Kidney,' *The Independent Magazine*, 25 November 1995.

PART THREE

•–•–•

# DIARY OF A
# SINGLE FATHER

# 1. WHERE'S THE BEEF?

—◆—

It's a family tradition to watch the Cup Final at Hendon with my dad. Seth humours us and agrees to join the party, though he's fifteen and a man about town (St Albans, that is, not London).

As we wait to turn right into Folly Lane a car pulls up alongside, on the wrong side of the road. We move out simultaneously, but the bend is in his favour. In an instant, mild-mannered Dr Sinclair has become wild-eyed Mr Sinbad. My hairy alter ego gives chase, honking like a banshee.

'What's the matter with you?' asks my son.

'I've got mad driver's disease,' I cry.

Seth resembles my dead wife, his late mother, never more so than when he is sitting beside me in the front seat of the car. 'For goodness sake, Dad,' he says, 'slow down.' Actually, I have to do more than that, because Dick Turpin has suddenly stopped in the middle of the road. He quits his van and marches in my direction. I lock the door. Fisticuffs, or worse, are not advised if you've recently had a kidney transplant.

'Let that be a lesson to you, my son,' I say sagely. 'Newton's Second Law of Dynamics does not apply in the quotidian. Actions do not always provoke an equal response; often they are greater, and, what's more, beyond your control.'

Seth was born in Santa Cruz, California. When he was twenty-six days old he saw George Best play for the San Jose Quakes. Alas, the magic didn't rub off. 'Who do you want to win?' he asks indifferently, as the 1996 final kicks off.

'Manchester United, of course,' I say.

'Why?' he asks.

'Because I'm Jewish,' I reply.

'I don't see the connection,' he says.

Footballers really need to know just two words, 'only connect'. They connect with the ball, I connect with the facts, which are these:

Like the Jews, Manchester United has its own creation myth. Instead of Jehovah and Adam, there was Sir Matt and the Busby Babes. 'Adam' means red. Manchester United are also called the Reds. 'Adam' also means man, as in Man. U. The Jews had their holocaust; so did Manchester United; the epicentre of both being Munich. The Jews rose from the ashes; so did Manchester United. The Jews had Abraham, Isaac, and Jacob; Manchester United had Charlton, Law, and Best. Redheaded Judas was regarded by many as evil incarnate, cf. the Red Devils these days. Their supporters are accused of being arrogant, triumphalist, and greedy for gold. Where have I heard that before?

The match, as usual, is a disappointment. 'Where's the beef?' asks Seth. Secretly, I sympathize. Too many processed emotions are generated by television, which has turned soccer players into actors, and the real thing into Pepsi. Instead of Brie, we're being served La Vache Qui Rit.

Not that cows have anything to laugh about, these days. 'Don't tell me,' says Seth, 'you're going to compare their plight with that of the Jews in pre-War Europe.'

'I wasn't intending to,' I say, 'but, since you mention it, the role of Germany is worth considering; whatever the problem, always ready with a Final Solution.'

'Dad,' cries Seth aghast, 'you sound like a Eurosceptic.'

'That was a low blow,' I reply. 'I would rather be reincarnated as a cockroach than a Eurosceptic.' In our house, Tories are considered the lowest form of life. An opinion confirmed when Mr Gummer re-enacted the sacrifice of Isaac, forcing his daughter to eat a hamburger to sanctify the Golden Calf. Since when we have eschewed its flesh. Now that Mr Major has declared war on the rest of the continent, we are, in effect, conchies. Surely it will not be long before beefy patriots with toilet-brush haircuts invent their own test of Englishness, and force-feed those who fail. And, when they have finished with us, there will be meatier enemies to face.

Victory in the World Cup is supposed to have assisted Harold Wilson in the polls. Unfortunately for Mr Major, England's team of graceless artisans (with exceptions, of course) has little chance of winning the European Championship. But that is no reason for the Tories to ignore the opportunities the competition provides. England's supporters may well triumph on the terraces, if not on the field of battle. I see them puffed up with prepackaged patriotism and shrink-wrapped burgers, all taunting the Froggies, Krauts and assorted Wops with their copywritten war cries: *Beef for Brits, Not Chicken Shits. Johnny Bull, Meat with Balls.*

Hitherto pariahs, but now licensed by the government and its propagandists, they will gleefully take on their traditional role of cannon fodder: as always, pawns in a larger game. Charging not at enemy guns, but at slices of beef which may or may not be the death of them. And all for a single cause, the re-election of a Conservative government.

But Mr Major had better beware, lest the ersatz autobahn angst he has provoked goes supernova; lest blood flows, blood that isn't only bovine. He must put on the brakes before it is too late. How? By making the supreme sacrifice. I'm not talking resignation; things have gone too far. There is only one way out; Mr Major must take the bull by the horns; must selflessly order a universal cull in the cabinet room itself. Only then will I be able to cheer England with a clear conscience.

'Dad,' cries Seth, 'you've gone too far. They'll hang you for treason.'

'Shut up and eat your tofu,' I say.

## 2. THE TRUTH IS OUT THERE

•◆•

'Do you mind if I go to a coeducational sleepover?' asks fifteen-year-old Seth.

'So long as I don't hear any accusations of date rape afterwards,' I reply.

'They're big girls, Dad,' my son replies, 'much more likely to ravish me than the other way round.'

My father, an octogenarian, telephones. 'Women!' he exclaims. 'I've just had a call from Lola, the one who went to Bournemouth. She wanted to know if I'd missed her. I said I had. That wasn't enough. She wanted to know if I had *really* missed her. I didn't know what to say.'

Nor do I. I'm piggy-in-the-middle and I'm envious.

'How's your love life?' asks the doctor, as he writes out a prescription for some new beta blockers.

'Since my wife died, non-existent,' I reply.

'Just as well,' he remarks. 'These are not exactly aphrodisiacs.'

So I name my penis Shimon Peres, in honour of the latter's limp performance in previous elections. But also in the expectation that, this time, he will at last rise to the occasion. No such luck; Peres loses for the fifth time. I should have known. His destiny is written on his face, which is not a vote winner;

too melancholy, too cerebral, no sign of telegenic sheen. We sympathize, my willie and I.

Actually, it is no dishonour to be shunned by the majority; on the contrary. For the election was but a rerun of a much earlier contest, also lost by the greater candidate. After Moses led the Children of Israel out of the Land of Egypt, they soon hit a few snags. 'A fine mess you've got us into,' wailed the ungrateful masses, unmindful of his great achievements, and suddenly terrified of the unknown. They rejected Moses, with his stammer, his invisible god, and his distant goal, flowing (so he stuttered) with milk and honey, and chose instead his smooth-talking brother, with his false assurances and his radiant god. The Israelites paid dearly for their error. Moses never led his people into the Promised Land, nor will Shimon Peres, but at least he has a vision of a New Jerusalem, a confederation of pacific states, which is more than can be said for Bibi.

Don't blame my Israeli friends, they all voted for Peres, as did Ruth Bondi, a friend of a friend. She is in St Albans for a couple of days, staying with a wine merchant and his wife. The lady pours wine from a bottle her husband cannot sell, not on account of its taste, but because it is called Château Tipsy. None of this is important; all that matters is the blue leather strap on her wrist. It has reawakened yesterday night's dream. I remember but a single image; a woman wearing a Tintin watch. I have such a timepiece; Seth bought it for my birthday. It too has a blue leather strap. 'May I see the face of your watch?' I ask the woman. She turns her wrist, and I discover the features of Thomson & Thompson, Hergé's incompetent detectives. 'Snap,' I say.

I tell the story to Seth. 'What does it mean?' he asks.

'Maybe there's a clue in the name of the *flics*,' I suggest, 'pointing my heart in the direction of your school.'

'Don't say it,' counsels my son firmly, 'don't even think it.'

'Why not?' I reply. 'Miss Thomson is a compassionate woman, and comely.'

'Dad,' cries Seth, 'please shut up!'

Relationships between parents and teachers are strictly taboo; better to sleep with your mother than with your son's teacher.

'Besides,' he adds, 'you're a cynic, you don't believe in anything, especially the paranormal.'

'You have stumbled upon a paradox,' I say, 'there is no one more superstitious, more susceptible to omens, than an atheist.'

'In that case,' says Seth, 'why do you keep mocking me for watching *The X-Files*?'

'Because its heroes behave like suspicious children,' I say, 'convinced that the grown-ups are withholding the truth, which is probably why you and your chums like it so much.'

'What's wrong with that?' asks Seth. 'Aren't most adults natural born liars?'

He's got me there. 'Even so,' I say, 'there's something rather disturbing about its paranoia, which bears a remarkable similarity to the world view of the freedom fighters who bombed Oklahoma. True, Mulder and Scully don't maintain that Washington is run by ZOG, the Zionist Occupation Government, but they know that someone, somewhere is pulling the strings. Nor do they trust the FBI any more than the militias do. Here's a good subject for an essay when you start Film Studies: *The changing image of the FBI in Hollywood, from saviours of democracy to Gestapo lookalikes.*'

'You're just trying to annoy me,' says Seth. 'Mulder and Scully are seekers after truth, not Fascists.'

Most of the girls in Seth's class fancy Mulder. 'What about Scully?' I ask. 'Do you think she's a babe?'

'She's cute,' he concedes.

'Apparently, the girls in Year 10 think you're pretty cute, too,' I say. 'I hear they're queuing to sample your charms, now that you've split up with Carrie.'

Unlike me, Seth doesn't require extraterrestrials to find him a girlfriend. He smiles. He dumped Carrie the other night. Just phoned her up and said he didn't want to see her any more. 'She cried,' he said, 'and she asked me why. She shouldn't have done that. A bloke would have had more pride.'

'No,' I say, 'she was right. The X-files may be fascinating, but the Y-files are the ones that matter. Keep asking the questions. Never vote for men who spread straight from the fridge.'

# 3. THE SPIRIT IS WILLING

—•—

I've nothing against ghosts personally; some of my best friends are dead. This does not make for an active social life, needless to say, but once in a while the departed do pay calls. These are always unexpected (for the deceased do not keep diaries) and usually occur at night. In fact it is after midnight when my late wife shows up. I can see at once that she does not know she is dead. Why should she? She looks in her prime. She has been absent for nearly two years; what else can we do but hug? I note that she feels unexpectedly solid. We continue in a conjugal manner, caressing and kissing, but I am restrained by the knowledge that the living cannot couple with the dead. My wife is hurt by my apparent reluctance. 'Go upstairs and wait for me,' I say. Meanwhile I sit on the sofa, at a loss how to proceed.

'What do you make of that?' I ask Seth over breakfast.

My fifteen-year-old analyst dips his spoon in the yoghurt. 'You miss Mummy,' he announces. 'But for some reason you also feel guilty.'

'That goes without saying,' I reply. Why guilty? Because I am a writer. Had I surrendered to the succubus you would have read all about it. Not that intimate descriptions were less of a dilemma in happier days. If the act were familiar, my wife would accuse me of sacrilege; if it weren't, she would wonder if I were researching elsewhere.

'I feel I know you very well,' a reviewer once said to her. 'Especially your organs.' Fran's look cut me deeper than a Sabatier knife. 'Yes,' he said. 'That Caesarean in your husband's new novel certainly read like an eyewitness account.'

Internal organs, not private parts! 'I invented the whole thing,' I replied, mightily relieved. 'Seth made his entrance through normal channels.'

'Is there nothing you wouldn't write about?' my son asks. Alas, I have no concept of the sacred. If it weren't for bad taste, I wouldn't have no taste at all. 'Nothing,' I reply, 'except perhaps the Holocaust.'

'What about other people?' he asks. 'Should they also maintain a dignified silence?'

A good question. Recently Elie Wiesel told an interviewer that as he recollected the unspeakable events he had witnessed as a child the manuscript became soaked with tears. This seems an entirely appropriate response, though perhaps the image would be more complete if the salt water cleansed the page of words altogether. Committing such memories to paper would thus become a Sisyphean task: a fitting punishment for writers who draw sustenance from the misfortunes of others. But how otherwise are memories to be preserved, historical knowledge transmitted?

'How about through the medium of synchronized swimming?' asks Seth. I try to fathom the *sequitur* in this response. The pool as a vale of tears? Unlikely. 'Are you taking the piscine?' I enquire.

'Of course not,' says Seth, somewhat offended. 'As it happens, the French Olympic team were preparing a routine inspired by the Holocaust.'

'You're kidding,' I say. So he shows me the evidence. It's there in the paper, in black and white. It seems that the all-women squad of precisely coordinated swimmers, presumably in fetching,

Frenchified costumes, were planning to goose-step into the water and then mime the selection, and worse. And afterwards, no doubt, wash the chlorine from their perfect bodies in the showers. I could only echo the words of a Jewish protester: 'There are subjects you just cannot deal with in a swimming pool.' Obviously the sirens begged to differ.

'No one complained last year,' they argued, 'when the Japanese team staged a re-enactment of the Kobe earthquake.' Nevertheless, they were ordered by higher powers to abandon the routine.

'What do you think, Dad,' asks Seth. 'Do you think they should have been censored?'

'Who knows?' I reply. 'Though I'm inclined to believe that suffering should not be turned into a cliché. On the other hand – or flipper – I can see no justification in limiting freedom of expression to sensitive types like me. Poetic licence shouldn't need an intelligence test.'

At which point – it being 8 a.m. – the letter box hiccups. 'I'll get the post,' says Seth. He returns with a manila envelope, postmarked in the usual manner, but also stamped with the motto, 'Working for English National Salvation'. It is another communiqué from the Dowager Lady Birdwood, recently hailed by a West Coast militia as 'the greatest living Englishwoman'. The mailing, as usual, contains an issue of her newsletter, essentially a digest of every defamatory article about non-indigenous life forms culled from the local and national press. In addition there is a leaflet which denies the Holocaust, the aim being to provoke an angry response, and thereby gain free publicity.

For a long time I assumed I received these reminders because I am listed in the *Jewish Year Book* as a writer and journalist. Recent events, however, suggest another possibility. I was watching the news with my father when the Dowager was featured, making one of her frequent court appearances for contravening the Race Relations Act. 'Good God,' cried my father, 'that's no Lady, that's my cousin Fima Smolensky.' Long thought to have been incinerated in a factory fire in New York, she had, it seemed, shed her former identity and built a new life in Acton.

## 4. THE SON ALSO RISES

•→•

Seth has spent the day on location with the BBC, filming a sequence for a long-running soap opera. It goes something like this. First a helicopter descends upon the Royal National Orthopaedic Hospital in Stanmore. Then an actor, strapped to a stretcher, is rushed to the spinal injuries unit. 'How serious is it, doctor?' he asks. 'Will I ever walk again?' The medic smiles. Good news, surely.

'Do you mind being back here?' I ask Seth, when I turn up in the evening to collect him. My son considers the question. 'No,' he replies. Why should he? How could anyone think unquiet thoughts on such a summer's night? The cerulean sky is simply too benign. Even so, I cannot help but recall a scene that occurred here two summers ago.

It happened in Ward 8. Fran – my wife, his mother, our holy ghost – had been resident since the previous February, when she had suffered a six-hour operation to remove an osteosarcoma from her sacrum. By June, despite a false spring, she was in desperate trouble. The consultant, Mr Pistol, asked to see me in camera.

'I'm afraid I didn't tell Mrs Sinclair the truth,' he said, holding an X-ray up to the light box. 'Look at this erosion. There is no doubt that the cancer has returned.'

'Does this alter the prognosis?' I asked. 'Is a cure still possible?'

Mr Pistol looked uncomfortable. No wonder so many people prefer soap opera to real life.

Seth's job is to assist the floor assistants, best described as personalities made flesh. Already he looks the part, sporting white T-shirt, Levi 501s (mine, actually), and a talkback (a headset with a tiny mike attached). Crew members approach and whisper: 'The kid's terrific, like a duck to water.' In reality Seth is still a schoolboy, and this two-week interlude merely work experience, but he has seen the future and he loves it. 'I only hope his dreams come true,' says my father, much moved by his grandson's enthusiasm. 'Tell me,' he says, 'how did you manage to get him into the BBC?'

'I slept with the right people,' I reply.

'People?' he says.

'Men, women,' I say, 'whatever it took.'

Seth is following a family tradition. As a young man my father frequented the studios at Elstree, pleading for a job; alas, he never got past the gates. As for myself, between visions of being the new Toulouse-Lautrec and a born-again Franz Kafka I considered becoming England's Ingmar Bergman. A visit to a theatrical agent put paid to that delusion. 'Are you ruthless?' he enquired. 'Are you a bully? Can you dominate a room?' Even then, I found it hard enough to be myself, let alone pretend to be someone I was not. Instead I elected to become a hermit and write books. My father, however, was more persistent.

'Have you heard of Paul Robeson?' he asks Seth.

'Of course,' his grandson replies indignantly.

'Good,' says my father. 'Not only was he a superb actor, singer, and athlete, but he was also a political thinker, a man of the left. In short, an authentic hero. Who is his equal today? Perhaps only Nelson Mandela. It's still difficult to believe that I actually trod the same stage as him.'

'You're joking,' gasps Seth, who has a proper respect for the giants of yore.

'It's the gospel truth,' says my father, 'it was, in some ways, the greatest night of my life. You must understand that in the 30s I was something of a political firebrand, eager to fight Fascism wherever it reared its ugly head. I didn't get to Spain, but I was at Cable Street when we stopped Mosley's blackshirts from marching. At that time a new theatre opened in St Pancras, called the Unity. It was a co-operative venture, dedicated to the cause. I joined as a stagehand, my main task being to lay out the costumes for the performers. It may not sound much, but it was quite important. At the beginning of 1938 we learned that our next production was to be an American play about working-class solidarity, Ben Bengal's *Plant in the Sun*. The sensational news was that Paul Robeson had agreed to play the lead, a character called Peewee. On opening night, I was summoned by Herbert Marshall, the director. He asked me if I was prepared to take a small part, which required me to learn two lines. The Goldington Street theatre was full of posh critics, more accustomed to West End extravaganzas. My heart pounded, my ears buzzed. "You bet," I said. The reviews were great, though none, I recall, mentioned me.'

'Wow,' says Seth.

Thanks to my son, I am allowed through the BBC's gates at Elstree. Unlike the pubescent girls who have gathered in their dozens. 'What are they doing here?' I ask the gatekeeper. He offers four words by way of explanation. '*Top of the Pops.*' Seth has been to a rehearsal, with his new friends the floor assistants. 'Paul Weller was great,' he informs me, 'but the others were disgusting.' As we drive out of the compound, and enter the gauntlet of jailbait, the precocious sirens all lean forward. Several wave their arms and scream.

'Who are they yelling at?' asks Seth.

'Not me,' I reply, as I turn left on to Clarendon Road. With the screams still echoing, father and son drive off into the sunset.

# 5. WHO LAUGHS LAST

Years ago, in the age of innocence, we would plug in the gramophone and play Seth old favourites. He loved them all, especially 'The Laughing Policeman'. I listened to it again recently, and wondered how I had failed to notice its decidedly sinister undertone. The lyric hisses with cat-and-mouse menace. Listen, if you dare!

'He opened his great mouth, it was a wondrous size. He said, "I must arrest you." He didn't know what for. And then he started laughing till he cracked his jaw. Ha ha ha ha ha ha . . .' Actually this is more like Kafka than Tom and Jerry. I question my motivation. Had it been my subconscious intention (against my late wife's better judgement) to turn our son into a tortured genius (like his dad)?

Ever since my wife's death, friends have been demanding a photo of her, an affectionate *aide mémoire*. Recently, I lighted on a picture that I liked. It was taken on an idyllic afternoon, a lifetime ago. Fran is sitting at the river's edge. She is wearing a purple T-shirt and shorts. Seth is holding a fishing net and wearing nothing. He is perched on his mother's lap, and his willy is at the exact centre of the composition. Worse, it is reflected in the water, doubling the offence. 'Would you mind if I have

this copied?' I ask the willy's owner. He takes a cursory look.
'Why should I?' he enquires.

Then it occurs to me that other folk might. Wasn't the
Hayward Gallery recently forced to withdraw a portrait of a
young girl from their Mapplethorpe exhibition because – as the
newspapers put it – she wasn't wearing any knickers?

I can already feel the horny hand of *le flic qui rit* pouncing
upon my shoulder, as I pick up the pix from Boots. 'I say, old
chap,' he purrs, 'don't you think you're showing an unnatural
interest in this young lad's private parts?'

'But, Constable,' I reply, 'the photograph was taken with love
and firm discipline within the family set-up.'

'In which case,' he says, winking at the assistant, and laughing
fit to bust, 'could you explain why you need twenty copies?'

Our next encounter is at the Mapplethorpe show itself, which
I attend with Seth. 'How old is that boy?' he asks.

'Fifteen,' I reply.

'So much for the innocence of youth,' he quips.

When I saw Mapplethorpe's X Portfolio at the ICA, x years
back, my biggest fear was that the sadomasochistic images would
turn me on, undermine my heterosexuality, and transform me
into one of the Village People. So I guess I am taking a bit of a
risk in exposing my son to the same in his formative years.

As it happens, he doesn't bat an eyelid. Even the image of a
biker using his lover's mouth as a piss-pot is sterilized by the
cameraman's classical aesthetic.

Seth's critical comment on that is brief – 'Yuck!' What does
disturb him is the fact that we are being trailed around the gallery
by a fellow who is probably not attracted by my looks. 'That
man is giving me the creeps,' he complains. It's time to go.

I certainly don't like the idea of a stranger stalking my child,
but I also wonder why paedophiles have suddenly become the
black sheep of the Zeitgeist, whereas the man who elects to use
the rod as a pedagogic tool is accorded heroic status. Surely the
loving hand, however misguided, is more benign than the agent

of pain? Not when you have a government which openly boasts of its sadistic skills. 'Yes, it hurt. Yes, it worked.' Words that hark back to Tom Brown's schooldays, when heads were heard to say as they whacked their pupils, 'This is going to hurt me more than it hurts you,' or, 'One day you'll thank me for this.' And they do.

It is the weapon of choice for the election of 1997. The Argentinians have been defeated, as have the miners; now it is the turn of Seth's less ruly contemporaries. The ploy may even work, given that the English resent children even more than they fear them; are, in a word, paedophobes. Consequently, the idea that their offspring should enjoy childhood is anathema. They are more comfortable with the vision of savages at war with civilization.

And so the Tories happily turn back the clock and revive the language of colonialism, transforming the younger generation into latter-day darkies, feral denizens of urban jungles. The fact that they have lived their entire lives under Thatcherism (both full-fat and semi-skimmed) is apparently irrelevant.

The Laughing Policeman flicks through his notebook. 'Investigations have revealed a dreadful conspiracy to poison childish minds,' he reads. 'As a result of which, all real teachers were secretly replaced by a pernicious bunch of hippies, pinkos, homos, and other weirdos, who worshipped the Antichrist, and preached anarchy.' Laughing his head off, he boasts, 'I arrested the whole lot of 'em.'

Having smashed their idols the conquerors must set about domesticating the natives. First, they will be stripped of their togs and compelled to wear the outfit of a gent's club. Thereafter, they will be civilized by missionaries, who will explain the difference between right and wrong, and instruct them in the teachings of Jesus Christ, with particular emphasis on the phrase 'suffer the children'.

# 6. GOOD GRIEF

Driving back from the Jazz Café on a Saturday night I observe that several lamp-posts have floral tributes attached to them. I turn to my companion, a psychoanalyst. 'What do you think about this new custom of turning a spot where a loved one met an immovable object into a shrine?' I ask.

'I'm all in favour,' she replies, 'if it provides people with a place where they can access their grief.' What is this thing called 'grief'? I picture it as some sort of internal acne, a pimple on the soul, which must be excised or let out, lest it corrupts the body politic.

'Even so,' I say, 'don't you find something distasteful in this colonization of public spaces? Don't you find this mania for display unhealthy? Doesn't it turn mourning into a cliché?'

'So what?' says my travelling companion, 'the purpose is to express feeling, not impress a passing critic.'

'Did you have a good time?' asks Seth.

'Junior Wells was great,' I say, 'even though he wore a toupee and kept forgetting the words. In fact, it didn't matter. The man obviously knows how to deal with pain. How was *Rabid Grannies*?' Seth and I tend to go our own ways on Saturday nights, though he is still happy to accompany me on my occasional jaunts abroad. So when an invitation arrived from our friend,

Professor Kenez, we both caught the next available flight to Budapest.

Peter and Penny Kenez live in California, Seth's birthplace, but were briefly resident in Hungary, Peter's native land. Their temporary home was a few yards from the Danube, where we promenaded as the sun descended. Later we celebrated our arrival at a posh restaurant, called Poski, which served a piquant stew of paprika and catfish. At the back of the smoky room, beyond the gypsy violinists and the plump singer, I noticed a menorah standing upon a sideboard, symbol of who-knows-what secret history.

After scoffing an order of strudel and sundaes at the Café Mozart on Erzebet korut we strolled the short distance to No. 26. Peter led us through a passageway that opened upon the interior courtyard of a five-storey building, housing some forty apartments. It was cream-coloured, with colonnaded balconies and classical ornamentation, the natural habitat of the middle class. Peter pointed to rooms on the fourth floor. 'That's where my grandparents lived,' he said, 'that's where I spent the last years of the war with my mother.' Being a shy man he added little more. I can only fill in the details because I have read his brilliant memoir, *Varieties of Fear*.

By 1944 there were forty-two people crammed into the apartment, and a yellow star above the gate. The children were not allowed out, so they ran along the balconies, and up and down the stairs, shouting their heads off. Could Peter still hear the cries, echoing through the silent afternoon? Or was he remembering a melancholy anniversary, that of October 1944 (after Germany had invaded its erstwhile ally), when home-grown Nazis, given the green light by the invading Germans, had herded the residents of No. 26 into this very courtyard and marched them to the nearby synagogue (still the largest in Europe), where they awaited their fate. In fact they were returned, without explanation, several days later. During the subsequent winter the army converted part of the building to a hospital. Since it was no longer possible to bury corpses, bodies and severed limbs accumulated where we were presently standing. Luckily it was a cold winter. Peter lived to tell the tale. How to commemorate those who didn't, without turning Budapest into Kitsch City?

Although Seth and I go our separate ways on Saturday nights, we spend the morning together. I drive him to the Liberal Jewish Synagogue in St John's Wood (picking up my father en route), where he attends Religion School. And so we are able to check out Anish Kappor's newly erected monolith.

'Does the world really need another Holocaust memorial?' asks my innocent boy.

'Certainly,' I reply, 'they make people feel better. A man visits one of them. OK, he thinks, I shouldn't have screwed my wife's best friend, but compared to what those bastards did to us it was a good deed. I call this Dr Sinclair's Law of Relativity.'

I see at once that this is different. Here you are not faced with evidence of depravity, but with your own image. The looking glass is a jet-black concavity, scooped from a massive block of grey limestone, and polished till it shines. This rectangular void, framed by the indifferent rock, inverts the image, turns the viewer into a denizen of a world turned upside down. The memorial is an invitation to remember, but it refuses to impose a collective act of remembrance. It requires the participation of the visitor. There is more. A window in the synagogue wall reveals that the memorial has been mounted opposite the ark, the holy of holies, as though the latter were being reflected in a darkened glass. Whereas the ark is filled with scrolls containing divine revelation, the memorial is as empty as a cenotaph. Thus the worshippers stand balanced between two polarities; between the positive word of God, and the negative deeds of man. On the other hand, it offers a generous niche, perfect for a vase of lilies.

# 7. MY BACK PAGES

**·–·–·**

'Did you remember the soup?' asks Seth.

'When you get to my age,' I reply, 'you start to worry about False Memory Syndrome. Was I actually abused by the au pair, or do I just wish that I had been? Did you really ask me to buy bouillabaisse because it looks like vomit, or am I going crazy?'

'Dad,' cries my exasperated son, 'did you or didn't you?'

I did. I went to the nearest supermarket and, having checked out the wholesome illustrations on the labels, and shaken the cans to ascertain consistency (can't be too runny), selected Tesco's own-brand vegetable soup as being most like the real thing. And so my son begins his acting career (as the legless groom in the St Albans Youth Theatre's sparky production of *Stags and Hens*) by spewing the aforementioned *potage* all down a fellow actor's trouser leg.

'Dad,' he asks on the way home, 'did you have a stag night before your wedding?'

'Certainly not,' I reply. 'As a matter of fact, I have participated in only one such event. It was the penultimate night of our undergraduate careers. So we all got a bit merry. Except for the husband-to-be who, as tradition demands, got blind drunk, threw up, and passed out. Next morning, he recalled that he didn't own a tie. Nevertheless, we got him, correctly attired, to the church on time. Fran was there, of course, though in those days she was neither your mother, nor even my girlfriend.'

At the end of that summer (the last of the 1960s), we travelled to the Isle of Wight together, to hear Bob Dylan and The Band. After that, we went our separate ways: Fran to St Vincent, to do good deeds, me to Santa Cruz, to further my education (and catch the Stones at Altamont). How, then, could I resist the lure of Bob Dylan in Hyde Park? In the absence of Fran, I took Seth.

A cold coming we had of it, though the month was June. Things warmed up quickly, however, when we were approached by a blonde. 'Have you journeyed far?' she enquired, revealing traces of an unidentifiable accent.

'A long way,' I replied, thinking of the Isle of Wight and all that happened after.

'Do you mind if I ask you some questions?' she continued.

Do I believe in free love? Sure. All sex should be gratuitous, otherwise it is prostitution. Dream on! The girl was from *People* magazine, and wanted to know if the tastes of a born-again hippie had been inherited by his progeny. Whereas all the man from the *Indie* wanted to know was her phone number.

Dylan, meanwhile, was roaring through 'Highway 61 Revisited', sounding like he'd just swallowed a Harley. Then he swung into 'Just Like Tom Thumb's Blues', with its evocative overture: 'When you're lost in the rain in Juarez, when it's Easter time too, and your gravity fails, and negativity don't pull you through . . .' Well, I found it evocative, having been in Juarez on Easter Monday myself. My first act, upon arrival in Santa Cruz, was to purchase a Ford Falcon. Some six months later, a group of us piled into it and lit out for the Mexican border. Among the number was Annette, dedicatee of my first novel (written after I had returned to England, and my muse to the southern hemisphere).

'Dad,' said Seth, as the old troubadour told how he started out on burgundy but soon hit the harder stuff, 'did you ever take LSD?' It was a question I had long been dreading, but in the end I had to tell him the truth, whatever it did to his image of me.

'No,' I replied. At least Dylan's reputation wasn't compromised by the presence of Prince Charles (patron of the charity we were supporting by our attendance). Bob's constituency consists of stoned heads, egg heads, bald heads, but surely not crowned heads. When the heir to the throne did show up, the VIPs in the corporation seats rose and clapped. Even the riffraff on the grass (there were 150,000 of us) waved and cheered. Cheer? I nearly wept. Instead of applauding, we should have been throwing rotten tomatoes and chanting Republica Britannica! Seth, knowing the consequences of treason, begged me to behave myself.

Hints from the Palace notwithstanding, I did not invite HRH to my recent book launch at Bernard Jacobson's posh gallery. It was an occasion for old friends, some of whom I no longer recognized, or mistook for other people. I bounced from guest to guest, like a pinball in a pinball machine, until a new arrival stopped me in my tracks, 'Hello,' she said, 'my name is Shael. I'm Annette's daughter.' Forget False Memory Syndrome; this was, in Kafka's miraculous phrase, a memory come to life. 'You look like your mother,' I said.

So does my son, lucky for him. 'I've just got a letter from Shael in Australia,' I announce over breakfast. 'The last paragraph concerns you. "I do regret not having spoken to Seth at the party," she writes, "but had to rush off to a show." Now she has a question for you. Would you be interested in writing to her little sister? Lorien — that's her name — is keen. Apparently, Shael fibbed and told her you were good looking. Well, what do you say?'

'Right on!' replies Seth.

## 8. JUST MY LUCK

—•—

'And there,' says my friend, pointing to yet another renovation, 'are the taps.' Not just any taps, of course. These, featured in a catalogue dedicated to the arcana of ablution, have been imported from Milano. I feign enthusiasm, but my friend sees through the disguise. 'Don't worry,' he says, 'the tour's over.' Why this lack of interest? Why, when our kitchen faucet suffered a fatal haemorrhage, did I send a plumber to pick the replacement?

To tell the truth, I have never been much of a fixtures and fittings man. Fifteen years ago, when we were between homes, my wife contacted the bivouac and said she'd found a house in St Albans. 'Great,' I said, 'make an offer.' She subsequently redecorated it; I merely picked the pictures. In effect, Fran was earthed, whereas I was a rootless cosmopolitan, ready to flee at the first hint of Cossacks without. I am, I suspect, the descendant of nomads.

I look at my son and wonder what he would rescue should the knock come at midnight. A photo of his mum? His Discman? Not forgetting the Leaning Tower of Pisa that accommodates his CD collection. It grows as quickly as Jack's beanstalk. 'Dad,' he said the other day, 'if you happen to be passing Our Price in the near future, could you buy me "Breathe" by Prodigy?' This is what passes for culture in Bedroom No. 2. Seth respects the written word, but tends to eschew the pleasures of bibliosexuality (that is, reading in bed), having heard that it can make you go blind. I worship the word, and read promiscuously.

The single, I discover, has a label affixed. It states: 'Parental Advisory: Explicit Lyrics'. I browse through the stacks, curious to see whether the opposite advice has been attached to the recordings of Leonard Cohen. I am joshing. I know perfectly well what 'explicit' is supposed to mean: rude words.

'I don't know if you ought to listen to this,' I say, handing the offensive disc to the sheltered lad. 'You have been taught to practise safe sex, perhaps you should start safe listening, too.'

'You're joking,' says Seth.

'Others aren't,' I reply.

'Why is it their business?' he complains. 'Why do they want to control what I hear and see?'

'They're frightened,' I say. 'They fear things are falling apart, but refuse to accept responsibility for the approaching chaos. So they point an accusatory finger at a portfolio of godless beliefs, spawned in the permissive 60s. "No wonder there is universal cynicism," they cry, when everybody else knows the true cause is that we are governed by a bunch of lying scumbags. Wittgenstein said that language limited his world. Our leaders have gone one better; they have created an alternative Britain, a logoland in which phrases like "care in the community", "flexible workforce", "falling unemployment", and "enterprise economy" have a correspondence in reality. Anyone who refers to the real world is denounced as a heretic. Unable to burn such types at the stake, they are using more underhand methods to defend the faith. Mark my words, the attack on "explicitness" is just the beginning.'

'So I can listen to "Breathe"?' says Seth.

'When you've finished your revision,' I reply. He is about to take his mock GCSE exams, and I have developed a split personality; I resent being an agent of the school, *in loco academia*, but I have also begun to exhibit symptoms of Einstein's Syndrome by Proxy.

It being quiet upstairs, I settle down to watch Manchester United play Rapid Vienna. Approaching half-time, the telephone rings. 'Answer it!' I shout.

'It's a man,' Seth informs me. 'He wants to speak to you. He says his name is Dick.'

'I don't know any Dicks,' I reply. I pick up the receiver. 'Hello,' I say.

'Hello, Clive,' he says. He clearly knows me, but not that well it seems. 'Do you have a big cock?' he asks, very polite, solicitous even. Just my luck: my first obscene phone call and it's a feller! He repeats the question. I am thinking: is this a chum having me on (a prick-teaser, as it were), or is it for real? Either way, the offer, when it comes, is admirably explicit. Either way, I terminate the conversation.

'Dad,' says Seth, 'what did he want? Why have you gone so white?' Have I? Is this how the easily shocked feel when pornography invades the living room? But they can always switch off the television or radio. Just as I put down the receiver. But there are differences. For one thing, I cannot stop the caller renewing contact. For another, the obscenity is personal, has my name on it. This is the real cause of my discomfort: the personalization, not the actual suggestion. Dick knows my name. That is the scary thing. And what do I tell Seth? The truth or an evasion (aka parental discretion)? 'It was the Boston Dangler,' I say. 'He made me an offer I was happy to refuse.'

'What do you mean?' demands Seth.

So I explain.

Much later that night, when we are both abed, there is a loud knock at the door. 'Who is it?' whispers Seth. I fear I know the answer without looking. At the beginning of the year I made a resolution to get laid in 1996. Admittedly, time is running out, but I am not that desperate to meet the deadline, nor did I have a man in mind. 'I don't know,' I reply, 'but I suggest we don't stay to find out. Let's grab our treasures and skedaddle.'

PART FOUR

⬩—⬩

# WRITERS AND ARTISTS

# 1. LOVE DEFINED IN THE FACE OF DEATH
### Review of *See Under: Love* by David Grossman

◦•◦

'My Momik,' David Grossman calls him, as though the epony-mous nine-year-old (the first section of *See Under: Love* is called Momik) were his little boy. He tells of how he recently took one of his little boys aside and, with some misgivings, told him about the Holocaust. And then I realize that Momik's desperate search for the facts about Over There is akin to another child's curiosity about the Facts of Life, and that Israeli parents (those whose roots are Over There) have two duties toward their children, to inform them about the Facts of Life and the Facts of Death, and that Israelis all have to live with this paradoxical knowledge, that every loving act has its dark shadow.

In one of *See Under: Love*'s most disturbing scenes Momik, now a married man, tells his wife of the education their son will receive at his hands. First thing each morning Momik will slap his face, so that he will learn that there is no justice in this world. 'Someday he'll slap you back, how will you feel then?' asks Ruth, his wife. Momik says he'll feel great, he'll know he's prepared his son for life. And she replies, 'But he may not love you for it much.' 'Love,' sneers Momik, 'I prefer a living son to a loving son.' 'Hitherto the Jews survived in order to live,' says Grossman. 'Now we live in order to survive.'

Momik has a mistress. Her name is Ayala. She is also his literary conscience. She urges her lover to take risks, to enter 'the White Room' containing the 'entire human, animal inventory, fear and cruelty and pity and despair, glory and wisdom, and all the pettiness and love of life, all that halting poetry', which she imagines to be the hidden heart of Yad Vashem, the memorial to the Holocaust in Jerusalem.

The author requires no such encouragement. David Grossman was born in Jerusalem in 1954. His father came from Over There, but as a child in the early 1930s. In short, *See Under: Love* is not autobiographical. The immediate details of Momik's life are not congruent with those of their author. Rather, the novel is an exercise in *impersonation*. Indeed, it contains a character called Malkiel Zeidman, a biographer, who is blessed or cursed with the ability to enter other people's lives at will – both a role model and a terrible warning.

This is not to deny that the novel lacks substance from the author's life. Grossman apologetically quotes an incident from his own wedding (which reappears in the book) when an elderly aunt, not wishing to cast a shadow upon the proceedings, arrived with a Band-Aid stuck over her concentration camp number. The plaster mesmerized Grossman, as the familiar tattoo would not have done. *See Under: Love* may be seen as a determined lifting of that plaster. Grossman has made a habit of peeling away the camouflage that obfuscates Israel's more painful wounds. His first book, *The Smile of the Lamb*, concerns the occupation of the West Bank, as does his third, *The Yellow Wind*.

For a writer of fiction, however, the Holocaust is a far greater taboo than the question of Palestine. When Aharon Appelfeld published *The Age of Wonders* Gabriel Josipovici declared: 'With this book post-war writing has come of age.' Appelfeld's novel (which Grossman also admires) is divided into two parts. The opening, a first-person narration in the manner of a *Bildungsroman*, tells of a boy's growing difficulties with his family and, more especially, with pre-War Austria. Such narratives are naturally optimistic. This one, however, breaks off suddenly: 'By the next day we were on the cattle train hurtling south.'

The concluding part begins with the legend, 'Many years later when everything was over.' The narrative, which has switched to the third person, describes the erstwhile storyteller's return from Israel to his native land. The voice is now jagged and disjointed, threatened and threatening. Blank pages divide the two sections. They convey the unbridgeable gap between before and after, and symbolize the missing link between European and Israeli writing. Was it not European culture that beguiled, then betrayed the Jews? Appelfeld's decision to maintain a fictional silence on the precise events of the Holocaust is doubly daunting; because of his great stature as a writer, and because he possesses the moral authority of a survivor.

Nonetheless, David Grossman has dared to fill in those blank pages. His purpose is not to add further details to a well-documented period, but to provide his generation with what he calls 'emotional facts', without which it cannot fully comprehend itself. Therefore Momik does not describe events so much as *re-imagine* them. In so doing he must become both murderer and victim, take the risk of releasing the Nazi Beast within himself (far from doing that he manages to discover a spark of humanity in the Beast itself). By writing *See Under: Love* Grossman-Momik has provided a novel that is both European and Israeli, the missing link itself.

The connecting figure is Bruno Schulz, 'Possibly the most important Polish writer between the two world wars.' Schulz was first brought to Grossman's attention by a reader who observed the Polish writer's influence in *The Smile of the Lamb*. Grossman subsequently devoured the unknown author's two surviving books: *The Street of Crocodiles* and *Sanatorium Under the Sign of the Hourglass*.

Bruno Schulz was murdered by the Nazis on 19 November 1942. To be specific he was casually shot on the streets of Drohobycz by a Gestapo officer named Karl Gunther for no other reason than he was the enemy of Schulz's protector, an SS officer called Landau. Having shot Schulz Gunther is supposed to have said to Landau: 'I killed your Jew.' To which Landau is reported to have replied: 'In that case, I will now kill your Jew.' Incidentally, this scene reappears in Philip Roth's *The Prague Orgy* and Cynthia Ozick's *The Messiah of Stockholm* (in which a Swedish critic fancies himself Schulz's long lost son).

Bruno Schulz can no longer assert his humanity, so Grossman has resolved to do it on his behalf. He rescues Schulz from the Nazis and has him jump off the pier at Danzig, whereupon he is transformed into a salmon. A salmon, writes Grossman in a miraculous phrase, is a journey incarnate. This image incorporates both the difficult return of the Jews to their place of birth and, more fundamentally, their return (against all of history's contrary currents) to Zion. It also represents the artistic derring-do Ayala has been demanding of Momik, the exercise that earns him the right to confront the Holocaust.

*See Under: Love* is divided into four parts. In the first (already mentioned), nine-year-old Momik, precociously bowed down by the inexplicable agonies that afflict his parents and their neighbours, desperately tries to reconstruct Over There and thereby comprehend the catastrophe that has rendered them inarticulate.

Out of the blue Momik's great-uncle is dumped upon his family by the authorities. This ancient revenant is even more silent than his peers and is regarded as a burden by all save Momik who, having just lost his last grandparent, looks upon the new arrival as a replacement. Once upon a time this dumbstruck witness was the writer Anshel Wasserman, popular chronicler of *The Children of the Heart*. Rooting in the cellar Momik discovers a fragment from one of his stories, and through that sees a way to recover the past. Hitherto his experiments have been zoological as much as literary. Hearing a neighbour talk about the Nazi Beast, he takes her at her word and tries to raise one from a menagerie of strays that he keeps underground.

The second part, the novel's heart, tells Bruno Schulz's fishy tale. It provides the inspiration for the third part, entitled Wasserman, in which Momik, mixing 'real' characters from his surrogate grandfather's adventure stories, recreates the old man's concentration camp experiences. Unable to die by gas or by bullet Wasserman ends up as the commandant's Scheherazade (though, as his name suggests, he is more of an Ancient Mariner), simultaneously reviving and entrapping the Nazi's soul with the story of Kazik, the marvellous baby who experiences a complete existence, from birth through maturity to death, in a single day.

The story is continued in the fourth part, though in a remarkable way. Here David Grossman weaves a coherent narrative out of an encyclopedia, to be precise The Complete Encyclopedia of Kazik's Life. Here Neigel, the Nazi, begs Wasserman – as a father – to spare Kazik and the other (now mature) Children of the Heart. Wasserman informs Neigel that he showed no such mercy when he shot his only child, a little girl, as heartlessly as the Gestapo officer killed Bruno Schulz. Neigel, humanized, can no longer live with such information. 'Believe me, Wasserman,' he says, 'I love children.' The penultimate entry is given to hypercritical Ayala who begs Momik to write with mercy and love. 'Not See Under: Love, Shlomik! Go love. Love!' Look under Love in the encyclopedia and you'll find, See Under: Sex. Look under Sex and you'll find, of course, See Under: Love. And yet Grossman–Momik has fulfilled Ayala's command, for the whole book is a brave and moving attempt by an outstandingly talented writer to redefine love, having looked the Facts of Death full in the face.

## 2. AN INTRODUCTION TO *ENEMIES: A LOVE STORY*
### by Isaac Bashevis Singer

•—•

'When I began to write myself, my brother, Israel Joshua, encouraged me and he gave me certain rules for writing,' Isaac Bashevis Singer once told an interviewer. 'He said: when you write tell a story, and don't try to explain the story. If you say that a boy fell in love with a girl you don't have to explain to the reader why a boy falls in love, the reader knows just as much about love as you do or more so. You tell him the story, and the explanations and interpretations he will make himself, or critics will do it for him. He had two words which he used: *images* and *sayings*. Sayings were for him essays, interpretations. He called sayings *zugerts*. It means you just talk, you just say things. You don't paint a picture, or bring out an image. He said, leave the *zugerts* to the others. You tell them a story.'

In *Enemies: A Love Story* he tells the tale of Herman Broder, who loved not one but three women. If you are impatient, and want the entertainment to begin, proceed directly to Chapter One. However, if it's *zugerts* that you want, read on.

Isaac Bashevis Singer was born on 14 July 1904 in the small Polish shtetl of Leoncin, where his father, Pinchos Mendel, was the unofficial rabbi. His early struggles are briefly sketched in an autobiographical volume entitled *A Little Boy in Search of God*. In this he tells how he quit the family home (by now in the 'half bog, half village' named Dzikow) and made his way to Warsaw, where his mentor, Israel Joshua, had become the co-editor of *Literarishe Bletter* (*Literary Pages*).

Another of the editors, a poet named Melech Ravitch, provided him with a roof. 'Ravitch believed with absolute faith that the world of justice could come today or tomorrow,' wrote Singer. 'All men would become brothers and, sooner or later, vegetarians too. There would be no Jews, no Gentiles, only a single united mankind whose goal would be equality and progress. Literature, Ravitch felt, could help hasten this joyous epoch.' Needless to say these optimistic sentiments do not inform *Enemies: A Love Story*, nor any of Singer's other novels.

Nevertheless, Ravitch had a profound influence upon his lodger (not least in his dietary habits), and they remained friends until the end of the former's long life. The epistolary evidence may be examined at the Hebrew University in Jerusalem, which was presented with Melech Ravitch's papers shortly after the poet's death in 1976.

To reach the archive, it is necessary to find your way through the windowless catacombs of the university's cavernous old library, until you reach an equally windowless room full of numbered boxes, one of which contains the uncompleted manuscript of a boulevard comedy, the joint effort of Singer and Ravitch. It is, as it were, the *Ur*-edition of *Enemies: A Love Story*.

Since Melech Ravitch left Warsaw for good in 1932, the play must have been written in 1931 at the very latest. The curator, who extracted the document at my request, possessed a tongue that could bring the dead to life. 'They wanted a money-spinner,' he explained. 'A hit. And how do you do it? By putting in a lot of hot stuff. Free love was a great fantasy for these boys from Hasidic or backwoods communities, and the drama was supposed to play out these fantasies – a lot of sex, night after night.'

The manuscript is mainly in Singer's own hand. He apparently wrote the dialogue, having a better ear for speech, while Ravitch provided ideas for the plot, which became so complicated that it would have taken five nights to resolve. There are notes on scraps of paper throughout the manuscript, as well as sketches indicating the actual staging. Its working title was *The Man with Three Wives*.

Closer investigation reveals this to be something of an understatement; the eponymous hero (the proto-Herman Broder) has at least four bedmates, the last being known as 'the fifth wheel on the wagon'. Alas, this heartless philanderer has a very low opinion of women (if not of human nature in its entirety); when he wants to test the fidelity of a favourite he does so by showering her with love, in the belief that this will inevitably prompt a perverse reaction.

Although the play was soon abandoned and never performed, it clearly made a lasting impression upon Singer; for polygamy was to become one of the dominant themes in his work, fully orchestrated in such masterpieces as *Enemies: A Love Story* and *The Magician of Lublin* (whose hero, Yasha Mazur, could never understand 'how other people managed to live and spend their entire lives with one woman without becoming melancholy').

A minor variation may also be found in a story entitled 'The Betrayer of Israel', one of an autobiographical sequence that relates to Singer's early years when his father was a poor rabbi on Krochmalna Street, in the heart of Warsaw's Jewish quarter. Young Isaac listens spellbound while the sins of Koppel Mitzner are enumerated. To be precise, Koppel has four wives. Finally, he runs off with the youngest, whereupon the rebbetzin gives her son an angry look, 'as if she suspected that I envied Koppel his journey, and, who knows, perhaps even his companion'. ' "Such depravities are not for you!" ' she cautioned. But they were − by the end of the tale it is not clear who is the bigger traitor, Koppel, or Isaac the future scribe, contaminated by association.

Sexual conquest and storytelling are thus intimately linked, both being irresistible but morally dubious, like the apple Eve handed Adam. Singer's father, that pious man who worshipped one God and had but one wife, called secular literature 'sweetened poison'. The description also serves to define his son's attitude towards women.

Singer's subject matter was clear from the beginning of his career – the conflict between carnal desire and morality. However, his means of expression was less certain. Obviously it was impossible to contemplate a boulevard comedy when, elsewhere, his fellow Jews were being made to wash the pavements. Instead he wrote a fierce novel about messianic fervour and sexual hysteria. *Satan in Goray* was published in 1935, by which time its author had left Poland for America, abandoning a wife and child – his only son – in the process.

There followed years of distress, during which Singer was unable to write anything except trivial articles for *Forverts* (Abe Cahan's great Yiddish newspaper). Under the pen-name of Warshavsky he scribbled sketches, under that of Segal he published pseudo-scientific pieces, which usually revolved around sex. 'Whatever you do,' advised Ravitch, recognizing his friend's despair, 'don't return to Polenu.'

After the war (and his brother's death from a heart attack), Singer wrote the following to his old friend and collaborator: 'Let's do something! Masada died a heroic death, let's also die a heroic death! Let's write the great books in this world – you, Melech Ravitch, you write the great poems, I'll write the great novels. Let's write the great stuff and die!'

As far as I know, Singer wrote all those great books on the same battered typewriter which he bought in 1935, immediately upon his arrival in America. I saw it once, when I visited him in Manhattan, a few months before he was awarded the 1978 Nobel Prize for Literature. 'It is barely functioning,' he told me, 'but it works. I compel it to function, because it's almost impossible today to get a Yiddish typewriter. When I go to Miami I take it, and I'm always afraid that it will be broken *en route*, because they throw valises here. But somehow when I arrive I take it out and I put it down and it still works. This typewriter is also very capricious. If I write a story which the typewriter doesn't like it stops working. It says: "It's not my duty to write such a story like this." That this typewriter can still do its work is to me really sometimes like a miracle.'

It was an excellent conceit. I regarded the machine with wonderment and forgot the man. This was a characteristic of Singer: he was a very great writer, but he also had a genius for evading responsibility. Just as he was happy to credit his typewriter for his successes, so he liked to blame dybbuks for the excesses which so outraged his Yiddish peers (who typically ascribed his universal popularity to the 'erotic-mystic short stories, that he understands so well to write').

Was he motivated by guilt, for favouring the vanity of art (as he often called it) over the sanctity of religion? Or did he simply rear the intolerable burden of personal responsibility? Even when he accepted the Nobel Prize in Stockholm that winter, he did so not in his own name but on behalf of the Yiddish language.

By the way, it is significant that he said *language* rather than *literature*, for he never had much contact with the tradition that his detractors all cherished. 'The truth is that the Yiddishists don't consider me a writer who writes in their tradition,' he told Irving Howe in 1973. 'The Yiddish tradition, in my mind, is a tradition of sentimentality and of social justice. These are the two pillars, so to speak . . . When I began to write I already felt that this kind of tradition is not in my character. I am not a sentimental person by nature. Neither is it my nature to fight for social justice, although I am for social justice. But since I'm a pessimist and I believe that no matter what people are going to do it will always be wrong and there will never be any justice in this world, I have in my own way given up. And because of this I had to create my own kind of tradition.'

An episode in a story entitled 'A Party in Miami Beach' neatly encapsulates the difference between Singer and his contemporaries. An old man is recalling his sordid wartime experiences, when he was trapped with five men and a woman in a cellar. He considers publication. 'God forbid!' says a Yiddish writer. 'You must leave this part out. Martyrdom and sex don't mix. You must write only good things about them.' The narrator advises otherwise: 'Write the whole truth.' For the narrator read Singer. It is an attitude endorsed by Leon Tortshiner, another survivor, in *Enemies: A Love Story*. 'In a hundred years, the ghettos will be idealized and the impression created that they were inhabited only by saints. There could be no greater lie.'

*Truth* here refers to historical embarrassments, which most would rather forget. But Singer was also concerned with another kind of *truth*, the stuff of theological debate. 'The truth', says the devil in 'A Crown of Feathers', 'is that there is no truth.' Singer was almost as sceptical *in propria persona*. At the end of the same story he notes, 'if there is such a thing as truth it is as intricate and hidden as a crown of feathers'.

There is, if nothing else, beauty in his uncertainty. Singer's father, the rabbi, entertained no such doubts; he was convinced that only the discipline of Judaic law stood between man and evil. His son would not have disputed that, but he also knew that love of life (not to mention women) was stronger than the love of God. Thus the *alter egos* that fill his books are possessed by passions they recognize as harmful, but even so are unable to resist.

Such passion, for Singer, was the harbinger of destruction (unlike their author, these *alter egos* were never allowed to evade the consequences of their actions); but the friction was also the beginning of fiction, and consequently the sine qua non of creativity.

In order to resolve this paradox Singer resorted to cabbalistic sophistry. *Tzimtzum* explains that God had to diminish his light (that is, admit evil) in order to create the universe, which otherwise would have been dazzled out of existence. 'I sometimes feel I am half a devil myself,' Singer once said. Half devil, half rabbi;

Singer also created a world out of the conflict. The devil tempts the denizens of this fictional domain and watches them fall, while the rabbi castigates their wayward conduct more rigorously than any Old Testament prophet, and punishes them more remorselessly than God.

Similarly, Singer is both a lover of women and a misogynist, compassionate and a misanthrope, an enlightened scholar and a hater of modernity. He makes his contempt for the modern world clear in the 'Author's Note' that accompanies *Enemies: A Love Story*: 'Although I did not have the privilege of going through the Hitler holocaust, I have lived for years in New York with refugees from this ordeal.' At the same time (ever mindful of the truth) he is careful not to blame the Nazis for all the deviant behaviour he depicts in the novel; his characters are as much the victims 'of their own personalities and fates'.

Having survived the war in a hayloft, Herman Broder makes his way to America, where he becomes – like the hero of that distant, innocent play – a man with three wives. His frantic efforts to keep this trio apart ought to be the stuff of farce, but the book somehow becomes a tragedy.

For a man with three wives, Broder is strangely unattracted to family ties. Above all, he is determined not to multiply. 'In a world in which one's children could be dragged away from their mother and shot,' he rationalizes, 'one had no right to have more children.' And yet, even before the death of little Yocheved and David, he had 'denied their existence and played the role of bachelor', abandoning them and their mother (as Singer himself had left Runya and little Israel). What had seemed harmless and humorous in the 1930s – a little inconsequential philandering – now appears but one step away from murder. By killing Broder's children the Nazis had blurred the distinction between word and deed, desire and action. What Broder had imagined, they had performed. What is the moral distinction? Broder can no longer tell.

In short, he sees himself as brother to the Nazis. He is 'without belief in himself or in the human race: a fatalistic hedonist who lived in pre-suicidal gloom'. Lacking the courage to kill himself he determines to deaden his consciousness, choke his memory and 'extinguish the last vestige of hope'.

It is hardly the tone of a boulevard comedy. And yet there is enormous vitality in this nihilism, much ironic laughter, even a perverse optimism. True, the novel contains a false pregnancy (like *Satan in Goray*) and a suicide, but in the end a child is born. Broder may have reverted to his hayloft somewhere in the States, but he has failed to extinguish the last vestige of hope.

Singer, too, has progeny in America. I have a theory which divides the great Jewish-American writers into fathers and sons. It is an unequal division. Only Bernard Malamud (author of 'My Son the Murderer') has a fatherly voice; the others – Saul Bellow, Jules Feiffer, Philip Roth, and Norman Mailer – speak through characters who are priapic, rebellious, and for ever burdened with Oedipal guilt. In my opinion the patriarch of these prodigal sons is that reluctant father, the author of *Enemies: A Love Story*.

# 3. BASHEVIS THE FIRST
Review of *The Certificate* by Isaac Bashevis Singer

•—•

According to Chone Shmeruk (the Richelieu of Singerology), *Scum*, the first posthumous addition to the canon, was in fact Singer's earliest attempt to write a novel about the Warsaw underworld (the later two, *The Guest* and *Yarme and Kayle*, remain untranslated, or at least unpublished). Dissatisfied with all three, Singer planned yet another, but the Great Editor intervened before he could begin.

Professor Shmeruk (of the Hebrew University, Jerusalem) gave the keynote address at the inaugural International Isaac Bashevis Singer Conference, which took place in London last March. During the course of his fascinating lecture, entitled 'A Childhood on the Krochmalna Street' (the site of Singer's childhood home in Warsaw, and the locale of much of his fiction), he also quoted from *The Certificate*, the second of Singer's 'posthumous' novels.

He read the extract in Yiddish, but thoughtfully provided a translation for those of us who did not understand the original. But even translations contain subtexts. By distributing his own translation (made for him by a colleague), Professor Shmeruk was conspicuously disassociating himself from the popular version which Leonard Wolf has produced for Hamish Hamilton. Afterwards, I asked him why. He smiled a scholarly smile. 'Where Wolf has understood the text, it is good,' he replied; 'unfortunately . . .' He then went on to list Wolf's faults which, according to the Professor, include misspelling the hero's name; apparently, it should be Bendiner, not Bendiger. The publishers obviously don't know whom to believe, since they spell it Shmeruk's way on the jacket, and Wolf's way in the text.

In fact, the two variants are consistently similar, save in the matter of proper names; for example, where Wolf has Gnoya Street, Shmeruk has Gnojna. The following extract will demonstrate the differences. Wolf writes:

Here was Yanush's courtyard, there was Number 5, where I had once been a pupil in the studyhouse of the Gradushisker Hasidim. It was said that the Kidushi Hari had lived here about a hundred years ago.

To which Shmeruk offers the following alternative:

Here was Janasz's courtyard, and there was Number 5, where I had my lessons in the Grodzisker *shtibl*. I had heard, once, that the renowned author of *Khidushei HaRim* had lived there, almost a hundred years ago.

As it happens, Leonard Wolf was also present at the Conference. A tall, courtly man of Romanian origin, he is not only the translator of *The Certificate* (and numerous other Yiddish classics), but he is also Singer's official biographer. He was the historical adviser to Francis Ford Coppola during the making of *Dracula*. Strange bedfellows, it would seem. In fact, there is an uncanny kinship between the Transylvanian bloodsucker and the Yiddish novelist, as we shall see.

Although Wolf had not actually been invited to read a paper to the Conference, he was still able to make his views known during some heated exchanges with Professor Shmeruk. He described his difficulties in deciphering the Yiddish original of *The Certificate*, which was nothing so grand as a typescript, but poorly copied pages from *Forverts* (the Yiddish newspaper where the majority of Singer's novels first appeared), which he was forced to scan as best he could with microfiche or magnifying glass. This, no doubt, explains the confusion over the hero's name, since the letters 'n' and 'g' are easily confused in Hebrew (Yiddish, of course, is written in Hebrew characters). A similar misreading has turned Gandhi into a hitherto unknown philosopher named 'Nogdehn'. The other errors are probably due to the subjectivity of transliteration, a real problem if the translator is a stranger to the proper names in their original language. Such unfamiliarity hardly mattered when Singer was overseeing the work. Now that he is unavailable, it would seem a sensible precaution for the publisher to provide the translator with a knowledgeable editor or, failing a Singer manqué, at least a fact-checker.

Underlying the spat between the Translator and the Professor was the more basic problem of the legitimacy of secondary texts. There are many Yiddish fundamentalists who still maintain that Singer cannot be properly understood in anything but the *mama-loshen* – the mother tongue – who question the authenticity of any translation, however brilliant. Whether Singer himself believed that is another matter. It is true that he once referred to his work as existing in Jewish and Gentile versions. On the other hand, his son, Israel Zamir (who came to the Conference from his home on a kibbutz), told how he once accompanied his father to *Forverts*. The printer took one look at the 1,500 words Singer had delivered and cried: 'You know it's not enough. You know each instalment must contain 2,000 words.' 'Give me a pen,' said Singer. He retired to a cubicle and, twenty minutes later, returned with the missing 500 words. 'Is this how a great writer produces his art?' asked his son, aghast. 'Ach,' replied Singer, 'this is just the first draft. When it is translated I'll have time to edit it properly. I'll soon dispose of all the padding.'

There are a growing number of Yiddishists, among them Anita Norich (author of *The Homeless Imagination in the Fiction of I. J. Singer*, 1991), who recognize the autonomous value of translations.

But who will do the quality control now that Singer is dead? It is no joke translating Singer these days. You must be bilingual, know Warsaw from A to Z, be familiar with the cultural milieu, be able to divine a dead author's artistic intentions and, finally, have good eyesight. Academic caveats notwithstanding, it seems to me that Wolf's translation is something of an aesthetic triumph, nicely steering *The Certificate* between the rocks of pretension and self-mockery. Thanks to him Singer's voice can be heard, loud and clear.

*The Certificate* was first published as a serial in *Forverts* in 1967. In a postscript to this edition, Wolf suggests that it was actually written much earlier, was in effect a young man's *Bildungsroman*. I remain unconvinced; it has nothing of the demonic energy that characterizes Singer's first novel, *Satan in Goray*. On the contrary (as Wolf himself remarks), it very much resembles the second volume of Singer's so-called spiritual autobiography, *A Young Man in Search of Love* (published as part of *Love & Exile* in Britain). As with his novels about Warsaw low-lifers (whom he regarded as the virtuosi of the modern city), Singer was not averse to re-using material.

In both novel and autobiography, a penniless young man returns to Warsaw from the Polish backwoods (where his father is a rabbi), determined to make a name for himself as a writer. David Bendiger's (or Bendiner's) role model is Knut Hamsun (one of the many writers Singer translated into Yiddish during his early years), and his struggles are certainly worthy of the hero of *Hunger*. David (like Singer) finds himself living in a cupboard and subsisting on handouts, and so is easily persuaded to accept the offer of a certificate that will guarantee him entry to Palestine. All he has to do is become the 'fictive' husband of Minna (Stefa in the autobiography), who will proceed to divorce him and marry her real fiancé once the couple have arrived in the Holy Land.

Woody Allen's joke, 'How do you make God laugh?' has the reply, 'Tell him your plans.' This turns out to be a variation on a Yiddish proverb quoted in *The Certificate*, 'He sits in heaven and laughs.' Needless to say, Bendiger does not make it to Palestine. Nor does he conquer the literary world. Worse, this naive Byron has discovered that modern woman is just as libidinous as he is. It should come as no surprise to the devoted follower of Singer to learn that his hero (like so many before him) is simultaneously involved with three women. Strindberg was right, thinks young David. 'Now suddenly I understood the tragedy of modern man. He had undermined his own foundations and turned the mother of his child into a whore.'

Then there is also the tragedy of the modern Jew, cut off from the past, but without a secure place in the present. Some (as David wryly notes) have replaced one orthodoxy with another, believing firmly in Moscow's new gospel. David remains unconvinced, even before he receives an eyewitness account from his brother Aharon (in reality I. J. Singer), who has returned to Warsaw with grim tidings from the new Socialist paradise. David is the very personification of the lost Jewish soul; sans home, sans belief.

The tragedy is that he still wants to believe. The most moving (and beautiful) scene in the novel occurs towards its end when David's ailing father visits the big city and forces his reluctant son to study and pray with him. 'Since we were reading from a single volume, I had to move close to my father. His beard touched my face. I smelled his cheap tobacco, his snuff, and some other odor that was at once familiar and long forgotten.' But it is not enough. Thoroughly disillusioned, David decides to retreat to the provinces. The novel ends with him queuing for a train. 'It was a crowded line but – since time did not cease – what difference did it make how long I waited?'

The reader knows that the story does not end there, that the hopeless *luftmensh* became not the second Knut Hamsun, but Bashevis the First. There is a feeling that the author knows this too, that he is smiling at his *alter ego*'s foolish attempts at fiction (he calls himself a 'fictive' writer), and that he is secretly apologizing for the fallout from a life devoted to art. After their 'fictive' marriage has failed and they have received a 'fictive' divorce, Minna (whose self-destructive obsession for another bounder gives the book its tragic core) smartly informs David: 'I think that you're not really capable of loving anyone. Or, to put it better, of *committing* yourself to anyone. That's what tells me you're really a writer.' Like Count Dracula, Singer drew his sustenance from those around him; they suffered, of course, but thanks to him they have become immortal.

# 4. FILLING THE EMPTY COAT

•—•—•

When it comes to missing persons a private eye is often more use than an art critic. I guess that's why Jacobson sent for me. My name is Smolinsky, Joshua Smolinsky.

He had a cute office in a ritzy part of the city. Cherubim stared down from the moulded cornices. The walls looked like they had seen too much; all as pale as ghosts.

'Don't you think this place could do with a splash of colour?' Jacobson asked. 'To tell you the truth,' he added, 'I'm off white.'

'I'm not without sin myself,' I said.

Jacobson ignored my remark. Instead he pointed to a brightly coloured print on the wall behind him. 'What do you make of that?' he said.

'To my untutored eye it looks like an advertisement for grass seed,' I said.

Jacobson snorted. 'If it was jokes I wanted I'd have invited Mel Brooks,' he said. 'Take another look.'

'Well, there's an open gate,' I said, 'but I can't say whether it invites the viewer to enter, or records the flight of the artist. It's what we (in the business) call an ambiguous sign. On reflection it may even refer to a far earlier drama, the expulsion from Eden. Either way, the garden beyond the gate is presently uninhabited. Looking closer it occurs to me that the two worlds, separated by the twin gates, are not entirely contiguous. Both have slightly different vanishing points. This is disconcerting, slightly reminiscent of that queasy feeling you get when reading a story by Poe; reality simply being an artifice, an illusion.'

Jacobson nodded.

'By the way,' I continued, 'wasn't it Poe who said that gardens always reminded him of "the fair forms that have passed there in other days"? Yes, the picture does have a spooky quality. I'm beginning to think that there may be something sinister hidden in the shrubbery. Where's the sky? There isn't any. If you ask me the biggest plant in that garden is claustrophobia. At its far end is a semicircular bed filled with yellow and pink blooms. Radiating from it, like green and golden spokes from the head of Apollo, are the lines of the immaculate lawn. It is the sun, domesticated, just as the garden itself is, nature tamed and trained. What do I make of it all? Remember, I'm a gumshoe, not John Ruskin. Speaking as such, I think we are being offered a glimpse into the absent artist's mind. I think we are being invited to infer, by analogy, that all the wildness has been cultivated, the seething discontents turned into foxgloves and golden rod. But I don't buy it. True, there are no weeds visible, but we all know they are biding their time beneath the surface. Likewise, the artist knows that repressions will out. Perhaps that is the real reason why the gate is ajar; as an escape valve for the invisible inner tensions. Many suburbanites, I am assured, feel trapped by their mortgages. In the same way this suburban garden – this advertisement for Englishness – is an elegant trap from which its creator absconds at the very last moment, disappears up his own vanishing point.'

'That's more like it,' said Jacobson, showing me a photograph of an empty frock coat.

'Don't tell me that the artist really has disappeared,' I exclaimed.

Jacobson laughed and said I shouldn't take things too literally. It turned out that I wasn't actually looking at a coat, but at a work of art. 'It's called *Houdini*,' said Jacobson. 'The guy who made it is something of an escape artist himself. I want you to pin him down for me. In particular I want to know whether he has abandoned the human form for good.' So it wasn't just one guy who had gone AWOL, it was everybody.

Nonetheless the starting point was the same; the artist Ivor Abrahams. It was summer 1976. London was hot, so was Abrahams. As well as the capital, he had exhibitions in Birmingham, Milan, and Malmo. He had certainly come a long way from Wigan, peerless Wigan where he was born back in 1935. After the war his parents had moved to Southport, seeking the comfort of other Jews. Abrahams was sent to *cheder*, but was quickly cheesed off. He preferred the beach. It was there, when he was twelve or thirteen, that he first experienced the transforming power of art.

'The element of surprise was the most astounding thing,' recalled Abrahams, years later. 'The sand had blown up, coming in from the sea – landward, as it were – so that the carcass was really half buried. It had sunk in, so that it was only on close inspection (as one would walking on a beach, looking at the objects around) that one realized that it was a pig, and worked out how it had got there. You could imagine those pigs getting out of their pen or sty or whatever it is, out on the back of those sandhills, which is a very curious place for a pig to be, in such a landscape, and then running wild. You know, the idea of pigs running away was a strong image – and the creature dashing into the sea, and panicking, and then drowning, before finally becoming the found sculpture on the beach.'

If it had been a vision it would surely be called prophetic, prophetic of battles to come in the name of art, Oedipal battles with the powers that be. Why else would the porker, king of unkosher beasts, the very hall-mark of transgression, be art's standard bearer? The psychoanalytically attuned observer might sniff a pun at this point. Say abracadabra over a hat and out pops a rabbit, say it over Abrahams and you'll get a ham. True, the porcine fugitive died, but it was a heroic death. Nor was death the end; varying light, shifting sands, decomposition – all ensured posthumous mobility.

It was like an image from the *I Ching*, the *Book of Changes*, which Abrahams picked up at about the same time. This oracle from the Orient used the perpetual fluidity of nature as a metaphor for human activity. In short, learned Abrahams, there is no such thing as stillness. Art catches its subject between changes, is redolent of the *before* and pregnant with the *after*. As a result, every sculpture contains a concealed history.

Anyway, the pig's sacrifice was not in vain; following his example Abrahams determined to dedicate his life to art and, like the pig, decided to flee Southport at all costs. Already a student at the local art school, where he had been studying window dressing or display (at the insistence of his father), before secretly switching to fine art (only to discover that he had inherited colour blindness from his mother), Abrahams did a bunk, set off for the smoke. He caught the London train from Lime Street Station, leaving his parents a farewell note pinned to the double doors of the television set. Surely that final filial gesture was in the back of his mind when, years later, he drew those open gates.

Abrahams was still young, about seventeen, but he already had a bulging portfolio, good enough to get him into St Martin's. At Southport he had studied anatomy, architecture, life drawing, perspective drawing, 'essential subjects that no one ever teaches in art schools any more'. He prospered at St Martin's – where, unable to mix colours properly, he concentrated more and more upon sculpture – but the fees were a problem. His father, unreconciled, refused to help. After a year, Abrahams moved on to Camberwell. Why Camberwell?

'All we did was study the figure,' remembered Abrahams, 'nothing else, a little bit of drawing, but most of it was doing life-size models, which you made for about five weeks, and then destroyed them. Then the Professor set another pose and off you went again; made the armature, modelled it, and you only got a bit of criticism every couple of weeks. It was quite hard, and there was no reward, you didn't make anything, you couldn't say to anybody, "I made this" – it was just hard slog. I mean, I don't regret it – you wouldn't have gone to that art school – Camberwell – at that time if you had not consciously required that kind of thing.'

The Professor was Karel Vogel, a refugee from Bohemia, 'a rather marvellous teacher' (to borrow a phrase from his star pupil). He took Abrahams under his wing and gave the fledgling artist a sound academic training. Vogel was in the old nineteenth-century tradition. He'd been a famous portraitist and had himself been a student at the Munich Academy, where he had studied under Adolf von Hildebrand, a seminal figure in the history of sculpture. Thus Abrahams had a direct link to the European tradition. Yes, the groves of academe were beckoning our boy. But he didn't enter. Instead he fell out with Vogel, and found himself in another acrimonious father–son relationship.

Strangely enough he sought refuge in the world of his real father, the world of window display. He began making manikins for a South African magician named Adel Rootstein; a brilliant woman, blessed with an uncanny knack of predicting next season's fashions, not to mention the shape of the women who would wear them. She briefed Abrahams as to the face, the hands, the position, and he set to work in his studio. 'I'd make the prototype and Adel would sell it,' he remembered. 'The more exclusive the shop, the more individual the manikin. It's called "kidology", as my father used to say. Considering my background my association with the retail trade was inevitable. A lot of things I've had to do in my life have been the result of being brought up by parents who had to run their own business. Consequently I have an instinct to be a seller of things, although my vocation is to be the maker of things.'

He made manikins from 1958 to 1960. Thereafter he moved around the Midlands, teaching in various art schools, until – in

1968 – he completed a sculpture, *Nude Standing on the Lawn*, his letter of resignation to the groves of academe.

'I took a malformed figure composed by a student and cast it in latex,' the disenchanted academician revealed to a questioner, 'added a drape, placed it on a base, and set it on a latex lawn, spraying the lawn a tone pattern. I later reworked the piece incorporating rayon flock in the lawn and bordering it with crazy paving. I had always used landscape or pseudo-landscape elements in my work and commemorative statuary is often situated in gardens. This work corresponded with a critical period in my personal life and when I came through it I found that I had discarded that statue and kept the garden.'

Maybe he had just lost faith in people; there was a divorce, a sacking, a nervous breakdown, and a car crash. Dope didn't compensate. Then, as he said, he made a new start. He even married again. Everything in the garden seemed rosy.

I checked them all out, those not-so-secret gardens. Some were like three-dimensional props from the landscapes of Claude Lorrain, but most were – like *Open Gate* – abbreviated representations of the English garden. Either way, arcadia was depopulated. Only three works – *Distant View*, *The Blue Lady*, and *Lady in Niche* – hinted at a counter tendency. In that trio the figure was actually in the process of disappearing or – an equal possibility – reappearing. Then I remembered my Ovid, and smiled.

'Jacobson,' I said to my client, 'we're not talking disappearance, we're talking metamorphosis.' He didn't look convinced. 'Listen,' I said, 'in the '50s manikins used to be made out of latex. Do you remember what Abrahams said about the stuff?'

Jacobson shook his head. 'Refresh my memory,' he said.

' "The thing with latex," said Abrahams, referring to the vulcanized sort, "is that you can paint it, put cosmetics on it, stuff like that."'

'Don't you see the significance of those words?' I cried. 'The rockeries, trees, terraces, ivy-covered walls, the shrubberies and gardens are nearly all made out of the same material. Thus the shop-window sirens, those pink-skinned lovelies who lured passing customers into Aquascutum and the like, were transformed – as were the vain beauties of Greek mythology – into *al fresco* ornamentation. In my opinion, that's what happened to all the figures.'

'So why did he do it,' said Jacobson, 'why did he bump them all off?'

'OK,' I said, 'let's put aside all these *trayf* myths, let's risk getting a little Jewish here. Didn't our hero's biblical namesake – old Abe himself – begin his career by smashing the idols in his dad's shop? Maybe that's what your man needed to do. And maybe he needed some peace after that, maybe he decided to cultivate his own garden, to regroup, to find his own way. Look, Mr Jacobson, I'm no expert but it wouldn't surprise me to see the gardens anthropomorphized, nereids and nymphs rise from the pools – the spell lifted, as it were – at some later date.'

I took a personal interest in Abrahams after that little episode. Of course I wanted to see if my prophecy would come true, but I had also developed an admiration for his strange work, which continued to haunt me. I decided to trail him, on a freelance basis, for my own amusement.

In 1979 he exhibited a group of bronzes, nominally bucolic, but – to my eye – chock-a-block with profiles and limbs. It was as though an entire population had been about to spring from the molten metal, only to be frozen *in situ* when it cooled. What remained were sensuous skins, voluptuous shapes, and the promise of change. It came, that same year, with *Effigies de Pays d'Oc.*

After that there were women everywhere; bathers, dancers, gymnasts, nymphs, and naiads. Some were cut-outs, others coloured silhouettes on paper; some were ceramics, others bronzes; some were individual statues, others were friezes. The sense of release, of perpetual motion, was palpable. Houdini was having fun. The *Open Gate* – with its English sunrise effect – was transformed into the *Large Gate*, which divided wilderness from wilderness in the Yorkshire Sculpture Park. The former had frowning brows, the latter was overflowing with *joie de vivre*, personified by athletic women. The first faithfully reproduced the buttoned-up quality of the English pastorals (though the unlatched gate gives a hint of rebellion, like an open neck at a black-tie dinner), whereas the second is loose-limbed, uninhibited, spontaneous, and very Frenchified. I'm not talking oh-la-la here, but Rodin, Degas, and Matisse.

Like Rodin before him Abrahams began working with dancers, intending to express their transient grace. He sketched, he sculpted, transmitting the visual stimulation to balls of wax or clay with intuitive ease. Dreamers display rapid eye-movement, or REM; Abrahams must have experienced something similar as his eyes absorbed and his fingers responded: RDM or rapid digital movement. He also used photography, following the example of his great predecessors, to arrest motion – as if it were guilty of breaking the law.

Actually, that was precisely what he wanted to capture, that moment when the dancer seemed capable of defying the law of gravity indefinitely. His problem thereafter was to express that freedom in bronzes that were themselves subject to the very forces the dancers were denying. It is not much use portraying matchless grace in pieces that won't stand up. His solution was to take liberties with anatomy, to charge hands and torsos with an overwhelming sense of compacted movement. The resulting show – named *Trente-Six* after the number of exposures on a roll of 35mm film – was as extreme as in earlier exhibitions. Those had excluded the figure; now it was Eden itself that was expelled.

A few of the dames looked as if they had been popping steroids – like shot-putters from the former Eastern Bloc – but most were blessed with the unselfconscious beauty of sprites. An inspirational line, written by Paul Klee, came to mind: 'To stand despite all possibilities to fall.' It took all my will-power not to palm a few of them. OK, I can pretend that I went to Languedoc in search of Ivor Abrahams, but between you and me it was a case of *cherchez la femme*. Why Languedoc?

Well, I figured that there surely had to be a synthesis on the horizon, a marriage of landscape and figure. And Languedoc, where the first effigy had been made, seemed the appropriate place to start. I wasn't the first to check it out. There had been a progression of ancient migrations and settlements, kingdoms had risen and fallen in blood and fire. The Greeks had built there, as had the Phoenicians, Carthaginians, Etruscans, Romans, Visigoths, Moors, and the heretical Cathars. What's more there was even a legend, attested to by some experts, of a Jewish principality called Septimania. I was sceptical, but that's where I went.

I took the TGV to Montpellier, then a slower train to Béziers. Opposite the station was a seedy garage that rented cars. There was a note pinned to the door, promising that the patron would return before the afternoon was out. It had been a long journey, so I stretched my legs in the adjacent park. A steep path led to the Plateau of the Poets, a grove filled with the busts of dead *belle letteristes*. Beyond that was a huge pseudo-baroque fountain, before which a chic wedding party was lining up for the official photograph.

I walked on and arrived at a monument to Jean Moulin, famous son of Béziers, who led the resistance to the Nazis and was done to death by the Butcher of Lyons. The dedication was inscribed in Roman letters on a large wall. Beside it sat a man with an unsheathed sword across his lap. He wore nothing save a pained expression on his face. 'He looks like he's battling constipation,' I said under my breath.

'It's all very well to be clever,' replied a fellow in a cloth cap, 'but you must remember that the sculptor was doing a difficult job. In its day this piece, which you find so amusing, was probably a sensation. A courageous break from the baroquery of Ingalbert, who made that fountain over there, and very probably had the rest of Béziers sewn up.' It had to be Abrahams! But why was he so upset? Because he identified with all who challenged their elders? Or because he knew how it felt to be a jobbing sculptor?

'In my opinion this piece is not really a memorial for Moulin,' I replied, 'but a faithful reflection of France's postwar self-image. France, through the figure, is represented as the last repository of the classical tradition. The man is naked and vulnerable, but muscular too. He sits like Rodin's *Thinker*, post-thought. His expression says that the time for meditation is over. The unsheathed sword, held horizontally, is about to become tumescent. He is, in short, the ideal Frenchman; the virile intellectual.'

'Whatever you say,' said Abrahams. 'I didn't mean to snap. I just overheard what you muttered and suddenly felt a bit protective. Let's forget it and have a drink.' We descended to the bar beside the garage, ordered Pernod, and thrashed the local champions at table football.

'Come,' said Abrahams, 'there's something I want to show you.' I picked up my Citroën and followed him down to the coast at Le Cap d'Agde, where we stopped outside the Musée Subaquamarin. It was out of season and we were the only two visitors.

The museum was filled with artefacts which archaeologists and local divers had fished out of the sea. There were dozens of anchors; the familiar cross and crescent combined, but also ancient Greek stone blocks, tapered rectangles, each with three holes. 'Eat your heart out, Henry Moore,' said Abrahams.

Amphorae were everywhere, stacked on the floor, pinned to the wall. Abrahams noted their feminine shape (something Moore also appreciated, having added – in a series of doodles – female attributes to their basic pattern).

Then we approached the museum's masterpiece; the *Ephebe*. A bronze statue of an Athenian youth, plucked from the river in 1964. Life-size, in its glass case, wearing nothing but its *chlamys* or cloak, missing only its extremities. Unable to stand upon its own feet it was mounted on a metal prosthetic. The angle offended Abrahams. 'It is not,' he said, 'correctly counterpoised.'

Hopping about he delivered an illustrated lecture on contraposture, demonstrating the correct stance with the aid of a much smaller *Venus* in another part of the building. This was clearly a man who loved sculpture. How could I resist an invitation to his studio?

It was a big basement, underneath his house, in the village of Castelnau de Guers. Luckily his street was steep, for a storm had developed and the open drain which ran alongside Château Abrahams was racing like a mountain torrent. The cellar, his studio, was in effect a museum of ideas. At that time it was dominated by a large plaster assemblage, consisting of an anchor, a classical bust, and a wreath or arch of fig leaves, destined – when finally cast in bronze – to be the centrepiece of his new show. Smaller works were scattered about. Sitting in the artificial light of that little Languedoc, Abrahams began to loosen up, to introduce me to the work-in-progress.

'All the small figures that you see – they're on the shelves – I made those when we first came down here. We went up into the hills where we purchased some very good clay – and I just sat down and day after day after day made myself a number of pieces. I finished up with about a hundred and fifty or something. Only a part of those were worth proceeding with. I then took photographs of them. There was a long period of waiting until we found a ceramic person to fire them – which was a bit hairraising, because I'm always frightened of them getting broken or something. You know once we started to get the firing in line and coloured them a little bit – they became my everyday material, really, my alphabet of shapes. Of course I added to the figures and objects – they range between plant forms, utensils, objects from the seaside, wave fragments, parts of the human body, people doing things, washing, elements from old sculptures, pastiches on modern art, architectural elements, fantasy pieces, mythological creatures, characters, boat yards, boat propellers, phallic lighthouses, vases of flowers, little men in boats sailing away, sphinxes, all kinds of things. I began to enjoy myself. It was only later that I realized that a lot of my figurations were obviously things that I was seeing around me all the time – I work completely non-referentially – just sitting down and deciding that day to make a bunch of grapes or an anchor or an arch or a ray-fish or some columns. Just trying to build the things up, obviously not wanting to repeat myself, but sometimes making variations on a theme, on a particular object, in order to improve it. Soon I had my basic imagery. Two-dimensional imagery – because I was very keen to record the things on film. And then I began to group them together, and to put them into little configurations that somehow worked – this is obviously an endless possibility. There are as many moves in this respect as there are in all the chess games put together. I made photographs of a few of the groups, and they got interesting, and from that point on I started to work in my sketchbooks, the sketchbooks providing me with more photographic material – and this became a con-tinuous toing and froing, referring back through the little models, back into my two-dimensional world. Thus was implemented a process that is still going on all the time. I'm still looking for new relationships, though at the moment I'm preoccupied with a number of groups that I've actually been able to enlarge, and make bigger versions of, which you can see around – these will be in the show. I also developed the pierced relief pieces from these images as well – again these come out of the sketchbooks, of which there are a large amount, covering an awful lot of ground. I go back over the sketchbooks, obviously, that's what they're for – sketchbooks are invaluable references because they do offer you an opportunity really to delve into and reassess, and in some instances develop further ideas that have been in one's mind at a past moment. They are the past, present, future tool of the artist, and as such are obviously of immense value, and central to everything – if we're talking about movement they're the springboard, I suppose. Subsequently I got more and more interested in the landscape, and I became aware of the relevance of a lot of my objects to my immediate surroundings – I've always had an interest in landscape, and as far as my work was concerned, in order to employ aspects of landscape in my plastic ideas. I've never studied landscape as such, so don't really think of myself as a landscape artist. But the ideas need to have grounds – the central theme of most of the historic painting in Europe for hundreds of years has been figure and ground, even up to Francis Bacon: it's a major subject, and this is obviously the subject I've been pursuing from time to time over a number of years.'

So my hunch was right! There was a synthesis in the offing.

'With this in mind I looked at the local landscape and started to take pictures solely of the landscape, and was able then at a certain stage – when I was ill with the flu – to begin to cut out my photographs of figures and superimpose them on the landscapes effectively scaling up the pieces from these tiny four- or five-inch things – even smaller than that – into monumental ideas, and this gave me an opportunity to sort of really project my pieces into a kind of appropriated classical world, if you like.'

He showed me some pictures of the pieces *in situ*.

'I like to think of them as illustrations to an undiscovered classical text,' concluded Abrahams.

That evening, over *coq au vin*, the sculptor's wife asked me what I made of her husband's work, especially the centrepiece. Caught off-guard I could only utter a single word, 'Enigmatic.'

Later that night, while my host and hostess were watching boxing on the television, I tried to solve the riddle, to unravel the enigma. I did so despite the suite of sexy naiads pinned to the bedroom wall.

What had I got to go on? An anchor, a female bust, and a wreath of fig leaves; a dreamlike association of apparently unrelated objects. How could I connect them? Absences! Perhaps the work was about absences? The anchor implied a missing boat, the bust implied an absent body, and the leaves were all that remained of a tree. They were positioned on platforms – the woman facing the anchor, the wreath behind – in such a way as to suggest that the boat had sailed along the channel between them and through the leafy arch. Nor could the boat ever stop, since it no longer possessed an anchor. Only that which earthed it – the anchor – remained. What, then, was the anchor? The symbol of ancient seafarers, long departed? Memory? The thing remaining when all else had gone. Something that functions in an alien element; iron in water, the past in the present? It was the spirit of the sculpture. The cross–crescent combination loaded it with religious significance. I could do better than that. Didn't it also resemble the ancient Egyptian symbol for life, coincidentally called the *ankh*?

The woman – looking across at it – was loss incarnate (or rather, disincarnate). The leaves were an opening to *pays inconnu*, from where no traveller returned (not even Houdini).

Was it the gateway to oblivion? But figs also had biblical (not to mention genital) associations, so that the opening could also be that of the womb. Death thus became rebirth. Don't forget the final touch. Those fig leaves (or their models) came from the tree at the end of the terrace, and therefore linked the whole piece with the House of Abrahams. There was something decidedly archaic at the heart of this post-Freudian assemblage, a harking back to the prehistory of sculpture. It felt like a memorial, a perennial landmark, a defiant buoy in the River Lethe. Right or wrong, my cynical old heart was moved.

'I know I am a detective,' I said to Abrahams the next day, 'and may, as a consequence, be too ready to spot a plot. But this speaks to me of a missing person.'

'You may well be right,' said Abrahams, 'my older boy died last year. The tragedy was certainly in my mind as I worked.'

He then told me that the woman's head had – without conscious effort on his part – come to resemble his mother. Many years before, in another part of France, an artist had picked up a piece of paper, whilst waiting in a queue, and begun to doodle

upon it. 'I drew without thinking of what I was doing, my pen
going by itself, and I was surprised to recognize my mother's
face,' wrote Matisse. 'I was struck by the revelations of my pen,
and I saw that the mind which is composing should keep a sort
of virginity for certain chosen elements, and reject what is offered
by reasoning.' Abrahams, it seemed to me, has reached a similar
conclusion. Anyway, the comparison was not unearned.

As it happened it was Hallowe'en, and Castlenau de Guers
was illuminated by a full moon. In the street, outside 2 Rue de
la Chapelle, an old Templar building, was a dead fish. A big fish,
like something out of a *nature morte* by Braque. 'That's the *curé*'s
house,' said Abrahams. 'Poor fellow, he's a demented soul. Keeps
ten cats, who shit where they please. No one is permitted to
enter, save the street sweepers, who go in every week or so
to fumigate the place.' But in his heyday, so I learned, the *curé*
was the cause of a miracle. He was preaching the Easter sermon
when the image of the Virgin appeared behind him. The entire
congregation saw her. The miracle was reported to the bishop.
Local entrepreneurs began producing relics. Investigation
revealed, however, that a protégé of the *curé* also happened to be
the projectionist at the village cinema. And so the matter was
quietly dropped.

I think I glimpsed a flicker of envy cross our hero's face as he
told this tale, but it didn't last a moment. He knew that artists,
not conjurers, were the true miracle workers and that, as a
consequence, he could never be dishonest with his talent.

'To carry on with this business,' said Abrahams, 'to keep going
at it, despite all the things that happen in life, with some success
and some failures, against all the odds, and against the better
judgements of many other people who are only too ready to say,
"I told you so, you should never have done that, that was silly,
what's the point of it? You can't make any money out of it,"
against all that, all that sort of thing, I'm very pleased to have
had the opportunity to be creative. Of course it's hard work, but
it does free you from a lot of the imprisonment of everyday life,

you know, the confinement of living a very materialistic life. Yes, I am a lucky man,' he continued, as we shook hands, 'because I don't know what would have happened to me had I not been an artist. I might even have been a master criminal.'

'I know how you feel,' I said, 'if I hadn't become a detective I could have been . . . I could have been an art critic.'

## 5. EATING OF THE APPLE

•◆•

As I wandered around the Mark Gertler retrospective at the Camden Arts Centre a pleasing conceit occurred to me. I decided that the artist must have obtained the apples, so prominent throughout, at my great-grandfather's greengrocery, which was located a few doors away from that of his friend and fellow-struggler, Isaac Rosenberg. I then thought how comparatively easy and pleasant it is to be an English Jew nowadays, even though we may not be universally admired.

It was much harder and more problematic at the turn of the century. Gertler was born in the East End in 1891 and named Max, thereby demonstrating the family's vestigial loyalty to the Austro-Hungarian Empire, whence they came and whither they briefly returned. In 1900 Max became Mark, signifying the family's final decision to assimilate here rather than there. Thus the trajectory of Gertler's life was fixed; from Whitechapel to Hampstead via Bloomsbury, rather than from the *shtetl* or ghetto to Vienna.

At which point it should be noted that this internal migration, this social metamorphosis, was not a betrayal of family or heritage, but the hoped-for end product of immigration. I pause at *The Rabbi and his Grandchild*, an emotionally charged painting dating from 1913. The eponymous rabbi, whose sad eyes look at nothing, is displaying his disdainful granddaughter. Where he wears a skullcap, she has a shiny cap of chestnut hair, where he has *peyot*, she has red earrings, where his lips speak of repressed tears hers pout with anticipated pleasure. She has clearly eaten of the fruit of the tree of knowledge. Gertler too had taken the apple and knew that there was no going back. Not that he wanted to; Whitechapel was no Eden. The rabbi's long fingers are beneath the girl's chin, but they do not touch; an unbridgeable gap has opened between them (as vast as that between God and Adam on the ceiling of the Sistine Chapel). The painting is a perfect emblem of assimilation, a visual reckoning of the gains and losses. The older Gertlers, for their part, presumably regarded the inevitable estrangement of their son, however hurtful, as a worthwhile sacrifice (there is pride as well as embarrassment in his portraits of them); after all, they were enabling him to lead a normal life – as he might have done, had he chosen a different calling.

In 1908, assisted by the Jewish Educational Aid Society, Gertler entered the Slade. The famous class photograph of 1912 is testimony to his success. There he sits in a foppish floppy hat, dead centre of the front row (David Bomberg in an equally dashing hat stands at the back among the professors, while the third of the so-called Whitechapel Boys, Isaac Rosenberg, is kneeling on the periphery and almost out of the picture). It was obviously a studied and well-liked pose, for something of the same raffish charm is visible in *Self-Portrait with Fishing Cap* (1908–9). Dora Carrington, for one, was captivated (she too is in the Slade photograph, as she is in the exhibition, looking like a pre-Renaissance prince). 'By my ambitions I am cut off from my own family and class and by them I have been raised to be equal to a class I hate!' he complained to his new mistress. 'They do not understand me nor I them. So I am an outcast.'

This perception did not stop him hobnobbing with the likes of Lady Ottoline Morrell, at whose house he met D. H. Lawrence (another attractive outlaw), Aldous Huxley, and T. S. Eliot. He obviously made an impression, becoming (so it is said) the model for Loerke in Lawrence's *Women in Love*, and for Gombauld in Huxley's *Crome Yellow* ('a black-haired young corsair . . . with flashing teeth and luminous large dark eyes'). Moreover, Gilbert Cannan ('a kind of Piccadilly Voltaire', according to Rosenberg) based an entire novel, *Mendel*, on his affair with Dora Carrington. Gertler returned the compliment by painting *Gilbert Cannan at his Mill* in the same year (1916).

The picture, which owes something to Rousseau (Gertler was bowled over by the Post-Impressionists), shows the long and lanky writer in front of his long and lanky house. He is flanked by his dogs, which look like creatures out of Hans Christian Andersen (especially the one with saucer eyes). They are also profoundly disturbing and seem to prophesy the madness that overtook Cannan shortly thereafter and – forgive me – dogged him for the remainder of his days.

On first viewing Gertler's most famous painting, *The Merry-Go-Round* (also completed in 1916), Lawrence declared it the 'best *modern* picture I have seen'. He regarded it as the end product of Gertler's 'inner flame', a 'terrifying coloured flame of decomposition'. At the same time, he saw fit to warn Gertler of the concomitant dangers: 'Only take care, or you will burn your flame so fast, it will suddenly go out. It is all spending and no getting of strength. And yet some of us must fling ourselves in the fire of ultimate expression, like an immolation . . . But do try to save yourself as well . . . I beg you, don't let the current of work carry you on so strongly that it will destroy you over-soon.' In the light of Gertler's subsequent suicide, these words also seem prophetic.

However, I think Juliet Steyn (writing in the catalogue) is correct to counsel against viewing his *oeuvre* as a 'witness of that death'. On the contrary, the work on show is a testimony to life: 'I have, underneath all, a certain undying impetus to paint and paint', he wrote. 'It is inexplicable, yet the most living thing about me.' Gradually the middle-European intensity that had so stirred Lawrence ('it would take a Jew to paint this picture') was replaced by French charm *à la* Renoir, and the symbolic apple gave way to the exotic pineapple with its green crown. Emotion was invested in the colour, rather than the content (actually this is not entirely true; the composition *Violin Case and Flowers* – done in 1930 – is full of foreboding). Perhaps by the end Gertler felt unable to sustain the necessary *joie de vivre*, nor could he summon up the demonic energy to create another *Merry-Go-Round* (he was, don't forget, suffering from tuberculosis). So he jumped off it instead. The year, after all, was 1939.

## 6. THE NAKED EYE:
## FRANZ KAFKA AND YOSL BERGNER

•-•

As a rule it is easier for a Czech to look Franz Kafka in the eye than read his mind. A situation the Communists were in no hurry to change. In 1965 they sanctioned a small memorial, which was attached to a house at the corner of Maislova Ulice and U Radnice in the Staré Město or Old Town. It was the first public acknowledgement (save for his tombstone in a suburban cemetery) that Franz Kafka had ever lived in Prague.

Admittedly Karel Hadlik was no Rodin, but his work is not without significance. The central feature of the memorial is Kafka's head, cast in bronze. Regarding a glum portrait, dating from his infancy, Kafka commented: 'At that time, that angry face was just for fun, but now I think of it as the secret truth . . .' Hadlik obviously took him at his word. His Kafka makes no effort to disguise his misery; on the contrary the corners of his mouth are firmly turned down.

Behind his head is a shield, decorated with broken lines. They hover between abstraction and representation. Are they the cracked shelves of a post-apocalyptic library, or the talons of the infamous harrow that inscribes a condemned man's misdemeanour upon his body (see 'In the Penal Colony')? Either way they bode ill.

Incidentally, the shield is concave, which creates a strange optical effect: Kafka's head seems to leap toward the viewer, like a disembodied spook in a 3D movie. This impression is emphasized by the natural tendency of bronze to turn green. It is almost as though the authorities had deliberately commissioned something to scare off potential readers. There is a brief inscription at the bottom of the memorial. It ought to say something like, 'Alienation is the fate of all pessimists'. Instead it merely informs the curious passer-by that Franz Kafka was born hereabouts on 3 July 1883. No mention is made of his occupation, or of his books.

However, by 1969 Kafka was considered sufficiently acceptable to appear full-face on a 2 koruna stamp. Moreover, he looks almost cheerful. True, his complexion remains pale, but at least it is white rather than green. He is even smiling, if the enigmatic expression pioneered by the Mona Lisa can be called a smile.

Actually, he rather resembles his own description of Charlie Chaplin:

> There burns in his eyes the flame of despair at the unchangeable condition of the oppressed, yet he does not capitulate to it. Like every genuine comedian, he has the bite of a beast of prey, and he uses it to attack the world. He does it in his own unique way. Despite the white face and the black eyebrows, he's not a sentimental Pierrot, nor is he some snarling critic.

Although Kafka obviously appreciated Chaplin's talent, he was suspicious of his chosen medium, which he regarded as nothing more than a 'marvellous toy'. When he heard that Gustav Janouch (his self-appointed Boswell) worked at the *Bio Slepcu* or Cinema of the Blind (so called because of the charity that sponsored it), Kafka burst into laughter: 'Every cinema should be called that. Their flickering images blind people to reality.' The viewer is led at dizzying speed from one image to another. 'Sight does not master the pictures, it is the pictures which master one's sight,' continued Kafka. 'They flood one's consciousness. The cinema involves putting the eye into uniform, where before it was naked.'

Alas, this philatelic endorsement of the unfettered eye was not destined for longevity. The obvious connection between Kafka's sweet features and Alexander Dubček's 'Socialism-with-a-human-face' was too provocative for the Soviet invaders. And so they made both disappear simultaneously.

When I visited Prague during the subsequent ice age, the streets were dominated by Communist iconography: sickles, hammers, red stars, red flags, pin-ups of Lenin. These days the city is full of huge posters for *Home Alone 2*. Wherever you go in Prague you see the brilliant image that is selling the film – the Statue of Liberty, her hands on her cheeks, obviously in shock (not, alas, at the liberties being perpetrated in her name).

Back in my room at the Interhotel Paříž, a sumptuous neo-Gothic building with numerous *Jugendstil* flourishes, I watch a feature on CNN about the merchandising of the movie, and learn that games and props specially made for the character played by Macaulay Culkin are now being marketed *en masse* to his contemporaries across the world.

As it happens, Franz Kafka is also being merchandised in his native city. The revolution has made him free (I mean spiritually, not economically). Unfortunately, the translation from German (Kafka's language) to Czech is a slower process than the transition from Communism to capitalism; which means that while he is now widely recognized, he remains little read. He is, in short, a commercial rather than an intellectual asset.

Curious, I pay my 10 koruna and enter the *Expozice Franze Kafky*. The atmosphere is strangely reminiscent of the Tintin shop in Covent Garden. There are certainly some display cases with contemporary photographs of the writer and his city, as well as a few *objets d'art*, but the true purpose of the venture (or so it seems to me) is to market Kafka's face. It has become an icon – the pale complexion, the high cheekbones, the dark hair, the black eyes. Oh, those deep, deep eyes! It is ubiquitous – on

T-shirts, on postcards, on posters, even on lapel pins. See how his disembodied face floats above the skyline of the city, like a guardian angel or the *genius loci*. The postcards, the T-shirts, the pins, and all the other souvenirs reproduce the same coda – Kafka, Prague. 'Prague doesn't let go,' Kafka once complained. 'This old crone has claws.' How right he was! And now, it seems, the names of Kafka and Prague are linked as firmly as Buda and Pest.

It is a phenomenon worth an explanation. Hermann Broch, Kafka's Austrian contemporary, wrote:

> The modern novel struggles heroically against the tide of kitsch, but it ends up overwhelmed by kitsch.

Even Kafka, that most austere of writers, seems to have been engulfed by it. Why? Developing Broch's theme, Milan Kundera argues that kitsch 'moves us to tears of tenderness for ourselves, for the banality of what we think and feel'. Accordingly, Kafka has been transformed and transfigured – from a proscribed writer into a patron saint. The locals look at his face and, weeping with self-pity, see only themselves. 'If we are all Kafkas,' they think, 'then our passion had meaning (albeit obscure), and our souls have depth.' It is no longer necessary to read Kafka; it suffices to wear him.

As I leave I catch sight of a first edition of *Die Verwandlung*, or *The Metamorphosis*. When Kafka heard that a famous artist had been commissioned to design the jacket, he pleaded with his publisher: 'The insect itself must not be illustrated by a drawing. It cannot be shown at all, not even from a distance.' Instead, Ottomar Starke produced a picture of a man staggering from a room, hiding his face behind his hands, not simply shocked but aghast. I feel as though I have just seen Kafka's ghost. No wonder he is in despair! He has been thrice traduced: personally, artistic-ally, and religiously. 1: Kafka was a pathologically shy man. 2: His writing was a mask, making it cruel and unnecessary to reveal the face beneath. 3: To worship St Franz contravenes the Second Commandment.

When Yosl Bergner first came to Prague in 1991, at the invitation of the Kafka Society, he was so distressed by the exploitation of the writer that he was ready to return to Israel without discussing the possibility of an exhibition. What changed his mind? Well, he decided that the wearers of Kafka T-shirts were, in the end, less harmful than the professors who anatomize the writer's *corpus* in order to expose his soul. Besides, he discovered that his hosts were kindred spirits. Indeed, they were attracted to Bergner precisely because of his one-line manifesto: 'I never had any desire to paint Kafka's portrait.'

The Kafka Society was founded in 1990. Its members are 'connected by their personal attachment to the work of Franz Kafka, but also by a desire to renew together the cultural traditions in Central Europe, and the atmosphere of humanism, tolerance and democracy.' The Society's logo is a jackdaw on an oak branch (Kafka means 'jackdaw' in Czech). It was first used by Hermann Kafka, that fierce old haberdasher, as his trademark. The coincidence is rather tactless (though preferable to using Kafka's head as an imprimatur). Franz Kafka saw his father as a giant, whose presence was inescapable. 'Sometimes I imagine the map of the world spread out flat and you stretched out diagonally across it,' he wrote in the *Letter to his Father*. 'And what I feel then is that only those territories come into question for my life that either are not covered by you or are not within your reach. And, in keeping with the conception that I have of your magnitude, these are not many and not very comforting territories . . .' Of course Kafka never delivered the letter. Yosl Bergner was less reticent. 'Read this,' he said giving it to his own father, 'and you'll understand me.' Lately, however, he has reversed his opinion: 'I think that it is up to the son to understand the father and not the other way round.' Concluding, as if for Kafka's benefit, 'It really helps, believe me.'

'The child is father to the man,' said the poet. Bergner paints a more vivid picture: 'We are all pregnant with our fathers.' His father also straddled the world, though in a more literal sense. Melech Ravitch was the unofficial foreign minister for Europe's Yiddish speakers, and, in the interwar years, scouted the globe looking for a Jewish homeland. He went as far as the Northern Territories of Australia (a curious expedition that has recently been re-enacted in Bergner's Tel Aviv studio).

Ravitch was also a poet, essayist, translator and editor. He was among the first to recognize Kafka's genius, translating 'A Country Doctor' into Yiddish shortly after the writer's death. 'His writing is like the peal of evening bells, whose sound will never fade,' he added in a short introduction. Much later he produced a Yiddish translation of *The Trial*. When it eventually appeared, it did so with illustrations by his son.

In 1937 Bergner followed his father to Australia (where he identified with the displaced aborigines and opened the eyes of the Angry Penguins). He also commenced a project that continues to this day. Some artists draw from life; he chose to draw from Kafka – in both senses of the word. Naturally the decision altered his relationship to the text. 'I told you that I feel comfortable with Kafka, that he's like a friend to me, a trusty witness, a witness to what I may want to hide from myself,' he said. 'Now I'll tell you, he's also my enemy. When I paint him he becomes my enemy. I mean what Bonnard said about nature – that it's the artist's greatest enemy. You cannot paint nature, you cannot follow in its footsteps, you have to find it a "form". Now to find a form for something with such a clear form as Kafka – that is the hardest thing.' He also needed a home.

Bergner left Australia in 1948 and slowly made his way to the newly established state of Israel. He was accompanied by his wife, Audrey, herself a distinguished artist. Needless to say, Bergner responded to his new environment, which was haunted by a familiar ghost. Uncle Monyeh had arrived in Palestine before the First World War, full of romantic illusions, but had ended up as a suicide in Vienna. Bergner became obsessed with the mad

dreams of the dead pioneer. At the same time he did not forget
Kafka. Initially he restricted his response to drawings, as though
not wishing to exceed Kafka's own doodle-like illustrations.

Bergner's confident lines have the spontaneous and exciting
appearance of ideas suddenly made visible. Indeed they are the
basis of all that was to follow. 'I found the subjects and sentences
which I most wanted to paint,' says Bergner, 'and which I have
since then painted over and over again.' Gradually he added
washes, as though transgressing by degrees. Only in the 1980s
did the fauvist colours flourish, and the canvases thicken with
oil. Meanwhile, there were exhibitions (for example in 1976 at
the Galerie Hardy in Paris), and publications (most notably the
magnificent *Paintings to Franz Kafka*, Tel Aviv, 1990).

Kafka is quoted by Gustav Janouch as saying:

> Jews are not painters. We cannot depict things statically. We
> see them always in transition, in movement, as change. We are
> storytellers.

I do not think Bergner (something of a writer manqué after all)
would necessarily disagree. However, there is a place where the
artist and the writer meet to create a dynamic synthesis. It is, of
course, the theatre.

Kafka's reservations about the cinema did not apply to the
theatre. He adored it, especially the Yiddish theatre, which he
first encountered in 1911 at the Café Savoy. He responded
enthusiastically to the melodramatic plots, as well as to the exaggerated gestures of the actors. He was fascinated by their
unequivocal Jewishness, and promptly fell in love with Mrs
Czyzyk, the leading lady. He also befriended another member
of the cast, Isaac Levi. Years later young Yosl Bergner also saw
Levi perform – in Warsaw (where Yiddish was no novelty). 'I
grew up with the Yiddish theatre,' Bergner explains. 'Like the
stage of this theatre, Kafka's stage was essentially small – not
the great world stage, only the actors were a lot bigger than their

stage. They are so big you cannot see their faces; their clothes, movements, all of these are described in immense detail. But instead of the face there is an empty space. For me, this means a struggle with the empty space.' Finally, Bergner feels that he has returned Kafka to the Yiddish theatre; that is, to the people. Professor Tuvia Rubner agrees: 'essentially they are theatre', he says of the paintings, 'the theatre of the heart'. As in all theatrical collaborations, there is both pleasure and pain, achievement and suffering. I can imagine Kafka and Bergner performing together in some vaudeville – a Jewish Laurel and a Jewish Hardy. I can almost hear Yosl say to Franz: 'This is another fine mess you've got me into.' He is probably referring to the exhibition in Prague.

'I must confess, that sometimes it looks like a very bad idea to use Kafka's name for some institution, because you all the time live in Kafka's stories,' wrote one of the organizers last March. 'Everything is a great existential problem. Also your exhibition. As you know first of all we wanted to arrange the exhibition in Kinsky Palais.' The Kinsky Palais is a handsome building on the Altstädter Ring. It housed Kafka's school and, later, his father's business. The plan was to restore Hermann Kafka's shop and hold the exhibition there. It didn't work. 'I am very sorry that everything is so complicated and that I am worrying you,' the organizer wrote a few days later, 'but it is both due to Kafka himself, and then due to the situation in Czechoslovakia, which is still too alive, too wild and far from orderly.'

At last new premises were obtained – the neo-Renaissance Ceská Spořitelna. Unfortunately, the revised dates were inconvenient. Moreover, Bergner became convinced that the location was too small. Reluctantly he decided to postpone the exhibition. 'Are you really sure with your todays decision?' replied the organizer, her emotions getting the better of her English.

Do you insist on it? Are you really sure you want me to go to artistic designer and took all materials for catalog out of her? . . .

Where did you find an idea that I did not see the exhibition hall?
It is the first thing I have done! I visited it with P. because he is
a specialist in arranging exhibitions. I wanted to be sure that the
space is enough large for fifty-nine pictures. He expertized
the space very seriously and said me his yes.

Eventually, Bergner also gave his assent. 'Yosl Bergner, Franz
Kafka' opened at the Karolinum (not the Kinsky Palais, nor the
Ceská Spořitelna) on 22 December. The Karolinum is the ancient
university, in the heart of the Old Town, where Kafka studied
law a lifetime ago. We approached on foot through the cold
night (passing the green-and-white Stavovské Divaldo where
Mozart's *Don Giovanni* was first performed in 1787) and, once
there, waved our invitations.

There was Professor Eduard Goldstücker, for ever associated
with the 1963 Liblice Conference on Prague's German writers,
which instigated Kafka's brief renaissance under Communism;
there was Jiří Dienstbier, signatory of Charter 77, and, more
recently, Foreign Minister; there was the Chief Rabbi of
Bohemia; there was the former director of the National Gallery;
there was the artist and his wife; there was the Ambassador from
Austria and the Ambassador from Israel (the first since '67), both
of whom had speeches in their pockets; and there were numerous
other dignitaries, journalists, a dozen of Bergner's cronies from
Tel Aviv, as well as countless members of the Kafka Society.

It would have been appropriate if some uniformed doorman
had refused us all entry, saying, 'No one but you could gain
admittance through this door, since this door was intended only
for you. I am now going to shut it.' But that would have been
to take Kafka too literally. Instead, we found ourselves beneath
gothic arches in cryptlike halls, illuminated by honey-coloured
light, and surrounded by nearly sixty pictures.

The main hall was dominated by a portrait of a red-robed
judge as meaty and vigorous as Soutine's *Carcass of Beef*. Alongside
was the accompanying quote from *The Trial*:

The strange thing was that the judge did not seem to be sitting
in dignified composure . . .

A young man stood before him, playing a little concerto on the
flute. Then came the ambassadors with their speeches. As it was
the fourth night of Hanukkah, the rabbi lit the appropriate
number of candles. Finally Bergner dedicated the exhibition to
the memory of Kafka's three sisters, Elli, Valli, and Ottla, all of
whom were murdered by the Nazis.

However, Ottla's two daughters, Helena and Vera, were both
present. Vera, in particular, resembles her uncle. It was uncanny
but also moving to see her, cradling a bunch of yellow roses,
standing before Bergner's version of Kafka's Hunger Artist. The
powerful image of the naked, dying performer seemed to speak
to her directly; its message was both specific and universal, concerning a man and his generation. His pale, emaciated arm was
raised. Her free arm also rose – an unconscious echo, an involuntary wave. It was a niece greeting her uncle, the living meeting
the dead.

The paintings had a profound effect upon us all. They quote
from Kafka, of course, and also from European painters such as
Soutine, de Chirico, Magritte, and Chagall, but the cumulative
vision belongs to Bergner alone. He has read Kafka with a naked
eye, and then looked within as mercilessly. The paintings that
result are truly (to quote Kafka again) the description of a
struggle.

One of the smaller halls was filled entirely with pictures
inspired by a fragment called 'The Vulture' (by coincidence, there
is a restaurant opposite the Karolinum called U Supu or The
Vulture). A gentleman comes across another whose feet are being
hacked to pieces by the eponymous omnivore. He offers to run
home, collect a gun, and shoot the bird. Alas, before he can
return, the canny vulture takes wing and flies like a javelin deep
into the narrator's mouth.

Bergner's paintings transformed the room into an intimate

theatre, wherein a brief but intense dramatic event was under way. As you turned your head, each vivid image slowly gave way to the next. There was horror, as the vulture and its victim both drowned in his blood. But there was also humour, and the feeling that the characters, having performed their roles, would all take curtain calls – vulture included.

The relationship – that between the vulture and its helpless victim – lends itself to many interpretations: for example, it serves my purpose to see it as the darker side of Laurel and Hardy, Laurel and Hardy with claws and a beak. I suspect that, deep down, Bergner sees himself as the vulture pecking at Kafka's innards. Guilt is another of his abiding themes. It is entirely unmerited. 'Yosl Bergner, Franz Kafka' is a revelatory exhibition, one that has opened Prague's eyes to the extraordinary power of its native son.

PART FIVE

·•·

OTHER PLACES

# 1. BELOW THE MORPHINE LINE

•—•

The man at the gates of the President's House asks me a single question: 'Do you have a gun?' He is smiling and I assume that he is joking. But this is Israel and he isn't. Since the intifada began, pistols have proliferated like the latest fashion accessory. I open my jacket to reveal nothing more vicious than a pen.

In the pioneering days the President resided in a shack, now he inhabits a palace. But things haven't become so decadent that his guests are served wine at five in the afternoon. There isn't even enough orange juice to go around.

President Herzog enters. As presidents go he looks a homely man. He welcomes us to the Fourteenth Jerusalem International Book Fair, which impressed him (as it depressed me) with its 'hundreds of square metres of literature'.

It obviously impresses the locals too, for they flock to the fair in their thousands. But only the most unworldly among them are blind to the occasion's ulterior purpose, which manifests itself when the President coyly greets 'those who are exhibiting for the first time'. He means the Russians, not to mention their satellites. A quartet of publishers has arrived from the Soviet Union, the same number from Poland and Yugoslavia, a score or more have come from Hungary, and there's even a couple from China. They may have come to discuss foreign rights but their attendance is also making a political statement that has nothing to do with literature, just as the absence of any Egyptian publishers (present in former years) attests to the current coolness between Jerusalem and Cairo. How could it be otherwise when their would-be hosts continue to crack Palestinian heads? This is the view from Cairo:

> In the West Bank and Gaza there are people who are lost in spite of the fact that they are living on their own land; land of their fathers, grandfathers, and great-grandfathers. They have risen to demand the first right secured by primitive Man; namely, that they should have their proper place recognized by others as their own. They were paid back for their brave and noble move – men, women, youths, and children alike – by the breaking of bones, killing with bullets, destroying of houses and torture in prisons and camps. Surrounding them are 150,000,000 Arabs following what is happening with anger and grief. This threatens the area with a disaster if it is not saved by the wisdom of those desirous of the just and comprehensive peace.

These are not the words of an Egyptian politician, but of an Egyptian writer. And not just any writer. I happened to be among the audience when Naguib Mahfouz's Nobel Prize lecture was delivered by the ailing Laureate's amanuensis in Stockholm last December. His words presented me with a dilemma; should I applaud them? On the one hand, I agreed with the general sentiments; on the other, I didn't want to be counted among Israel's enemies.

I happen to believe that the government of Israel is misleading its people. I believe also that the Israelis made a terrible mistake in returning Mr Shamir to power. But I do not believe that they did this because they share his ideology. I think they did it because they are frightened. They are frightened of history repeating itself. When viewed from Jerusalem, those 150,000,000

Arabs, many of whom are still fighting the Crusades, seem anything but disinterested observers.

The overzealous followers of the Prophet who sustain the jihad against Israel have, on occasion, turned their wrath on Mahfouz himself. Now, it seems, the novelist has made his peace with his antagonists, and he is advising Israel to do likewise. But it is the peace of an old man who, having nearly been strangled, speaks of Islam's tolerant embrace. This is literature dressed up as politics and, as such, will convince nobody. Why did Mahfouz outrage the faithful? Because the words of a writer are invitations to think, not to act. Because they speak of unmade worlds, not of the world as it is, and, as such, deal in possibilities not certainties. Therefore they cannot expect to be heeded when they start to offer certainties. This is not their territory. It is the territory of their other natural adversary: the politician.

By coincidence Yasser Arafat was also making pacific overtures that same week in another part of Stockholm, a week in which Dr Moshe Yegar had the bad luck to commence his career as Israel's Ambassador to Sweden. I met the latter, a sophisticated man, a few days later at a Christmas party. What did he think of Arafat's apparent recognition of Israel's right to exist? Not much, it turned out; nothing more than prestidigitation and propaganda. Mere words! Israel had defied the laws of probability in all previous crises, he maintained, and would continue to do so in the future. Although married to a historian he seemed to believe that Israel, alone among nations, could indefinitely defy the logic of events. And maybe the Israelis were able to do so in the past but, from the vantage of Jerusalem, it seems to me that they have lost the will to do so once again.

The common currency of the word intifada provides the most striking evidence of this loss of authority. For the first time the Israelis have been unable to impose their linguistic hegemony on local history, have had to concede the naming of things to the Arabs. In *After the Last Sky* Edward Said acknowledges the importance of such verbal niceties: 'The standard Hebrew method for transliterating Arabic words and names has now completely taken over the American press; this enrages me to an absurd degree.' The controller of Israel's State-run television is no less sensitive; he recently directed his newsreaders to refrain from using the word intifada. To no avail; hardly anyone uses *hitna-arut*, its Hebrew equivalent.

The stones of the intifada also have their symbolic weight, which frightens the soldiers more than the weight of the stones themselves. Because the stones are the land itself. If the soldiers step back under its assault they will be demonstrating that the land is stronger than they are, and that it is in the hand of another people. So they do not retreat. Because they do not retreat their lives are in danger. Because their lives are in danger they are permitted to open fire. And the number of Palestinian martyrs grows, and the intifada continues.

Yosl and Audrey Bergner, two considerable painters, recently took a taxi from the centre of Montreal to the airport. 'Where are you from?' asked the driver. 'Israel,' they replied. The driver didn't say another word and, upon arriving at their destination, refused to lift their bags from his car, as though they were personally responsible for the sufferings of the Palestinians. Had he bothered to solicit their opinions he would have learned that like many of their fellow citizens they are deeply disturbed by the performance of their government, a government that has made a mockery of democracy.

I do not know whether Shimon Peres led the Labour Party into junior partnership with the victorious Likud after the last election because he wanted to spare Israel from the excesses of a right-wing coalition, or because he was power mad. Either way, those who voted for a 'land for peace' compromise – over one third of the electorate – do not have effective representation in the Knesset. They have heard Arafat's words and are ready to call his bluff, to find out if he really means what he says, but there is no leader prepared to take the risk on their behalf. The consequence is a sense of helplessness mounting to desperation. Nor is this attitude confined to the intellectual community.

'Move your ass,' shouts the taxi driver at the crowds who spill out of Tel Aviv's bus station. 'Are you American?' he asks, turning on me. 'English,' I reply, but I confess that I lived in California for two years and at once he assumes that we're on the same wavelength. 'After the army I thought, what the hell, I want to see the world,' he says. 'I spent a year in England, working in an Israeli restaurant in the Finchley Road. Maybe you know it? After that I washed dishes in a whorehouse in Hamburg, worked for an Israeli shipping company in Napoli, and cleaned the roads after the grand prix in Monte Carlo. Altogether I spent two years in Europe. Then I went to America, where I lived for fifteen years; New Jersey, Houston, and Pensacola, Florida. Eight months ago I came back here to get married and now I'm stuck, because my wife won't leave. So I must make a sacrifice. You see, I hate this country. Don't get me wrong, the people are OK. I don't mind the army, or doing reserve duties. I don't even mind the taxes. It's the system that's so rotten. You know what I call this place? El Salvador. There they don't have a Minister of Agriculture. They have a Colonel this or that. So do we. They have their peasants. We have our Arabs. They are our slaves. I cannot stand it here. It's like living below the morphine line – after the morphine has worn off. Every day I spend here is like a year of my life.'

Back in Jerusalem I stand outside the Binyanai Ha'ooma Convention Centre, home of the Book Fair, waiting for the bus. It is pouring and every so often someone from the queue breaks ranks to hail a cab. Thus a woman steps forward, raises her arm, and a long Mercedes glides into the lay-by. A few yards down the road there is a religious gentleman who also wants a taxi. He assumes that the Mercedes has stopped for him, and is outraged to see the woman about to enter it. Wild noises fly from his mouth as he sprints up the road, his black gaberdines flying around him, and pushes the unfortunate woman out of his way.

He gets in himself and, slamming the door, issues the driver instructions at the top of his voice. We all boo at his performance. Every incident in the quotidian life of Israel seems to reflect upon the macrocosm: this episode could, for example, be used to illustrate how the religious parties are seizing control of the State from under the noses of the secularists – which makes it an effort not to read the place as if it were an open book.

By the time I reach the university my feet are soaking. I don't want to catch pneumonia so I hang my socks over the radiator in Aharon Appelfeld's office. Aharon, a distinguished novelist, is one of the judges who dispensed the 1989 Jerusalem Prize, given every two years (at the time of the Book Fair) to the author whose work best expresses the idea of 'the freedom of the individual in society'. It is a condition Appelfeld continues to associate with Israel, so it pains him to tell me that the first question to be asked whenever one of the judges nominated an author for the prize was: 'Will he accept such an award from us?' He professes to being a little flattered that Israel, the land of Jews, should have been so demonized, but in fact he is deeply shocked. He knows the army is behaving badly, but it is far from being world-class in its brutality. Having lived through the Holocaust he sees other forces at work against Israel. After some sandwiches he settles down to study, accompanied by two scholars from America, Bialik's great poem, *In the City of Slaughter*, the subject matter of which is the pogrom in Kishinev. 'Come,' he says, 'let us all sit in a row like *yeshiva* students.'

When it is suddenly announced that Ernesto Sabato, the recipient of the Jerusalem Prize, will not be coming to Israel to accept the award in person, there are suspicions that his absence, like that of the Egyptians, has a political basis. None the less, the ceremony goes ahead, as it did in Stockholm. Twins, a pianist and a cellist, begin the evening with a lively piece by Granados. Then two of the three judges, the Minister of Education, the *Chargé d'Affaires* from the Argentine embassy, and the Spanish Minister of Culture, all shuffle toward the stage. While they take their places various groups of photographers and video cameramen take theirs. Alas, several of the former block the view of the latter and refuse to move aside when requested to do so, thereby provoking harsh words and fisticuffs among the rival media men. Meanwhile Jorge Semprun, the Spanish Minister of Culture, tries to deliver a speech in his native tongue, but the civil war in the pit proves too distracting, and his words are lost. Then the lights dim and Ernesto Sabato appears on film. He is sitting on a chair in his back garden. He apologizes for his absence. 'With all my heart, I long for the day when peace will finally find a home in this sacred area, and when the two peoples who today are locked in such tragic antagonism will live securely side by side, fulfilling in brotherhood and harmony their national aspirations and their historic destiny,' he concludes. 'To this ideal I dedicate the prize that is awarded to me here.' Sentiments that seemed out of place in Stockholm now appear entirely appropriate.

I make a last visit to the Binyanai Ha'ooma Convention Centre. Writers should not really go to book fairs. I want to behave like a bull in a china shop, but feel more like a heifer at McDonald's. I stumble through the maze of book stalls until I eventually reach the one I seek. I have a lunch date with Niva Lanir, Editor-in-Chief of Keter, Israel's largest publishing house. As we walk through the rain to the Hilton she tells me that after the boom years the book trade is in dire straits. In other words, I cannot expect to grow fat on my royalties from her. We enter the hotel to find a table. I order a frugal bowl of soup.

Like many of her fellow citizens Niva is a chain-smoker. The cigarettes she smokes are called Time. What does this signify? I settle for: Time is catching up on the Israelis. Niva probably wouldn't disagree, though she professes a curious optimism, which has its origins in defeat. The argument goes something like this. We have lost. The Palestinians have won. But they have only won what we were formerly prepared to give them. So we have not lost everything. On the contrary we have only lost our madness. For this we should thank the Palestinians, who have restored our sense of reality. All that remains is for our politicians to recognize what has happened. Niva knows Yitzhak Rabin, the architect of Israel's response to the intifada. Her friends castigate her, a leftist, for still speaking to him. 'Why shouldn't I,' she replies, 'when you are prepared to talk to Arafat?' She remains convinced that Rabin has already recognized the inevitability of the outcome.

Niva is also in frequent contact with Arieh Der'i, the Minister of the Interior. He has been putting pressure on Keter – informally of course – to abandon its plan to publish *The Satanic Verses* in a Hebrew translation. The Minister speaks for a coalition of clerics – Muslim and Jewish – which is anxious to set a precedent that may be followed on all future occasions. Otherwise . . . apocalypse now. The security services, however, take a less serious view of the consequences of publication; no armageddon, not even any bombs. The extremists are always trying to blow us to bits, they say, they don't need an excuse. Go ahead and publish. It won't make any difference. Some peaceniks are not so sure. They fear that the moderates will lose control of the Palestinian masses who, in their new-found fervour, will renounce all possibility of compromise. Such a suggestion incenses Amos Oz and other like-minded writers, who remain absolutists in their support for Salman Rushdie.

Maybe I was wrong to be depressed by the sight of so many books at the fair, maybe I should take comfort from the vast number of authors there seem to be in the world. Counted separately we may have our individual faults, but taken together we are more beneficial than most. Our potential for good comes from this collective impact, from which it follows that every loss diminishes the rest of us. That is why it remains vital not to abandon Salman Rushdie and his book to Islam's tolerant embrace. As for me, I shall not abandon Israel either, although I reserve the right to use my pen in whatever way I see fit.

## 2. THE EL-AL PRAWN

—•—

I first sighted the thing in 1991, the year Zbigniew Herbert won the Jerusalem Prize. I was on flight LY315 out of Ben Gurion, returning from the book fair. We were flying over Greece or maybe what was once Yugoslavia, at a height of 39,000 feet, and were dealing with the usual dilemma: beef or chicken? The hors d'oeuvre, however, was mandatory. It came in a plastic container with a transparent lid – rather like a specimen box – and my neighbour (obviously less Hellenized than I) was regarding it with appropriate caution. Was it a crooked digit, beckoning him to apostasy? It was as large as an index finger, aggressively pink, and curved like a comma. The sort of thing you try not to look at in public urinals. Whatever it was, it certainly did not look kosher. 'Don't worry,' said the air hostess reassuringly, 'it's only a replica made from fish.' My neighbour was not convinced; he prodded the ersatz crustacean with his plastic fork, but did not taste of the forbidden food. I had no such qualms. The El-Al prawn had the springy texture and sweetish taste of the real thing, but left a slightly polluted aftertaste, nothing like the sharp salt-waterish side-effect of a well-bred shellfish. Even so, it wasn't a bad simulacrum. The question was: why bother to make a counterfeit prawn in the first place?

Those were the days of Yitzhak the Flinty (who was succeeded by Yitzhak the Martyr, Shimon the Unelectable, and Bibi the Shmoozer), when the land of Israel was afflicted with a strange mood; a mixture of shame and self-righteousness, best exemplified by the following construction: 'We have animosity towards the Palestinians, but only because of what they are making us do to them.' Put another way: our boys may look like standard-issue thugs when they break the bones of our enemies, but rest assured, they take no pleasure in their work. Or: they may look like goyim, but they are not. In short, the El-Al prawn was the culinary equivalent of a border guard thumping a Palestinian; it looked unappetizing, but was acceptable in the eyes of God.

There were other reasons for the prawn's existence. In the days of Yitzhak the Flinty the gentile world was regarded as essentially hostile and anti-Semitic, but was also full of desirable goods and lifestyles; fast cars, mobile phones, fancy restaurants. The false prawn was born to feed the appetites of these pseudo-sophisticates; the symbol of a generation that had lost its self-respect, and doubted its unique identity. It could even be argued that the El-Al prawn was, *pace* the stewardess, not really kosher, since its very presence dared the consumer to try the original.

As it happens, I have never seen a prawn manqué in all its naked shame since that flight. It would be pleasant to conclude that its absence marked a return of self-confidence, and a greater sense of security, but the fact is that the supermarkets of Israel are now stocked with a breaded variety; for example, Shrimp Style with Sesame Coating. No preservative, low cholesterol, guaranteed kosher by the rabbinate of Nahariya. Its chief ingredient is *dag zahavon alaska*. So, if you fancy processed Alaskan goldfish, mixed with water, soya protein, potato starch, corn starch, sugar, sorbitol, vegetable stabilizer, vegetable oil, flavourings, salt, monosodium glutamate, and natural colouring, you too can mimic the habitués of Fisherman's Wharf without risking the eternal barbecue. The titbit goes well with the likes of sweet and sour sauce, and Thousand Island dressing. In fact I

can picture the ideal consumer. I can even picture how he
acquired the taste in the first place. I see an air hostess – let's call
her Sara – approach a porky lothario – let's call him Bibi – with
the aforementioned delicacy, saying: 'Eat.' I see him smacking
his chops.

# 3. ALL THE WAY TO HEBRON

•-•-•

The only Palestinian my friend ever sees is her gardener, and she doesn't see him any more now that the border with Gaza is closed. She feels sorry for him, but really she is more worried about her lawn. In truth the wild women of the coastal strip are not political animals; Rio rather than Jerusalem is their natural habitat. The gym not the synagogue is their temple. My friend worships the body beautiful (hers) on a biweekly basis.

'Can you keep a secret?' she asks.

'Only if it's boring,' I reply.

'It isn't,' she says, 'but I'll tell you anyway. Here's the picture. It's workout time. I'm on my belly, shifting weights with my feet. Believe me, it ain't easy. "Come on," says a meaty voice in the background, "you can do it." And I do; five times, ten times. Then I let go. "Atta girl," says Mr Beefy, laying his hands upon my legs. He has the touch of a miracle worker; his fingers reach through sinew and muscle right down to the bone. I'm snoozing in the sauna, a few days later, when I feel familiar hands on my calves. "That's good," I murmur, without looking up. Yesterday, after a particularly sweaty session, a girlfriend says, "See you in the sauna." "Can't," I say, "no bathing costume." "So," she says, "wear a towel." I knot it above my breasts. It turns out that my friend has forgotten an important appointment, so I go in alone.

I have the place to myself. After a while I hear the door open and close, but it's too steamy to see if anyone has entered. Someone has. The Man with the Hands. This time they do not stop at my knees. It is clear they are intending to make *aliya*. "Whoa!" I exclaim, "I've got nothing on beneath the towel." But he knows that. His hand is already inside me. So he also knows that I am very excited. "What's to stop us," he whispers, "what's to stop us going all the way to Hebron?" Nothing, as long as my hubby remains in blissful ignorance, and I'm not going to tell. So I roll over and let him bury old Abraham in the Cave of Machpelah. I was dead right; he was a miracle worker.'

Note that while the current preoccupation – will Netanyahu continue the withdrawal from the West Bank? – is not even a minor component of the intercourse, it nonetheless colours the vernacular.

'Did you exchange names and addresses afterwards?' I enquire.

'There was no need,' she replies, 'I recognized him at once. He lives next door.'

Such things never happen to me (save in dreams) so why do I have such a strong sense of déjà vu? I'll tell you why. What I have just heard is, in its bare essentials, a contemporary reworking of the infamous seduction of Bathsheba by King David. (David, you'll recall, spied Bathsheba bathing on her rooftop and immediately resolved to have her.) My brazen Bathsheba may be Brazilian in spirit, but even she cannot escape the gravitational pull of her homeland. This is both a blessing and a curse; a blessing because it creates an uncanny sense of belonging, a curse because it also establishes a claustrophobic atmosphere of historical determinism, as though every biography were inscribed in stone, every life a repetition. As a diaspora Jew, whose life story seems writ on water, I have always considered that the blessing of being part of the whole outweighs the curse. Let me be frank. I am glad the lovely storyteller is not my wife (I have not forgotten what happened to Uriah the Hittite), but I confess that I am envious of her conqueror, am jealous of his effortless self-confidence, his ability to turn desire into reality; in short, his Israeli identity. Compare his relentless advance upon his private Hebron with my own failure to get further than the outskirts.

It happened in 1986, when I set out to attend a Peace Now meeting at the Park Hotel, birthplace of Hebron's Jewish renaissance. I never arrived. At a village called Halhul I ran into a jumpy army patrol. 'The demonstration is over,' snapped a soldier, 'go home.' Meekly I obeyed. Now I am back in the promised land, determined to complete the journey. Although it is midwinter my comely friend is wearing a loose-fitting vest and shorts. When she leans forward to switch on the television, I am afforded a glimpse of her breasts, which are like twin fawns, feeding among the lilies. 'You must watch this,' she says, '*Hartzufim*. What's that in English? Crappy faces? Anyway, it's our version of *Spitting Image*.' Bibi and Yasser are lovers, it seems. Anyway, they are in bed together, humping and grunting beneath the heaving sheets. 'We have here a couple who haven't reached a climax in eight months,' explains the master of ceremonies, 'despite maintaining full relations.' 'This is nothing,' says my friend, 'when Netanyahu started to get cold feet about quitting Hebron they showed Arafat clutching his manly parts. Whenever Bibi said "no more concessions", Yasser would give them a squeeze. Poor Bibi. He can't stay, but he can't bring himself to leave either. Even Amos Oz – our most famous dove – feels the "anguish over parting from Hebron". On the other hand I wouldn't go there now, not for all the tea in China. You're crazy to even think of it.'

An acquaintance, a writer for the *Jerusalem Post*, offers to accompany me. We set a date; Thursday, 2 January. 'See you tomorrow,' I say, replacing the receiver. Unfortunately, while we are talking, a third party puts his own plan into action. Jon calls me back thirty minutes later.

'I've got to go now,' he says, 'there's been a shooting. Do you still want to come?'

'Has the shooting stopped?' I enquire.

'As far as I know,' he replies.

I pause. Am I a man or a mouse? 'Count me in,' I say.

Ten minutes later there is a third call. 'It seems it's much more serious than I thought,' says Jon. 'A soldier went berserk. Seven Arabs wounded. Two seriously. The situation is completely unpredictable. In the circumstances I cannot be responsible for your safety. You can still come, but you would be taking a risk.'

I am a single parent. My responsibilities are scary enough. I have second thoughts. I curse Noam Friedman, the mass-murderer manqué, who opened fire 'for the sake of Hebron, the historic city of our fathers', and to avenge the death of a more successful assailant, Baruch Goldstein.

Unlike Goldstein, Friedman is quickly disowned by his ungrateful beneficiaries. No wonder! He is bathos personified; more buffoon than homicidal maniac. It seems he attempted to adopt a sniper's pose, but took no account of his borrowed weapon's powerful recoil, and ended up on his backside. As a consequence every bullet missed its target, the actual wounds being inflicted by shrapnel and other flying debris. Although injuries are exclusive to Palestinians, the local branch of Paranoia U Like can still see only Jewish blood. Displaying a supernatural inability to empathize with his neighbours, Rabbi Moshe Levinger (a founding father of Kiryat Arba, the adjacent settlement) maintains that he is really the injured (or potentially injured) party. 'If our army were not here,' he argues, stirring the toxic logic, 'it could have led to a pogrom.' Eh? Consider the *mise en scène*, as pictured by the rabbi. Friedman pops a few Arabs. Unfortunate, but no doubt he has his reasons. Being essentially unreasonable the Arabs don't want to know; forget explanations, they want blood, you-know-who's blood. Unhindered by their own police (who are – this is common knowledge – really terrorists) they storm the settlements and butcher all the inhabitants. Without the army, concludes the gun-toting rabbi, we are at their mercy. QED.

Fortunately no Arabs succumb to their wounds, nor are any
Jews murdered, so there is no reason not to go to Hebron on
the morrow. We set off as originally planned. Since 1986 a new
road has been built, bypassing Palestine. It is known as the
'apartheid road' because only residents of Israel proper (and
the settlements) are permitted to use it. Our first stop is Kiryat
Arba, which turns out to be an antiseptic community with a
poisoned heart. We stop outside Meir Kahane Park, named in
honour of the late rabbi whose party – Kach – was banned on
account of its racist credo and violent methods. It is a small park
with a central avenue. The avenue ends with a circus, like the
dot at the base of an exclamation mark. A rectangular block of
Jerusalem stone rests upon it. Beneath lies the body of Baruch
Goldstein. It is more a shrine than a tomb. The stone is guarded
by a pair of lanterns, sources of perverse enlightenment. Flanking
the grave are two benches, where the overcome may regain
strength, or the perplexed develop courage. Beyond the circus,
on the borderline between the park and the wilderness, is a
receptacle for candles (which bears an uncanny resemblance to
a concentration camp oven). Beside that is an alfresco bookcase,
filled with prayer books. The inscription of the tombstone
begins, *Hakodosh Dr Baruch Goldstein. Hakodosh* means 'the
blessed' or (believe it or not) 'the martyr'. The good doctor, let
me remind you, murdered 29 Muslims at prayer, wounding a
further 125, before meeting his maker. Needless to say the
inscription makes no mention of this detail. Instead it informs
the passer-by that the deceased 'gave up his soul for the people
of Israel, its Torah, and its land'. Thus the assassin regains his
innocence, and the victims grow guilty. Local legend has it that
they were planning a genocidal pogrom, which would certainly
have succeeded, if not for the doctor's sacrifice. A woman – her
face freakishly white, like a nun's – prays at the graveside. She,
in turn, is filmed by a news hound with a video.

The name Hebron is apparently derived from the Hebrew
*chaver*, meaning 'friend'. Al-Khalil, as the Arabs know the city,

also translates as 'friend'. It is, presumably, a divine joke. We park near the Cave of Machpelah, where the bones of Abraham, Isaac, and Jacob are deposited, and enter the souk on foot. But the shoppers are gone, and the shops are closed. Only a vendor of sweetmeats remains at his post. 'There are no customers any more,' he laments, pointing to the parallel lines of shuttered stalls, 'so most of us must look for jobs elsewhere. But I know nothing, except how to make my Turkish delight.' It is ironic that there are no souvenirs on sale in a city devoted to remembrance, in which every citizen is a repository of ancient wisdom, and more recent grievances. The last trader turns toward the copper vats, trays, and presses at the back of his shop. 'Without peace all this must go,' he says. I buy two boxes, though I hate the stuff. It is my small investment in the future. I want him to remain open, to sweeten the lives of his fellow citizens, to fill them with dreams of the good life to come, to anticipate banquets that will begin with mezze and inevitably conclude with bitter coffee and Turkish delight. Surely he is a more appropriate ambassador for Hebron or Al-Khalil than the fratricidal descendants of Abraham, the friend of God. Better cavities in the teeth than the body.

In Gross Square (named by the settlers after a murdered *yeshiva* student) it is possible to see exhibit number one, a metal sheet perforated by yesterday's avenger (in fact ten of the twenty shots discharged hit this accidental target). It stands, no more than knee high, propped against a market stall. This part of the kasbah is crowded with greengrocers and their customers. The sky is a flawless blue, and the sun unseasonably warm, adding lustre to this little Eden, in which death also dwells. An old man, shaded by his chequerboard keffiah, slices an aubergine, purple as a bruise, and offers raw segments to potential buyers. High above, on a rooftop, two Israeli soldiers watch the transaction indifferently. Atop an adjacent building another sign is even more threatening, 'This Market Was Built On Jewish Property Stolen By Arabs After The 1929 Massacre'. The subtext being, 'We want it back.' Noam Friedman's bullets were the deposit; twenty pieces of lead.

There is a rumour that Friedman is shortly to re-enact his crime (a peculiar requirement of Israeli law). And so an audience assembles in Gross Square. Gross Square is not well named, being more a natural amphitheatre than an achievement of town planning. Nor is 'audience' *le mot juste*. If anything it is a crowd in search of an author. The characters are already in role, they just lack a script. The soldiers man the pillbox in the centre of the square, and patrol the periphery, keeping their antagonists in place. These are nearly all boys or young men. Some stand in front of the vegetable stalls, others perch on the cemetery wall opposite. Journalists have replaced tourists in Hebron. They are ubiquitous, with their videos and their cameras, their notebooks and their mobile phones, their courage, their coats of many pockets. A few settlers wander around, like raptors, ears and eyes alert, awaiting the occasion to express their righteous indignation. Not that they have a monopoly on anger. Every so often an elderly resident pauses centre stage to deliver an impassioned monologue on the perfidy of the Jews. Immediately he is surrounded by photographers, who obtain picturesque shots of the Levantine Cicero. The atmosphere, according to Jon, is unusually relaxed. It is, in truth, rather pleasant, like being back stage before an amateur production of . . . you name it. The trouble is that there are too many guns (and stones, I suspect, behind the cemetery wall). Chekhov said that if you introduce a gun in the first act, you are obliged to make it go off in the third. Yesterday turned out to be a rerun of *Uncle Vanya* (Vanya, you'll recall, also fires and misses), but another time it could just as easily be a Jacobean tragedy. The mood can change in an instant, as quickly as a bullet can end a life. We wait for several hours but – like it or not – there is no performance today.

Walking back to the car, along a narrow alley newly restored with Saudi money, we approach a boy carrying a large drill on his shoulder, as if it were an Arriflex. When he sees us it undergoes a metamorphosis, however, and is reinvented as a rifle. With a barely perceptible flick of the wrist and a bat of the eyelid he shoots me and then Jon. Lucky for us he's only Marcel Marceau.

So I have been to Hebron, and come back unscathed. Has the experience changed me? Am I ready to surprise my uninhibited friend in her bathroom? In my dreams! Having returned to the diaspora I learn that Bibi's manhood has been restored, and the agreement initialled. Sneaking into the Prime Minister's bedchamber *Hartzufim* is able to show the long-delayed consummation, after which a flushed Arafat giggles, 'Oh, Bibi, I adore those withdrawals of yours.' But the important question remains unanswered; will Hebron be a one-night stand, or the beginning of a beautiful friendship?

## 4.  $E = MC^2$

◆

Tomorrow they fly, but tonight they are on the beach at
Ashqelon. There are five of them: the Lone Ranger and his
sidekick, Seth, plus his Israeli friends Pamela and Jonathan, and
their daughter, sweet Ma'ayan. The coast is curved like a
longbow; on the southern tip (some ten kilometres away) the
lights of Gaza burn, to the north are the cities of Zion. A crescent
moon lies low over the land, like the illuminated toenail of a
recumbent deity. They, too, are reclining, faces turned heaven-
wards, hoping to spot shooting stars. 'The firmament remains as
indifferent to my existence as Michelle Pfeiffer,' laments the Lone
Ranger, 'as does the inky sea.' A few days earlier he took Seth
to gaze upon the Dead Sea Scrolls at the Israel Museum in
Jerusalem, where they had also seen a manuscript of the First
Theory of Relativity (in Einstein's own hand). Though they
couldn't understand a word of either exhibit, there was inspiration here: both, in their different ways, had attempted to
decipher divinity's teasing code, the stellar hieroglyphics
embossed upon the velvet sky.

These were night thoughts. During the day the Lone Ranger
would have been contemplating those more material mysteries
concealed by bikinis. He is feeling philosophical – well, guilty –
because the vacation has passed and he hasn't written a single

postcard. However, he takes comfort from complying with King David's royal edict: 'Publish it not in the streets of Ashqelon.' Anyway, the flavour of the ancient city can be easily savoured elsewhere, for Ashqelon is a word that may be eaten with relish. That essential ingredient of *coq au vin*, the shallot, derives its name from *Ascalonia*, an onion the Romans cultivated hereabouts.

The previous Wednesday, the same company took the night plane to Amman, formerly a forbidden city. In the old days, it seems, every town had to have its resident strongman. Ashqelon boasted Samson (who ended up eyeless, down the coast), while Amman co-opted Heracles. At the omphalos of Amman is a hill, called Jabal al-Qal'a, or the Citadel, upon whose summit stand the ruins of a Roman temple dedicated to the mythic superhero. Far below is the 6,000-seat theatre built by Marcus Aurelius when Amman was known as Philadelphia, the city of brotherly love. It was the Umayyads who renamed it, recognizing its ancient name, Ammon. Now the city is in the hands of the Hashemites, and its *genius loci* is King Hussein. He is every citizen's household god; his portrait ubiquitous. Even so, the itinerants never felt Big Brother was watching them. If anything, the diminutive monarch resembled Sean Connery's kid brother.

The Lone Ranger wondered at the vast size of the Roman Empire as he contemplated the ravished splendour of Jarash, some fifty kilometres north of Amman and about 4,000 kilometres east of contemporaneous Verulamium (latterly St Albans), his home. The ruins of Verulamium are circumspect, neat masonry protruding apologetically from the greensward, but those of Jarash are an eloquent display of Levantine excess. Indeed, the regular rows of honey-coloured columns could be the exposed skeleton of some colossal ichthyosaurus. What can one say of such a place save, ichabod, the glory has departed? So, too, did they.

The Arabs, who replaced the Romans as local overlords, constructed a castle on a hilltop at Ajlun, from where, on clear days, it is possible to look down upon both Syria and Israel. 'It was built in 1185 by Izz ad-Din Usama, cousin of the more famous

Saladin,' explained the guide. 'See how strong the walls are. Sandstone is a much better building material than semen.'

'Does he remind you of anyone?' the Lone Ranger asked Pamela.

'Benny Hill,' she replied without hesitation.

'Uncanny, isn't it?' said the Lone Ranger.

He wandered off to take some photographs and, upon his return, was astonished to hear the local Benny Hill quoting Robert Frost. ' "The woods are lovely, dark and deep," he quoth, "But I have promises to keep, And miles to go before I sleep . . ." Those lines always make me think of tourists,' he continued, 'as they flit from one beauty spot to the next, without ever penetrating the surface . . . My philosophy is: live for the moment, seize the day.' As they handed him his tip, this Ettrick Shepherd shyly confessed that he too wrote poetry. 'Of course, it is in Arabic,' he said. 'However, I'll translate a few lines for you. The subject is a spring which rises near the castle in the rainy season and descends into the valley below. The water flows simply to express itself. The frogs in the valley wait for it. The sheep on either side of the dry bed also await its coming.'

The Lone Ranger recalls those lines on the beach at Ashqelon as the relentless sea advances and withdraws.

## 5. BULGARIAN OPTIMISTS

▬•▬

At the heart of Sofia, midway between the erstwhile palace and the cashiered Party building, stands the statue of Nikolai Vaptzarov, poet and national hero. He leans against a shovel, symbol of his trade, while writing in a notebook, symbol of his vocation. His career seems to have been the norm for a Bulgarian writer; early promise followed by an unnatural death. Elias Canetti is the exception, not Georgi Markov; the rule is, death before prizes.

In advance of my departure for Sofia I do my homework. I read a couple of copies of *Obzor*, 'A Bulgarian Quarterly Review of Literature and Arts', which I pick up at the Embassy along with my visa. Two writers stand out; Viktor Paskov and Geo Milev (aka Georgi Milev Kassabov). The former is the author of a novella entitled *Ballad for Georg Henig*, a bitter-sweet tale of a violin-maker who makes his last instrument for God. It preaches the spiritual value of art, as opposed to the material (not that Bulgarians have much option, as I discover) and concludes thus: 'Holy, holy, holy is art . . . Alleluja! Alleluja! Alleluja!' I like it. His photograph shows a man in his early forties with a dark moustache, longish hair, and the specs of an intellectual (I later learn that his hair — rather than his life — was forcibly cut short in 1968 by barbarous cops in the cathedral square). If Geo Milev wasn't a genius, I'll eat his hat (the peaked cap of a Bulgarian officer). His photograph was taken in 1916 shortly after the poet and philosopher (aged twenty-one) had lost an eye in battle. He sports a pince-nez, apparently a prop from *Battleship Potemkin*. His good eye stares at me unflinchingly. It is a memorable image (unlike a wishy-washy portrait by Dechko Uzounov, which is also reproduced). Milev lost his life in the following manner. In 1925 a group of revolutionaries assassinated a general and planned to blow up the King himself when he attended the former's funeral. The bomb exploded but the King was unhurt. Nevertheless the local Fascists decided to take revenge on his behalf. Among those who disappeared was Geo Milev. His remains were found years later at the bottom of a dry well and identified by the glass eye still lodged in the skull. Accompanying the photo are fragments of prose which read like prophetic utterances. 'Nevertheless', he wrote, 'any time of tyranny, no matter how black, is just a comma in the historical development of mankind, never a full stop.'

When I first met Roumen Mitkov, in the summer of 1989, such sentiments seemed like wishful thinking. I had received a letter from the Great Britain / East Europe Centre. 'Mr Mitkov,' it said, 'a member of the Bulgarian Translators' Union, has made a request to meet you . . .' So I invited him to see me in London. Now, in turn, he has invited me to Bulgaria. Of course much has changed; Milev was right after all, even Communism was only a comma. The cheerful stewardess on flight LZ496 hands me a copy of the English-language edition of *Sofia News*. The lead story concludes (beneath a photograph of a queue for petrol): 'Bulgaria is probably approaching one of the harshest and darkest winters in its modern existence — a winter in which the question of questions will be how to survive, rather than how to get out of the crisis.' The crisis is easily defined: Bulgaria is short of everything. Nevertheless no one I meet regrets the passing of Todor Zhivkov, the erstwhile dictator. Indeed, as I discover, most people date their reawakening from the day of his fall; 10 November 1989.

Roumen Mitkov meets me at the airport. He leads me to his car. One morning, within the past week, he must have risen before dawn and waited for several hours in order to have enough petrol to drive me around the city.

Roumen lives with his wife and two children on a shabby estate, though their apartment is cheerful and well furnished. On the walls of the living room are posters of John Lennon, Jimi Hendrix, and the portrait of Geo Milev by Dechko Uzounov (which I recognize thanks to *Obzor*). It turns out that Diana, Roumen's wife, is Milev's great-granddaughter. His daughter, Leda Mileva, also became a poet. In the 1950s she published a poem for children called *The Uncle from America*, which is as well known locally as *Alice in Wonderland*. The pictures tell the story. A wealthy uncle arrives from America loaded with gifts and pity for his Bulgarian relatives. Imagine his surprise when he discovers that they are not poverty-stricken, that their tables are heavy with meat and wine, that consumer durables are abundant, that the countryside is idyllic and that health care is free. Nowadays the book looks like satire or sick humour (among the most distressing sights in Sofia are the ubiquitous memorial notices that are plastered to every wall, many of them lamenting the premature death of youngsters). Hospitals are running out of medicine. Supermarket shelves are bare, save for bread and compote. Cheese is rationed, as are eggs. Despite all the evidence to the contrary (not to mention six years in Paris at Unesco) Diana's grandmother remains a dedicated Communist, representing them in parliament to this day.

Unlike his wife, Roumen was not a banana-kid (as the children of the *nomenklatura* are called). He remembers how his father would queue for bananas on rare days of availability and buy them by the kilo. These would be placed prominently in the kitchen where Roumen and his brother would find and devour them. Their father never ate one, sacrificing that rare treat for the sake of his boys. This seems to have been the story of his life. He was born in Macedonia, and nearly died there. His own father was murdered and his mother – left with five children – was unable to cope. One day she stood on the banks of a river with Roumen's father in her arms. Luckily his sisters saved him from a watery grave. He eventually received a good education and became an accountant with a large firm in the west of the country, a job that came to an end when he refused to join the Party. Determined that his sons would have the opportunities that he lacked he moved to the capital and took a job as an engine driver, thereby establishing residency (without which he could not bring his family). His sacrifice bore fruit; Roumen is now the editor of a new magazine called *Logos*, while his brother, Zdravko, is a director at the Theatre of Satire.

Zdravko began his career at the National Youth Theatre, presently being reconstructed (like the State itself). It is so behind schedule that, on the projected day of completion, the actors organized a mock celebration beside the rain-filled hole that should have been the stage. The director, wearing waders, walked to the middle of the giant puddle and, cutting a ribbon, declared the building officially open.

Roumen informs me that Julian Barnes is in Sofia to promote the local edition of *Flaubert's Parrot*. On Friday he read to a full house at the Translators' Club. On Monday I get an audience of two: a reporter from Radio Hristo Botev, and a second-year law student named Radoslava Veleva. I am not offended, on the contrary, the empty seats make me feel like an honorary Bulgarian. The reporter, plugging in his tape-recorder, commences to ask me a series of political questions, the point of which I do not see. On the other hand, the girl, disillusioned by the recent election (which the Communists, under a new name, somehow won) and the subsequent stalemate, would rather talk about literature. It seems that they both attended Barnes's reading, though the reporter does not appear to have learned much, for he keeps referring to a book called *Baudelaire's Parrot*. Fortunately the charade is terminated after twenty minutes when the Translators' Club is plunged into darkness by a power cut. We all depart; the writer and his host, the reporter and the girl. The streets are dark, like a blacked-out city in a time of war. People drift past silently. Only the trams, rattling on their tracks, make any noise. 'What did you think of Julian Barnes?' I ask the girl as one rolls by. She only hears the first syllable, and assumes that I have asked her about the Jews. She proceeds to express a great interest in them. This is just as well because (unable to find a restaurant) we all end up at the 12th Jazz Meeting Sofia '90 where we hear the first Israeli band ever to play in Bulgaria. They are rapturously received, especially when the guitarist announces that he has just seen his Bulgarian cousins for the first time. This is, in fact, another manifestation of collective recall, for Bulgaria had all but forgotten its Jewish community (which had migrated to Israel *en masse*). Now they were reunited, as they had been in the 1940s, when the admirable Bulgarians had saved their fellow Jews from the Nazis.

Mrs Nikolova, Editor-in-Chief of Inter Press '67 (the erstwhile mouthpiece of the Central Committee of the Communist Party and the Ministry of Foreign Affairs, now on the lookout for new authors), says: 'Please present yourself.' I tell her about my books. She seems attracted by *Blood Libels*, especially by its hypochondriac narrator. She informs me that she is preparing two new series: *Man and Health* and *Man, Cosmos, Harmony*. The latter will explain how to cope with the stresses of life.

'That's certain to be a bestseller,' I quip.

'This is impossible,' says Mrs Nikolova, 'we simply do not have sufficient paper.'

As I am preparing to rise from my chair she makes an unexpected diagnosis – it is not only the State that is sick; it seems that I have a very bad cold which is on the point of turning into an even worse cough.

'Do you want me to cure your cold?' she asks, walking around the room.

'Why not?' I say, uncertainly.

She stops behind me and suddenly grasps my jaws with what feels like a pair of pincers. 'Do you have false teeth?' she asks.

'No,' I gasp.

'Good,' she says, proceeding to squeeze my back teeth as hard as she can. 'Does that hurt?' she asks.

'Yes,' I say.

So she squeezes even harder. Having rendered my jaw numb she begins to apply similar pressure to the bridge of my nose. She then stands back, like a bomb-disposal expert. I sit still, waiting for something to happen. 'In a few moments your head will be clear,' she assures me. Nothing happens. Not wishing to disappoint her, however, I pretend that it does. Much encouraged she sets about readjusting my shoulder blades. It is universally acknowledged that some publishers massage figures, but this is the first time I have heard of one massaging an author. Roumen explains, *en route* to our next appointment, that faith healers and other alternative practitioners are proliferating in Bulgaria, as though the failure of the Communist prescription had sanctioned the use of less scientific remedies, both for the body and the body politic.

Bozhan Hristov, a gentleman with wavy white hair and a dark blue blazer, is the Deputy Editor of a magazine entitled *Panorama*. *Panorama* was founded ten years ago by Diana's grandmother, the author Leda Mileva. Its aim was to let in the light from the outside world. Needless to say, the light Leda Mileva admitted was somewhat diffused; no eroticism, no deviance, no Judaism. Naturally Bozhan Hristov and his colleagues are more liberal. Roumen has translated a section from Kazuo Ishiguro's *The Remains of the Day* for their latest issue. They are even prepared to consider my own *Cosmetic Effects*. I ask about the state of Bulgarian literature. 'It is going through a crisis,' says Bozhan Hristov, 'just like the Bulgarian economy.' He explains that there was no samizdat culture in Bulgaria, no Bulgarian equivalent of Milan Kundera or Ivan Klima (the only contender, Georgi Markov, having been murdered). Instead of producing manuscripts for 'the bottom drawer', the good writers devoted their energies to translation; Valery Petrov, for example, dedicated two decades to rendering Shakespeare into Bulgarian (with great success, by all accounts). Now they have freedom of expression but, ironically, no paper on which to express it. 'Newsprint has already risen nearly ten times in price,' he complains, 'and it is continuing to rise.' Consequently the next issue of *Panorama*, which is ready, cannot be printed.

'Do you know the difference between a Bulgarian pessimist and a Bulgarian optimist?' Bozhan asks.

'No,' I say, 'tell me.'

'Well, the pessimist maintains: "The situation is so bad that it cannot possibly get any worse." To which the optimist replies: "Oh, yes it can." '

Finally I am taken to Narodna Kultura, publishers of *Flaubert's Parrot*, also Roumen's former employers. Rada Sharlandjieva is Editor-in-Chief. She has short black hair, wears tight pants and a sloppy joe, and sits in a chilly office with a leather jacket draped over her shoulders. The room is foggy with cigarette smoke. In short, she is a woman of the world. Before the changes of 10 November, there were twenty-seven publishing houses in Bulgaria, all State-owned. Narodna Kultura was the second biggest, concentrating on the translation of foreign literature. Now Narodna Kultura is taking steps to become independent by buying out the State's share. Alas, this new-found freedom has coincided with the paper shortage. Three years ago they were responsible for 180 titles per annum, now the total is down to 80. The phone rings. It is Julian Barnes. After dinner she is taking him to a party at the home of Ivailo Ditchev (that seemingly rare thing, a Bulgarian writer). 'You must come too,' she says.

We dine at the Budapest Restaurant on Stefan Karadja Street, opposite the Theatre of Satire. A few minutes after our arrival there is an unexpected power cut, and for some time we sit in total darkness. The management lock the doors, refusing to let any customers out lest they sneak away without paying. This means that our other guests are left standing on the pavement for nearly an hour. Eventually they are permitted to join us; they are Roumen's brother, Roumen's wife, and Nevyana Nikolova (a former colleague from Narodna Kultura). Nevyana talks about her fears, for example her fear of bringing another child into the world. It is not simply the uncertainties of life in Bulgaria that frighten her; she is scared of life itself. Somehow the name of Kafka is invoked. Nevyana reveals that her father published a book about him, long ago, in the 1950s – 'shortly before his suicide at the age of thirty-six'. I feel like a spectator in the Theatre of Satire who has suddenly realized that the blood on the boards is real. I have reached the borderline that jokes cannot cross, the iron curtain beyond which laughter does not redeem. In this far land people experience psychic power cuts and, fearing that the light will never return, end their lives with a bare bodkin or whatever. There is a real possibility that this dangerous phobia will become an epidemic as winter approaches and the hours of darkness increase. Fortunately Nevyana has already obtained her copy of Freud's *Introductory Lectures on Psychoanalysis*, freely on sale for the first time. It is a melancholy edition. The ink is of variable quality, being either smudged or faded. The paper is thin and multi-coloured; some of the signatures are off-white, others are yellow, brown, or blue (as though the various stages of Freud's career were colour-coded). Nevertheless, the book exists, and with it the possibility of enlightenment.

A tall man with unkempt hair and the manic eyes of a chess player approaches our table. He is wearing a sweater and jeans (beneath an Israeli anorak). 'Is it true that we have a parliamentary crisis?' shouts Zdravko, as the newcomer reaches the adjacent gypsy band. 'No,' he replies, taking his seat, 'but we have decided to simulate one tomorrow.' His name isn't Abbie Hoffman but Solomon Passy, and he is a member of parliament representing the UDF (Union of Democratic Forces). His table manners are those of an eccentric Grand Master (in fact he is a

mathematician); he habitually wipes his mouth on the tablecloth.
It was Mony (as he is known) who first proposed sending Bulgarian soldiers to the Gulf. Some say the President endorsed the
proposal in order to curry favour with Saddam Hussein (while
seeming to support the Americans), it being well known that
whichever side Bulgaria backs in a war is necessarily vanquished.
But a serious point is also being made; if Bulgaria helps defend
Kuwait then – just possibly – other nations will help Bulgaria in
a Balkan crisis.

There is no music at Ivailo Ditchev's party; just cigarette
smoke, alcohol, and talk. I find a seat on the sofa between him
and Julian Barnes. But even in the scribe's quadrant the talk is
of politics rather than of literature. I want to know what has
happened to Communism. Where has it gone? The machinery
of State oppression seems to have disappeared as absolutely as the
red star from the top of the Party building. I mention the pathetic
*gendarmerie* I saw outside their scorched headquarters, sitting on
a bench, killing time. They looked helpless. 'You are right,'
replies Ivailo. 'It has vanished completely. Last night I was at
work when the electricity was cut off. Naturally the words
disappeared from the screen of my computer. When paper burns
some ashes remain, but Communism has gone the way of my
words – leaving not a trace behind.' It seems to me, however,
that this little incident has an even greater weight, symbolizing
as it does the new dialectic between Western materialism (the
computer) and Bulgarian idealism (the uncertain power supply).
In the understandable rush for a synthesis much may be lost. It
is up to the likes of Ivailo Ditchev and his guests to ensure the
quality of the words that eventually appear on the screen. I am
therefore flabbergasted when he asks some questions of his own.
'Tell me,' he says, 'I've often wondered how you know . . . how
you recognize one another. I mean, how did you know that
Mony was a Jew? Did you give each other signals, or are there
secret signs, or what? I mean, what do you do when you are
introduced?' This is surely not the voice of Ivailo Ditchev, writer

and member of the faculty of Philosophy at the University of
Sofia, but that of the old hermit (who surely did not know the
difference between a Jew and a freemason) I saw in the pseudo-
Byzantine vastness of the Alexander Nevsky Cathedral. He had
long snowy hair and a flowing beard. He was wearing a brown
coat fastened with string. His feet were bound in white cloth.
Maybe this is the true reflection of Bulgaria, what Rip Van
Winkle himself would see if he glanced in the looking glass.
Perhaps even among these intellectuals a struggle is taking place
deep within the psyche, where superstition (the size of a sumo
wrestler) grapples with knowledge (emancipated after its long
fast). I raise my trouser leg. 'That's what we do,' I say, 'we show
each other our cloven hoofs.'

There is a Jewish story which tells of an ancient sage who fell
asleep for seventy years. Upon awakening and realizing what had
happened to him he begged God to either send him friends or
let him die. God, in His mercy, allowed him to die. Bulgaria,
likewise, needs friends. I now count myself among that number,
though I think they would do better with Uncle Sam.

## 6. AN IMPERFECT DESTINY

—•—

I have arrived too late for the formal opening of the XXVIIIth
October Writers Meeting at the Serbian Assembly, but I am in
time for the Second Plenary Session at the National Library.
Wrong! There is no Second Plenary Session; it has been cancelled
due to a scarcity of speakers. 'Last year there were two dozen
writers from abroad in attendance', the Hon. Sec. says sadly,
'three dozen the year before that, and nearly one hundred the
year before that. Alas, this year there are hardly any.'

But there is Bernard-Henri Lévy! Even now the famed French
intellectual is speaking at the Bookshop Montparnasse in the
centre of town. What are we waiting for? The Hon. Sec. leads
me through the clammy night. We hit the main drag, a wide
boulevard, that still bears the name Maršala Tita. The shops are
handsome (especially the secessionist-style apothecary) and aglow
with parrot-red paprika, *sljivovica*, sausages, patent-leather shoes,
even quails' eggs. None of the windows are taped, nor are
sandbags in evidence. The atmosphere may be tense, but Belgrade
feels secure.

BHL is sitting in the corner of the bookshop, dressed in black.
In mourning for Yugoslavia? Anyway, he does not look happy. I
can barely hear his mellifluous French, nor can I comprehend
his Serbian interpreter, but it isn't necessary to be polylingual to

deduce that the encounter is acrimonious. Finally BHL arises and leaves, accompanied by a single friend. He walks one way, the rest of the meeting another. The latter are going to a pre-arranged room at Francuska 7, where the philosopher is also expected. However, the crowd waits in vain.

Next morning I am afforded an explanation of BHL's behaviour. It sounds like the plot of a French farce. The comedy began at the airport where the Association of Serbian Writers, under the impression that BHL was their guest, gathered to meet him. BHL, however, thought otherwise. He dodged the welcoming committee and slipped away with his cronies. And so, after a fruitless wait for the wayward genius, the local writers returned empty-handed. At the bookshop, so I am told, BHL delivered an ultimatum; the Association of Serbian Writers must denounce the invasion of Croatia or else BHL will have nothing to do with them or their Meeting. What vanity, what chutzpah! Did BHL really believe that the Association of Serbian Writers – which clearly regards itself as the *vox populi* – would abandon the national struggle in order to listen to a French popinjay? Of course not! BHL may be vain, but he is not naive. Hence his subsequent press conference at the Hyatt Hotel, where his intended audience isn't a few unenlightened Serbs, but the wider world.

Even so I confess that his public proclamation has left me feeling very uncomfortable. Like BHL I do not consider myself to be a guest of the Serbs, who actually invited Martin Amis, Doris Lessing, and Seamus Heaney. Having been refused by all three they turned to the British Council who, in turn, asked me. Nevertheless, I now feel that my presence is an unambiguous signal of acquiescence. Moreover, the subject of the Meeting – 'This year we will talk about survival' – hardly lends itself to farce, given the present circumstances. No, it is not sufficient to merely mock BHL. And so, that day, I speak my mind, not at a news conference, but at a sparsely attended round-table discussion in the National Library.

Although we are nominally writers, talk quickly turns to history, the Serbs being very anxious to impress on us the details of the conflict. Wandering around Belgrade I have observed hirsute brigands in battle fatigues selling monarchist insignia on stalls in the ritzy arcades. Needless to say, the writers are more sophisticated and persuasive than their hairy brothers, but they come to the same conclusion. In short, the Serbs, like the Jews, are victims of history. The hammer of Dubrovnik? Us? You must be joking! On the contrary, the Croats are all born-again Nazis! Our Chairman removes some pamphlets from his briefcase to prove the point. One describes the concentration camp run by the Ustashi when Croatia was a Fascist republic (where hundreds of thousands of Serbs were butchered). The other, as if to emphasize that leopards never change their spots, details more recent persecutions of Serbs on Croatian land. It is, in effect, a *casus belli*. As it happens, I am not unfamiliar with these stories (years ago, when I was on the Writers in Prison subcommittee of PEN I declined to correspond with a Croatian nationalist on account of them). Yet there is something in the manner of their retelling that disturbs me. Nor am I alone. Enter Miodrag Pavlovic, an elegant Serbian poet in late middle age, who supplies *le mot juste*. 'It is a great pity that our language lacks an equivalent of your *self-righteousness,*' he says, 'for self-righteousness is our national malaise. We are always ready to blame the outside world for our troubles – not to mention the Croats! – but never acknowledge the faults within. Just as every human being has to live with a permanent sense of injustice, the sense of a destiny imperfectly achieved, so must we – the Serbian people – learn to live within unjust frontiers. We may be self-righteous, but we are not gods, we cannot have everything our hearts desire.' Alas, this is not the voice of the consensus, not this morning at any rate. His fellow writers feel an obligation to express the will of the nation, as they see it. For my part I have always believed that a writer's job is more modest. I paraphrase Kafka's famous rejoinder to the Zionists: 'How can I be for you, when I am not even for myself?'

'It seems you think otherwise in Belgrade,' I continue. 'Perhaps I was foolish to expect anything different. You are recovering from a Communist winter — which isn't over yet — and your thoughts remain fossilized.' Popov is not flattered. He has unkempt grey hair, a thick beard, and favours Levi's. Sure enough he speaks with the exuberance of a beat poet. 'I have never supported the Communists,' he says — the usual opening. But, having been a journalist for many years, he is well acquainted with their machinations. As a novice on a newspaper he poured his heart out and, consequently, had his copy cut to pieces by the censor. Subsequently he became smarter and learned to outwit the censor, at any rate his copy was returned unamended. Popov pauses. He is no fool. He wants us to know that he has been compromised, that all he has really earned is a first-class degree in auto-censorship. Now he declares himself, or seems to. 'This war is a bloody thing,' he says, 'a stupid, bloody thing.' He speaks of Tito's private zoo on the island of Bironi, where the old dictator kept lions and tigers. According to Popov these represented the national passions he had tamed. But now that Tito is dead and buried the Presidents of Serbia and Croatia, both former henchmen, have entered the garden and unlocked the cages. Popov quotes some graffiti he saw recently: 'Separatists of the world unite!' We all laugh. But then his mood suddenly changes. 'I have admitted my errors,' he says, 'but why won't the rest of Europe? Why does it continue to believe such lies about the Serbs?' And so he too begins to relive the ancient feud. There is great irony here; irony in the fact that all these avowed anti-Communist intellectuals find themselves justifying the excesses of Slobodan Milosevic, one of the last Communist presidents on the continent, simply because they are unwilling to contradict his neo-nationalism. Or dare not. There is fear in the land, fear of what may happen when Yugoslavia finally disintegrates and the *altneu* states are reconstituted. Fear that other commissars will appear, pseudo-priests who will oversee the new orthodoxy, who will pursue all utterances for evidence of scepticism, mockery, or irony (not that there is much in evidence at present).

Alas, my interventions fall on deaf ears. When the Chairman sums up the proceedings of our group at the Final Plenary Session he ignores my contribution entirely. 'If anyone feels that I have missed anything out,' he says pointedly, 'they are welcome to make their own statement.' To tell the truth, I lack the confidence to preach to the unconverted, not in the main hall of the National Library of Serbia, not after the corpulent gentleman with the porcine features and a jacket worn in the style of Alexi Sayle has laid into BHL. 'I do not want to say more than is necessary about the unpleasant business with Bernard-Henri Lévy,' he began, '*but* I must make a few remarks. The Serbs didn't accept ultimatums from Hitler or from Stalin, and we won't accept one now from Lévy. Nevertheless, we must thank Mr Lévy for making it so clear to us that we are losing the war where it really matters – on television. Those of us who are failing to present our case to the world are traitors. Yes, *traitors*. If we continue to do nothing the soldiers who return from the front will want to know why we were silent.' He looked up menacingly. 'And they will be right to ask, and right to demand punishment. We have no choice. We must conclude this Meeting with an appeal to the world. We must demand a fair hearing and justice for all Serbs.' Shall I disclose this orator's name? Why not? When my neighbour (an American scholar) asks him for it he is handed not a calling card but the academician's latest opus, a volume that outweighs the Belgrade telephone directory. As it happens, I have heard the likes of Krunoslav Spasic many times before. After Israel's calamitous invasion of Lebanon Anglo-Jewry wrung its hands and cried: 'Why are they traducing us?' It seems that the Serbs are more like the Jews than they imagine.

The local Jews, however, do not welcome the comparison. They are, ironically, the last Yugoslavs. How much easier it was to be a Yugoslav – an equal among equals – than a Serb or a Croat (to name but two). Now the Jews must prove their loyalty

to their new homelands, lest they stand out as aliens, as rootless
cosmopolitans. If history is any precedent the Jews of Croatia
have more reason to be frightened than their co-religionists in
Serbia (needless to say, the Ustashi massacred Jews as gladly as
they did Serbs). Consequently the Croatian Jews have recently
declared war on their Serbian counterparts. An exchange of
letters, taken from the *Independent*, gives some idea of the nastiness
in the air. Lea Bauman writes from Zagreb: 'I have to say that,
as a Jew, I am afraid of Serbian aggression against Croatia, not of
Croats in Croatia.' She does not defend past crimes (they are 'a
fact that nobody is denying') but she wants to tar others with
the same brush: 'Sixty thousand Jews were transported from all
parts of Serbia to three concentration camps where they were
exterminated . . . The actual killing was done by Serbs.' 'I am
aghast at the allegations of Lea Bauman that Serbs destroyed the
Jews in Serbia during the Second World War,' replies Aleksandar
Demajo from Belgrade. During my stay in the city the Jewish
community holds a stormy assembly, at which the provocation
from their co-religionists in Croatia is discussed. It was the elders
– the grandfathers and the grandmothers – who were the most
belligerent, who wanted to declare reciprocal war upon their
fellow Jews in Zagreb. 'Hold your horses,' came the reply, 'it's
not your blood that will be spilled. The army will send you away
because you are too old to fight. Instead they will conscript us,
the young men. And we are not prepared to lay down our lives
for a Greater Serbia.'

Afterwards I have a meal at a popular restaurant with one of
the participants: a writer, translator, and the exhausted father of a
new-born daughter. 'The nurse told us that she has never seen
so many baby girls before,' he says. 'It is as though the people
were suddenly afraid to have boys.' I am partial to David because
he has translated some of my stories, but I like him anyway, and
accept what others have told me about the quality of his work.
However, I cringe when he admits that he supported BHL. Of
course he did! David is an outsider, having left the Association

of Serbian Writers, but is not yet a dissident. He is involved in the formation of an alternative forum, one that will have a basic charter but will thereafter refrain from political arm-twisting. He is not optimistic. He does not want to leave Yugoslavia – or even Serbia – but, as they say, his suitcases are already half packed.

Others have developed angina. Pasha is pear-shaped, with brown eyes and bushy brows. He resembles an owl; in appearance and in wisdom. His apartment, to which he is confined after a recent prostate operation, is full of Judaica. It is in the same street as the synagogue, now locked for reasons of security. I am fed lemon tea and plum strudel by his wife who refers to herself as the 'house nigger' (certain of our verbal sensitivities have evidently not reached Yugoslavia). Pasha eats dry biscuits and drinks an antiseptic potion to disinfect his waterworks. We talk about the difficulties facing the Jews of Serbia, how they must overcome the temptation to become more Serbian than the Serbs (lest they appear less), how they must refuse to be used as instruments of political propaganda. But it is equally clear that my friend's ailing body is weighing heavily upon his mind. He moves with great difficulty, and only to pass water. It seems that he began pissing blood soon after the operation. This was a side effect of the pills he was taking to ease his angina (which, by enlarging his arteries, promoted the bleeding). 'You cannot afford to lose so much blood,' declared the professor in charge of his case. He put an immediate end to the internal strife by placing an embargo upon the cardiovascular pills. 'The bleeding has stopped,' the patient concedes, 'instead I am blessed with daily bouts of angina pectoris.' He places his hand over his aching heart, thereby providing me with the emblem of my visit. Pasha is the personification of the Yugoslav body politic. If it is to survive in any shape at all it must surely experience similar heart ache. Each of the nationalities must follow the Professor's prescription (not to mention that of Pavlovic) and accept an imperfect destiny. At least then the blood will cease to flow.

# 7. SWEET WATER AND BITTER WATER

‧—‧

'And now, my dear Clive,' says the Chairman of the opening symposium of Stockholm's Jewish Cultural Week, perhaps you'll begin by explaining why you became a writer.'

'Oh, for the very best of reasons,' I reply, 'Freudian ones. I wanted to attract women, and found I operated better at a distance. My first attempts were therefore letters. Then I surmised that the recipients would be even more impressed if I could get these efforts published. Only much later did it occur to me that my ambitions were somewhat limited. Now I want to seduce the world.' Though I'll settle for the audience this morning, hence my careful preparations on their behalf.

But the thought given to my appearance is as nothing compared to that given to his by Bernard-Henri Lévy, but then he is a philosopher. His clothes doubtless represent his Manichaean world view, being black and white, though what the upturned shirt collar signifies is beyond me. Bernard-Henri Lévy is French and, like me, was born in the year that Israel was refloated upon history's deep waters. There the resemblance ends. He is about six feet tall and has thick black hair which he habitually combs with his fingers. His features are sharp, the sort that appealed to the late François Truffaut.

Bernard-Henri Lévy is not only a philosopher, he is also an

orator. More than that; he is a personification. Thus, when called upon to speak by the Chairman, he begins by announcing: 'We were Maoists, we were Leninists, and those of us who were Jews were Sartrean Jews.' 'We' does not indicate some royal delusion, but refers to the generation of '68. A Sartrean Jew is one who is dependent upon anti-Semitism for his identity. Judaism was therefore regarded by the generation of '68 (as personified by Bernard-Henri Lévy) as a hindrance to genuine self-expression. Or so Bernard-Henri Lévy thought when he sat down to write his first philosophical text. It went swimmingly until he came to the subject of evil. 'That chapter proved impossible to write,' he says. 'Each day I tied it up, and each night it undid itself.' It is a problem he has since solved, not with modern philosophy, but with ancient Hebrew texts. Yes, Bernard-Henri Lévy is a *baltshuve*, a born-again Jew; though, because he is a philosopher, it is his thought process rather than his behaviour that has been altered. He still acts like a Frenchman.

The third member of our panel is Janina Bauman, whose book, *Winter in the Morning*, describes her childhood in the Warsaw ghetto. She did not, in fact, leave Poland until 1968. Her English, though fluent, betrays this late arrival. Otherwise she seems a well-adjusted woman, afflicted with nothing worse than nicotine addiction. Although she is here on account of her book she has not adopted the hangdog appearance of the professional survivor, nor has she adopted the pulpit-patter that usually accompanies it. Her subject is the universal application of the Holocaust experience. Unlike some I could name she does not dwell upon the moral superiority of the Jew. Actually I do name Elie Wiesel, and not to give him compliments.

This enrages Bernard-Henri Lévy, much to my surprise, who looks upon Wiesel as a saint. He says it is our sacred duty to memorialize the dead whom Wiesel (a fellow personification) speaks for. I am accused of wanting to forget about the Holocaust. This, in turn, enrages me. 'I said I didn't feel inclined to write about the Holocaust,' I reply, 'not that I didn't want to know

about it. You are a thinker, you are supposed to know that there
is a big difference between fiction and history. The former being
lies.'

By now the audience of critics, artists, and assorted intellectuals has begun to take sides. I look around and observe that
most of the women only have eyes for Bernard-Henri Lévy.
What these moist orbs express is not hostility. In fact the cerebral
osteopath has both sexes in the palm of his hand. Take that lady,
a buxom film-maker, very popular in Sweden, who has been so
moved by Bernard-Henri Lévy's confessions that she wants to
share her dreams with us. When she was a kid, she reveals, she
was very proud of the drawings she did at school. So much so
that she showed them to her dad, a stern critic, who told her to
put them in the dustbin. 'Since then,' she says, 'I have not
touched a pencil.' At least, not in the flesh. In her dream-life,
on the other hand, she has a fat portfolio. Sage rabbis encourage
her to fill it, paternal disapproval notwithstanding. These are, she
has been reliably informed, Jungian archetypes. And it is her
duty to follow the rabbinic advice, as Bernard-Henri Lévy has
done in his own way, to find herself through Judaism. According
to her analyst there has been a veritable epidemic of such anti-
assimilationist dreams in Stockholm.

The headquarters of the Jewish Community, the Judiska For-
samlingen, and its neighbour, the Great Synagogue, are built,
like the rest of Stockholm, on islands. The mud below their
particular island is not especially stable, so much so that the
building opposite looks as if it is auditioning for the part of the
House of Ussher. To forestall similar occurrences on the Semitic
side of the street piles are being driven down to reinforce the
foundations of Wahrendorffsgatan 3. It is in the Judiska Forsam-
lingen's library, a long room lined with dark wood and books,
that the Jewish Cultural Week is to be officially inaugurated.

We are all here, of course, the controversies of the symposium
still as fresh as the salmon we're being offered as an hors d'oeuvre.
For some the main course is fish roll in cream sauce, for others

– notably the speaker himself – it is Bernard-Henri Lévi's lecture. Accordingly he excuses himself from the table and repairs to a small room, wherein he may prepare himself. When he returns it is in the guise of a romantic hero; his dark hair is swept back, his dazzling white shirt unbuttoned to the *pupik*. 'Do you know the first question he asked me when I collected him from Arlanda?' whispers one of the Cultural Week's organizers. 'How many reporters are coming to my lecture?'

Bernard-Henri Lévy needn't have worried. The hall, which seats 250, is packed. Writers, journalists, artists, starry-eyed women, all quiver with expectation. Outside people are being turned away. 'His bag was filled with twenty-five kilos of papers, just so that he could carry on with his book in Stockholm,' adds my Swedish informant, anxious to correct any wrong impression he may have created. 'It was so heavy I could hardly lift it.' If those are the volumes he requires for two days in a foreign capital, who can measure the burden of his mind, now in its fourth decade? He must have devoured more books than are housed in this building, library and all. Indeed, he quotes from most of them in his lecture, as erudition pours from his tongue like lava.

He leans upon the lectern, and speaks in confidential tones of his past mistakes (Mao, Lenin, Sartre), until he knows that his audience forgives him, then he tells of his repentance, of his Jewish renaissance. Finally, with a smile, he concludes that literature itself, by dint of its Talmud-like nature, is also Jewish. I join the applause, for it has indisputably been an excellent performance, to have spoken so fluently in a foreign tongue (English being our lingua franca) with only a few notes to guide him. Bernard-Henri Lévy, now leaning Chopin-like against the grand piano, absorbs the adoration. A born performer, without a trace of self-doubt, he will certainly be a hard act to follow.

In his closing remarks the Chairman offers the French philosopher's chameleon ability to change his convictions from day to day as proof positive of his genius, but a fierce woman in the

row behind me remains unconvinced. 'He is so impressed to
have a genius as a friend that he has lost his sense of judgement,'
she says of the Chairman. 'He is like a lion tamer in a circus
who boasts, "Ladies and gentlemen, here is a wild beast I have
pacified for you," and then proceeds to put the animal through
its paces. And naturally the genius obliges.'

Stockholm is a watery city, there's no escaping that. Near the
parliament building are the locks where the salt licks of the Baltic
meet the sweet inland waters. Here fishermen stand all day in
their sou'westers, casting long lines in the hope of landing
salmon. I know just how they feel.

My lecture is indebted to Paul Klee, who wrote: 'To stand
despite all possibilities to fall.' This, I explain to my audience of
forty (which does not include the philosopher, who has returned
to France), describes not only the Jewish nation, not only this
building, but also my position at the lectern. Defying gravity I
compare myself to the fishermen of Stockholm, as I try to pull
a prize from my swirling inheritance of English culture and
Jewish history. Both streams – sweet words and bitter experience
– influence my writing; language enables me to pursue each
image to its logical conclusion; history, a more physical proposition, forces me to judge this and every act by its most extreme
consequence.

# 8. METAMORPHOSIS

•—•

## WINTER

Bror had a beard like Solzhenitsyn, but a much kinder face. He was our man in Stockholm. The weather was generous too. Milky light fell upon the Old Town across the water. A group of anglers, with precisely waved grey hair and pencil moustaches, were naked to the waist. In October! They looked incongruous, like refugees from the waterfront at Riccione, and seemed more interested in chewing the fat than catching fish. Beside them was a more convincing native, dressed in a tweed overcoat and plus fours. The Saltsjön was glutted with fish, and he obviously wanted the lot. His line shivered with golden hooks and shiny weights. No bait. The hooks sufficed. Often there were three or four quicksilver sprats attached when the line resurfaced. 'Soon the water will be frozen,' said Bror, 'the forecasters warn us that winter will begin next week. I hope you have warm coats.'

We returned to Uppsala, our temporary home, to our art-decoish apartment on Kyrkogårdsgatan. Although a river, the Fyris, ran through the city, and woods were no rarity, we preferred to plunder nature at the Saluhallen, a spacious food hall which hawked everything from sugared almonds to shanks of reindeer. In the kitchen my wife artfully synthesized the newly acquired raw materials, both inanimate and formerly animate, into local dishes such as *gravadlax* or *ärter och fläsk*. The kitchen faced Uppsala's medieval cathedral. At sunset jackdaws flew in from their diurnal perches and circled its twin spires, as though they were penitents vainly seeking readmission. Our front windows had a more scientific aspect, which included the university's old observatory, a white cylinder with a hatband of red stars, much like an ocean liner's funnel. In short, we were poised between two celestial transmitters: the Voice of Prayer, and the Voice of Reason. Perhaps that is why the Swedish language has two tones: to symbolize the inner struggle between these conflicting voices.

Lest we got heady on this ethereal duet our address – literally, Church Yard Street – and the eponymous cemetery across the road (which accommodated the bones of Dag Hammarskjöld among numerous notables) kept us earthed. On All Souls' Eve the living lit candles within its leafy precincts, which flickered all night like will-o'-the-wisps. In the small hours a noise within the apartment awakened me. I arose reluctantly to investigate, and upon opening the bedroom door found myself face to face with a rough-looking bruiser. A second glance disclosed his identity: D. H. Lawrence, staring out head-high from the open end of a bookshelf. Later, when I wrote about the episode, I deleted Lawrence and inserted Strindberg, the latter being more likely to haunt Uppsala, whose bourgeois values he despised.

The nearest Shakespeare ever got to Uppsala was Elsinore, even so he is one of the *spécialités régionales*, thanks to my friend, Professor Gunnar Sorelius, known affectionately as Gunnar-Sit-Right-Down-And-Write-Myself-A-Letter. His book – *Shakespeare's Early Comedies* – certainly explains a lot about the plays, but also reveals much about the Swedes. He identifies Ovid as a great influence upon Shakespeare. But the Swedes are no less attuned to the Roman. They too understand that the world is in a state of perpetual flux, that metamorphosis is the norm. Who is more sensitive to the brevity, the fragility of a midsummer night's dream? Who is more aware that when chaos gives way to order, chaos remains in the wings? All the plays, says Sorelius, have a Janus-like quality; which is to say that July always implies January.

Bror's meteorologists were right, needless to say; it was snowing by the end of the week. One of our new friends rejoiced, and gleefully described the pleasures of cross-country skiing. 'The paths are enlightened till past nine o'clock,' he assured us. 'And when it is below minus five you can see ice crystals form in the air. It is almost like a drug. In fact a doctor assures me that the cold acts upon the brain in a similar way. It certainly makes you feel high!' Of course he should have used 'illuminated' rather than 'enlightened', but it was a delightful error, which expressed to perfection the Swedish attitude to the natural world; both enlightening and controllable, like LSD taken in laboratory conditions. But even in the most ordered of societies things can get out of control, whereupon the strange and terrifying beast that lurks beyond the circles of enlightenment makes an appearance. Darkness is its name. It may be found in the deepest part of the forests that girdle most Scandinavian settlements, but its true habitat is the Scandinavian winter.

Long before Uppsala became the national omphalos of theology and learning – Sweden's Canterbury and Oxbridge – it was the haunt of the Svea, the proto-Swedes. They worshipped Odin and feared that a wolf would swallow the sun. In order to avert this catastrophe animals and humans were sacrificed every ninth year, and their remains hung from trees in the sacred grove. On snowy evenings, among the copses and burial mounds of Gamla Uppsala, we could all but hear the echoes of those pagan cries and whispers. The language remembers too; *vargtimmen*, the hour of the wolf, is the darkest part of the night. It is also the title of an Ingmar Bergman movie. Driving the film are these words from *The Magic Flute*: 'O dark night! When will you vanish? When shall I find light in the darkness?' Bergman was born in Uppsala. Indeed, his parents were married in the cathedral. His mother was a local girl, raised in a grand house on

Trädgårdsgatan, where Bergman also spent his formative years. He shot his last film, *Fanny and Alexander*, on location in the city (where he was 'ogled and applauded like royalty'). He is Uppsala's *éminence grise*, geographer of its inner space.

As Christmas approached it seemed that every home, however atheistic, had advent candles burning in the window. Even the schools, the very fundament of the secular society, celebrated St Lucia's Day. At *Eriksskolan* the boys, our seven-year-old among them, donned the red tunic of a *tomten*, and danced attendance on their female classmates, all of whom were dressed as vestal virgins. Heading the procession was a girl crowned with a circlet of candles, 'to light the darkness'. Another acquaintance, a professor of theology, offered this explanation: 'Many of my fellow countrymen have lost faith in a personal god. But they mark the absence with sacred artefacts, they continue to struggle in the language and symbolism of religion.'

However, this takes no account of the equally insistent need to control nature, to uncover its inner workings; to restore reason's crown, and thereby banish irrational fears of the void, not to mention irrational behaviour. A few kilometres across the plain from Uppsala lies Hammarby, summer residence of Carl Linnaeus, the real *genius loci*, 'the most renowned scientist in Uppsala's five hundred years as a university city'. The house and its outbuildings sit modestly upon a cultivated corner of the rocky landscape; indeed they are a variation upon it, being made of local timber and, in one instance, roofed with turf. The neat walls are the colour of bloodstone, being plastered with a ruddy paste that is produced when the waste of local copper mines is mixed with linseed oil. In the brilliant light of an autumn afternoon those russet walls glowed like the skins of ripe fruit. Hammarby's owner was surely the ideal Swede, for his greatest achievement was the *Systema naturae*, an attempt to fix the identity of all living things, the rationalist's antidote to Ovid's *Metamorphoses*.

It seems that eighteenth-century Uppsala was teeming with

such encyclopaedists. For example, in a neoclassical house on Svartback Street, the astronomer Anders Celsius perfected the scale – centigrade – that would thereafter keep winter's measure. Thanks to him we could be certain that the first day of December was more than usually chill, was in fact minus 22. Like every Swedish residence ours had a thermometer affixed to an exterior wall. It was practically a civic duty to consult it on winter mornings, so that you did not go insufficiently clothed into a hostile world. The local paper, noting a preference for style over substance, delivered a fierce jeremiad. 'Today's fashion of wearing just a headband instead of a hat is deplorable when attempting to stay warm in very cold temperatures, such as the ones Uppsala is experiencing at the moment,' it scolded. 'To venture outside without a hat represents a threat to one's entire organism.'

The temperature was still well below freezing when we rode the train to Stockholm a week later. From the Central Station we hurried across the bridge into Gamla Stan, the Old Town, and clip-clopped our way up quaint Västerlånggatan until we reached Stortorget, the Great Square, where we entered the gilded and colonnaded hall of the venerable Bourse; not only the Stock Exchange, but also the Swedish Academy. There we heard a very dapper Egyptian (whom I was to encounter again at a conference in Mexico) deliver the Nobel Prize lecture on behalf of Naguib Mahfouz, a reluctant traveller. We emerged to discover that the temperature had risen unexpectedly, causing the snow to thaw with great rapidity. During the night, however, the temperature once again plunged below zero, and by morning Uppsala was transformed; ubiquitous ice made the city look like an exquisite ornament, as though the Snow Queen had commissioned Fabergé to electroplate its trees, shrubs and streets with silver. Despite their best efforts, the townspeople couldn't keep their feet, causing the hospitals to treat a record number of broken wrists, sprained ankles, and concussions. Knowing the precise temperature was of no assistance. It was a flawless demonstration of essential instability.

## SUMMER

By contrast the temperature on 4 July 1997 is nearly 30° centi-grade. The two of us – father and son – are returning to Scandinavia for the first time in nine years. Bror, our man in Stockholm, is on vacation, as are all other middle-aged Swedes; either in their dachas or in the warm south. The city has fallen to the young; my eyes are partial, so all I see are armies of nubile girls patrolling the streets in their summer suits of cotton and skin. They are certainly dressed for the weather, though not all would regard their attire as sensible. Alas, as far as they are concerned I am the Invisible Man. Except to the receptionist at the Lydmar Hotel, where we have reservations. Our room has a double bed. 'No way,' says my travelling companion. I return to the reception desk. 'The young man is my son, not my catamite,' I say, 'is it possible to have a room with twin beds?' We are offered an alternative. No time to relax. The phone is ringing. The receptionist. 'I have a fax for you,' she says. 'I'll be right down,' I reply. She hands me the single sheet without a word. It's from a friend who promised an introduction to Swedish exotica. 'Sorry,' it begins, 'I misinformed you. *Condominion* is in Amsterdam, not Stockholm. You'll have to get your novelty rubbers elsewhere. However, there is a gay beach at Kärsön; a beautiful island, I'm told, with woodpeckers and deer, who, I presume, are also gay.' In order to establish my heterosexual credentials I leave the book I'm reading in a conspicuous position; a 60 pence extract from amorous old Ovid, *Orpheus in the Under-world*. Only later do I read how Orpheus consoled himself after the loss of his wife. Apparently paedophilia was unknown in Thrace until then.

On just such a summer's day in 1628 the *Wasa*, flagship of Gustavus Adolphus, began its maiden voyage from the quay near the King's palace. In fact we would have had an excellent view from the Opera House, where we have just booked dinner. We would have seen her towed out into the Saltsjön, her sails set: foresail, foretopsail maintopsail, and mizzen. We would have been dazzled by the woodcarvings on her poop and bow, swaddled like toffees in goldleaf. Roman emperors flanked the figurehead, supposedly His Majesty's ancestors, while gaudily painted warriors in ancient armour guarded the upper galleries, ever ready to smite the foe. 'Look,' I would have said, as the great galleon swanned by, 'there's Hercules with Cerberus, terrible guardian of the underworld, chained at his feet.' But as the ship left the shelter of the cliffs a sudden gust caught the canvas and she heeled to port, righted herself, then keeled over completely. 'All were in a state of confused terror,' wrote Ovid of another shipwreck. 'Their seamanship deserted the sailors, their spirits sank, and a separate death seemed to be rushing upon them with each oncoming wave.' She went under within minutes, 'pennants and all'. Only then did Neptune show compassion. The *Teredo navalis*, a termite with a taste for wood, was banished from the Baltic, permitting the *Wasa* to gently marinate like a monstrous herring on the seabed, until raised intact in 1961. Now she is on display in all her former glory; a unique relic, a gigantic fossil.

The Opera House has two restaurants: the Opera Café and the Operakallaren. We are patronizing the former. I remember eating in the grander establishment, some time ago, with my friend Lena, arts editor of *Affärer*, and devotee of August Strindberg; though I remember the conversation better than the cuisine. It was Lena who introduced me to the *Blå Tornet*, the spectacular art nouveau tower where Strindberg spent his last years, and the Intimate Theatre, where his chamber works were belligerently enacted. Strindberg was not sympathetic to the combination of drama and food, scoffing at 'tittering diners'. But we're excused, our tickets are for tomorrow night. The Opera Café gleams with *fin de siècle* splendour, a cross between the Café Royal and the bar at the *Folies Bergère*. Our first course, a selection of Swedish hors d'oeuvres, resembles an artist's palate, one with a preference for flesh tones. There's a dab of pink – the prawns; orange – the lumpfish caviare; rose madder – the *gravadlax*; burnt umber – the roast reindeer; grey – the marinated herring. I look up at the ceiling wondering whether any part of the enormous fresco requires restoration, perhaps some naked torso with divine bosoms, but all I see is bereaved Orpheus strumming his lyre. We have swordfish and steak for the main course, and wild strawberries for desert.

After the meal it is still light, of course. In fact you begin to wonder if it will ever get dark. The sky is iceberg blue, overlaid with strips of smoked salmon. Hot-air balloons drift overhead like hard-boiled eggs. 'The night is young,' I say to my son, 'the world is our *smörgåsbord*. What shall we do?' We hike the length of Kungsgatan (i.e., the King's Road); past concert halls, past multiplex cinemas, past nightclubs, past alfresco cafés, past the twin towers that seem common to all great maritime cities, past a duo singing 'Dust My Broom' (in Swedish), past the thousand smiles of a summer's night, until we reach *Fasching*, reputed to be the best jazz club in town. The doors are open and we can hear the mambo rhythms of a Latin American combo. We can also see the audience, most of whom look younger than my son. 'Another time,' he says sympathetically. There's more jazz at our hotel, and waitresses whose chests clearly say — albeit in a muffled voice — 'Hello boys!' Rather, *boy*. I retire gracefully, switch on CNN, and wait for Sojourner to send back pictures from Mars.

Stockholm stands where the sweet waters of Lake Mälar mingle with the bitter brine of the Baltic. It is a series of skerries stitched together with bridges, a patchwork of water, wood, and stone. Reflective surfaces are everywhere, but this is not a city of narcissists. Stockholm's beauty is natural, and unselfconscious. Indeed, one of the islands, Djurgården, could stand as an idealized self-portrait; not only the capital, but the country in microcosm. Formerly a royal hunting preserve, it now contains numerous museums, including one which preserves the complete range of Swedish domicile; from Lapp croft to mansion. There's also a zoo, filled with every variety of indigenous creature, and a much larger nature reserve. Djurgården? Better call it the Republic of

Linnia. It is certainly a likeness, but it is not the living image. There was a joke I once heard. 'What's the difference between Sweden and a pot of yoghurt?' 'I don't know. What's the difference?' 'Yoghurt's got culture.' This may be true of Linnia, but it slanders the real country.

To prove it we are travelling in the opposite direction; a ferry is taking us across the lake towards the island of Lovön, where the royal family built its modest Versailles: Drottingholm, a Frenchified palace, with formal gardens, ancient statues of men behaving heroically, and an eighteenth-century theatre attached. The latter is neoclassical, sweetly proportioned, perfectly symmetrical, and the colour of butter. If you've seen Ingmar Bergman's film of *The Magic Flute*, you'll be familiar with the interior; with its contemporary scenery and stage machinery, dating from the days of Gustav III (the one who was assassinated at a masked ball). Tonight they are performing Jacopo Peri's even older *Euridice*. How could we resist? Orpheus and his bride appear, and a chorus of nymphs and shepherds sing, 'the sun never saw such a loving pair'. But, woe, their happiness is short-lived. A messenger enters to report the death of the heroine. Consternation. Orpheus performs a heartbreaking *lamento*. Venus, moved, obtains a visa for the Underworld. Orpheus descends, and begs Pluto for the return of his beloved. Pluto obliges and the lovers are reunited. The opera concludes with joyful choruses and dances. Eh? Who is Peri kidding? Everyone knows that Orpheus looked back and lost Eurydice. But not tonight. The false ending is the perfect icon of the Swedish summer, when everyone acts as if the light will never die, even though everyone knows that the season is two-faced, and that winter is approaching.

# 9. BABYLON VISITED

·•·

'Take a look at New York,' says the pilot, 'you're never likely to get a better view.' Thousands of feet below, the lights of the city form geometric patterns; gold out of black. A landscape by Piet Mondrian. It is like much modern art; striking but incomprehensible.

At immigration the girl asks me, 'You here on business or pleasure?'

'Both,' I reply.

Fran is waiting for me in the reception area. We embrace. It has been a long separation.

It's about 90 degrees tonight; thick drops of moisture dribble from the atmosphere like condensation in a steaming kitchen. The City Bus is already half full of elderly ladies forlornly fanning themselves with copies of the scandalous *National Enquirer*. I have read somewhere that the *eshoba* or fly-whisk used by African leaders is really meant to brush off evil spirits, and I rather suspect that these superstitious New York matrons are playing the same game.

The agency has booked me into the Hotel R——, but we decide upon an extravaganza and spend our first night at the Algonquin. In the dazzling dining room a waiter approaches us, and like all great waiters he makes his obscure European origin obvious. 'You are ready, yes?' he says. He stands over us, pen on paper, like a student awaiting a comment from his professor. I say, 'We'll begin with the vichyssoise and the escargots, and then I'll have the Long Island duckling and the lady will have the scallopine of veal.' 'Thank you,' says the waiter; I hope that I have not disappointed him. He walks studiously away and we sense we're in for a long wait. Soon I find myself eavesdropping. Such is the reputation of the Algonquin that you listen in constant expectation of a priceless epigram. The two ladies next to us are involved in an intense conversation. Their voices remind me of English actresses who play in Henry James serials on BBC2; certainly both speak with the appropriate degree of gravity.

'I have a very dear friend I want you to meet,' says A, 'she works in television.' 'My boyfriend is writing a novel,' B says, not to be outdone, 'he's written fifty pages, and he's got another hundred to go. It's about this man who is taken by his lover to a big house full of women and used as a sexual plaything by them all. He has to do whatever the women want.'

'That sounds like a very good idea. What happens in the end?'

'More women come bringing other men, and they don't need him any more. Tastes change, so he's abandoned.'

'Does he lose his masculinity?'

'Oh, yes. They dress him up in women's clothes and all things like that.'

'Tell me, is there one woman who makes statements on behalf of the others?'

'I'm not sure of that.'

'Why?'

'Because he hasn't got to that bit yet.'

And so they go on, earnestly discussing a book that does not actually exist. I am superstitious, I do not like discussing anything I am working on, and I feel a tinge of sympathy for the unknown writer. Americans are often in a hurry. They tend to anticipate reality, they grow impatient quickly. Not us, we wait patiently for our slow snails. Eventually our Continental waiter returns bringing cold soup and escargots.

We have come to the Algonquin straight from Kennedy Airport, and in a way we are still in transit. We'll be gone tomorrow. But tonight we are happy to respond to the literary history of the Algonquin, to honour blind Thurber and dumb Harpo Marx and other jousters of the Round Table (third on the right in the Oak Room). We try to trace thematic connections between here and Kennedy's Camelot, but nowadays the mythologist has given way to the muckraker, and it is better not to look too closely at America's past because all the straight lines get twisted and everyone turns out to have been bent. *Sic transit gloria mundi*, also.

Sitting in the lobby I ping the bell that's attached to our table. A waiter appears and we order chocolate cake. 'Of course, sir.' There are no inconsistencies inside the Algonquin, nothing to disturb the culture, everything works to order. The chairs are soft, 'coolly slip-covered in summer', the walls are panelled in seventy-five-year-old oak, and the tables are just big enough for coffee and cakes or neat whiskey and nuts. Intimacy is encouraged. People speak dialogue. It all reminds me of my favourite magazine, *The New Yorker*. That attention given to detail, the care taken over appearances. I have never seen a misprint in *The New Yorker*. An article that describes some beastliness in Vietnam will, nonetheless, look extremely elegant. If the United States cannot impose democracy with an army, at least *The New Yorker* can superimpose the order of good English. In a sense it is a missionary magazine, holding the old rationalist belief that man is not necessarily corrupted by the filth he experiences. It uses grammar as a charm against chaos. Though I wonder if merely naming the thing *lupus* will really keep the wolf from the door.

In Room 1112, later, I quote John Donne.

> *Licence my roving hands, and let them goe*
> *Behind, before, above, between, below.*

*Oh my America, my new found lande,*
*My kingdome, safeliest when with one man man'd,*
*My myne of precious stones, my Empiree,*
*How blest am I in this discovering thee.*

The Hotel R— is very big. The lobby is full of people on the move; they will not stay still long enough to meet your eye; there is no way you can invite intimacy with any of them. They are all in transit between roles, in limbo land between being an insurance salesman and a loving husband. This hotel clearly isn't a safe base where you may nurse your neuroses; on the contrary it is a place where you dare not stop to think for fear of what you might conceive. We register. 'Mr Sinclair of Young & Rubicam.' I am glad Fran is with me, for I know that otherwise I should be very lonely here. The Hotel R—, however, has anticipated this loneliness and provided for it; the management have taken advantage of a recent New York statute which forbids any massage parlour to operate unless it is part of a larger establishment and opened one of their own. On the mezzanine we glimpse rangy girls in sparkling bikinis strutting inside the Leisure Palace. Beside the door, illuminated by concealed neon lights, is this promise. 'What hasn't your woman done for you lately? Come be part of the way of life you fantasize. Submit to delights always imagined. Sensually the cool hands of our magnificent ones slowly anoint your tense body with exotic oils, stroking to a rhythm of inner excitement. Your body tones are prepared by mistresses of the vibrator.' What a vision for the weary traveller! An Amazon holding aloft a liberating vibrator beside a golden door! The Leisure Palace is open twenty-four hours a day. Just the place to seek refuge from the hour of the wolf.

There is no daylight in the corridors, only artificial glows and deep shadows. Jimmy, the porter who carries our cases, is a small man in an untidy uniform; greasy haired, sharp featured, an obscenity hanging like a drip on the tip of his tongue. He pushes open the door of our room. The bed is unmade. There is a tray, full of dirty dishes and broken toast, among the blankets. The plates are all sticky with jelly. A single fly buzzes, disturbed by our entry. The porter is angry, but his anger is not directed at the mess in the room, nor even toward us for having seen it, he is just angry – period. He hollers, 'Sadie!' Down the corridor, in a pool of light, a door swings open. A fattish black woman in green overalls appears. 'Whaddya want?' she yells. She swaggers over, muttering, to see for herself what the fuss is all about. 'Shit,' she says, 'I didn't know 558 left already.'

Back in the lobby a complete airline crew – pilots, stewards, and glamorous stewardesses in butter-brown buttock-tight skirts – is checking in. A black man in a different uniform – custardy-cream in colour, with gold braiding along the collar and cuffs – rotates in through the whirling doors. Air Ghana? But he is followed by another black man in exactly the same get-up, and another, and another, until twenty-five have entered; and they are followed in their turn by an equal number of black women in starched white dresses and Sunday hats. The precise nature of their union is a mystery, but since they are all sporting badges with Brother This and Sister That spelt out on them we conclude that they must be either a religious or a Masonic or a patriotic society. People passing stare at them as if they are an invading army, probably envious of their kinship, of the identity they draw from the group. They all amount to something. It is odd that a nation which preaches the predominance of the individual, that has motivated the myth of the loner, should set so much store on the recognition of others. Still we all of us need this external identity. Fran provides mine. I am her lover. I am lucky. However, Jimmy (who is carrying our cases along the corridor for the second time) wears his uniform like a mark of shame. To be a porter at the Hotel R— excites envy in no one. That makes him angry.

On our bed is a yellow card bearing the encouraging title, 'Hotel Security and Safety Precautions'. It contains 10 Alwayses and 7 Nevers: 'Always keep the door locked while you are in your hotel room; when retiring for the night use the double lock and chain'; 'Never invite strangers to your room.' It reads like an incantation to ward off bad luck. At the bottom of the card there is a black spot, like on those 'Accident Black Spot' road signs you see at dangerous corners in England. It effectively reduces your area of safety to a single room, it implies that the City of New York (which begins on the other side of the door) is full of people just waiting to get you. So what can a person do here? Left alone in your room chances are you'll lose your mind and blow your brains out, venture outside and you'll probably be murdered before you've gone fifty paces.

We share the elevator with another couple. The lady is a middle-aged plump one who looks as though she has been well-cared for.

'You are English,' she says.

'We are.'

'Do you know how I guessed?' she says. 'Well, I heard you say *post* rather than *mail*. You see, I know your country very well. I love it. We used to visit at least once a year.'

The man, a little bald chap in a short-sleeved shirt, explains.

'This is the widow of Oliver Hardy.'

'The late Oliver Hardy.'

'The late Oliver Hardy,' he says, corrected.

'This is my present husband,' she says.

'Pleased to meet you.'

The man smiles proudly. It is good to be somebody. Later we hear on the radio that the widows of both Oliver Hardy and Stan Laurel have been awarded all the royalties accruing from the use of their late husbands' names.

'The great big city's a wondrous toy, just made for a girl and boy, we'll turn Manhattan into an isle of joy.' Right on, Ella! We decide to take a ride on the Staten Island Ferry. How to get there? Fran, expert map-reader, plots a route. Along Madison Avenue. Madison Avenue! Wow! Left on East 42nd Street. No joke, I'd be lost without Fran. Down the steps into Grand Central

Station. Old black men in red blazers, hair all grizzled, offer to shine your shoes; pale men in light summer suits stop and sit in state reading *The Wall Street Journal*. Right foot out, left foot out. The duster see-saws to and fro. From all four corners people teem down the stairs, painted orange by the overhead lights, hurrying, pleased to be travelling to their appointed places. Squares of bright kiosks sell magazines, cigarettes, chewing-gum, Kleenex, and other necessities of city life. Down more stairs into the subterranean subway station; concrete platform, grey columns, disappearing forest-like into the distance; scores of people wandering through the semidarkness. A rush of air. A clattering. The silver train approaches. Covered from roof to wheels in multi-coloured multilingual graffiti, layer upon layer, an archaeology of discontent. Starting from the general, the witty statement or the straightforward obscenity, moving to specific grievance – Attica, Vietnam, Gay Lib, Libido Lib, Chile, Czechoslovakia – and the exhortation – clickety-click, clickety-click, Pray for Peace – to the most basic statement of all, the writer's name, Joey or Mario or Huey's only available expression of individuality. People's art. Great. I'm all for it. Norman Mailer has written a book in favour of it. Why not? Think of London's tube stations plastered with posters advertising mouthwash, movies, and merchandise of every description; better by far 'Advertisements for Myself'. The train rattles off down the track, stops at stations: Park Avenue, Brooklyn Bridge, Wall Street, Bowling Green; people get on, people get off; blacks and whites and yellows; men and women, some in suits, some in denim; it all seems very normal, another working day for the folks. No one molests us. We arrive at South Ferry safe and sound. And here, right at the subway entrance, the invisible hand of some underground wit has sprayed, in letters of blazing red, *mene mene tekel up arsin*. The original writing on the wall.

Now that we've reached the shore the sky looks like it's full of tissue paper, grey-white clouds hanging there just waving gently in the breeze. We're in Battery Park, on the southern tip of Manhattan Island, where the Hudson River and the East River begin to go their separate ways. But people are meeting here; lunchtime lovers walking hand in hand, older couples sitting on the benches munching salami sandwiches and throwing crumbs to the cooing pigeons. Parks are fun, one of the few places in the city where you can wander around without any ostensible purpose; their peripatetic therapy enables you to return refreshed to the city proper. Looking back from Battery Park we can see the first wall of skyscrapers, windows glittering in the hazy sunshine, and we feel the mythic strength of New York, a city paned with gold. Helicopters whirligig their way around the tops of the buildings and swoon away out over the coast. The stories we've heard! And here it all is, shimmering. It gives off a kind of medieval splendour, all the cruelty of a castle; it is a city full of lords and vassals, of safe refuges and wildernesses, of priests and poets, of minstrels like Dylan, of robbers and wild bands of outlaws. It is full of tribes. No wonder my grandfather, a cobbler in a *shtetl*, situated some way beyond the pale (near Smolensk), dreamed his bold dreams of America. For his whole generation America was the Promised Land, the Golden Land. Here they are described by an enthusiastic editor of *Tageblatt*, a contemporary New York Yiddish newspaper:

> Millions of yearning eyes are peering ... towards the fair lady who stands in New York Bay holding aloft her beacon of hope to all who seek liberty, to all who seek opportunity. In millions of hearts there throbs one hope: the speedy coming of the day when they shall be able to flee ... and find shelter beneath the folds of the Statue of Liberty. For them hope is spelled A-m-e-r-i-c-a.

But in coming to America they became so anxious not to appear as greenhorns that they shaved off their beards and earlocks, forgot their religion, lost their identity, and bred a new generation of perplexed writers. Some got the gold, it is true, but many others simply became jaundiced. This misfortune, of course, came as no real surprise to my pessimistic people; indeed in Yiddish *Goldeneh Medina* means not only a Golden Land but also a Fool's Paradise. I belong to a tribe of suffering jokers, to borrow a phrase from *Herzog*.

Abraham Cahan, founder of *The Jewish Daily Forward*, and the first of the Jewish-American novelists, describes, rather ironically, in *The Rise of David Levinsky*, an immigrant's arrival in the New World.

> I conjure up the gorgeousness of the spectacle as it appeared to me on that clear June morning: the magnificent verdure of Staten Island, the tender blue of sea and sky, the dignified bustle of passing craft – above all, those floating, squatting, multitudinously windowed palaces which I subsequently learned to call ferries.

Well, the Staten Island Ferry we ride on isn't exactly up to that standard, but it is big and multidecked and bright yellow, and we stand up at the front and watch it churn its way out of the harbour, leaving behind foaming water and squawking gulls. There's the burr of the motors and the wind tugging at your hair. We lean forwards against the rails. Most of the other passengers are sitting down inside reading their papers; this journey being part of their regular commuter run, they do not bother much with the view. The light slants through the windows making dark triangles on the floor and ceiling, an expanding band of light that gives the populous interior the quality of an old photograph.

The enormous Statue of Liberty is green, going mouldy. And the words that launched a thousand ships (copy by the immigrant poet Emma Lazarus) are as stale as an old ad. 'Give me your tired, your poor,/Your huddled masses yearning to breathe free,/ The wretched refuse of your teeming shore./Send these, the homeless, tempest-tost to me,/I lift my lamp beside the golden door.' Who believes that now? And yet when you look back at the Island of Manhattan and see those various skyscrapers balancing there, blue-grey in the impure light, seemingly untouched by decay or decadence, as beautiful as Venice, all the terrors you know lurk in their shadows seem to dissolve and you are left with the feeling that New York is a marvellous and hopeful place. I know it is an illusion. 'You are a stranger in a strange land,' I tell myself, 'also with an expense account. You have Fran. What do you know?'

Think of Henry Roth's sad brilliant novel, *Call it Sleep*, the story of David Schearl, an immigrant boy growing up on the Lower East Side. Nothing optimistic here. The novel begins with David's arrival in America. But Roth uses the Statue of Liberty as a grim, forbidding symbol; 'her features were charred with shadow, her depths exhausted, her masses ironed to one single plain.' I detect a bitter joke about the masses cast into the melting pot. But now we are two generations on, and the fiery furnace ain't quite so hot. Where is the all-American jockstrap boy, the Wasp in his land of milk and honey? No longer in fashion, especially in New York, that's for sure. Nowadays, according to no less an authority than Philip Roth (no relation) all 'those bland blonde exotics called *shikses*' have the hots for 'none other than a brainy, balding, beaky Jew, with a strong social conscience and black hair on his balls, who neither drinks nor gambles nor keeps show girls on the side; a man guaranteed to give them kiddies to rear and Kafka to read – a regular domestic Messiah!'

On terra firma now, at the corner of Canal and Mott. And since we're in Chinatown we're thinking about sweet and sour pork. Nothing particularly noteworthy about this Chinatown; the usual parade of inscrutable restaurants, the interesting array of groceries selling strange ingredients, the misshappen ducks hanging in windows, the old parchment-coloured men wrapped up in their cardigans sitting on stools on the sidewalk gossiping to cronies, the bun-haired women scurrying by in tunics and trousers, a stray drunk from the Bowery smashing a bottle and swearing, the not knowing where to eat. On the wall facing us is a huge poster advertising the Dumpling House; above it is a poster-portrait of an obviously popular Chinese gent with the legend, 'You have a friend in Chinatown'; but above them both is a giant poster which reads, 'Ask for Hebrew National Kosher All Beef Frankfurters (100% government inspected), it's good for you.'

New York has turned out to be the largest Jewish city outside of heaven. Its mayor is a Jewish boy from Bournemouth, beaming Abe Beame, a sensible man, unglamorous, nothing like Lindsay, the handsome *shaygets*, who made so many promises but brought only *tsuris*, trouble. And its favourite son is Woody Allen, a red-haired owlish comedian of no great height, a suffering joker, whose latest movie has opened to wild acclaim – 'Woody Allen's imperially funny new picture', says *The New Yorker*. We join the queue outside the Sutton, at the junction of 3rd Avenue and East 57th, a point which appears to have been deliberately aligned with the midsummer sunset. We are all ablaze with the sun's final rays, our shadows extend eastwards. The movie is set in Russia. As expected the audience, which consists mainly of the children and grandchildren of Russians, laughs continuously.

At midnight, outside the Hotel R—, an extraordinary Volkswagen pulls up. It has been sprayed gold and the front has been raised to accommodate the radiator grille from a Rolls Royce (winged lady and all). The doors open and three svelte black whores in silver mink stoles emerge, followed by their super-fly chaperone, himself resplendent in full-length waisted coat and broad-brimmed white fedora. They are instantly recognizable for what they are, this impressive impresario with his trio of star-spangled cunts, their glamour is outrageously artificial, about as appealing as gold teeth. I feel I should approach them, Gladstone-like, waving, in place of a religious tract, this prize-winning advertisement culled from *The 54th Art Directors Annual*:

### 'WHEN I GROW UP I WANNA BE A PIMP LIKE
### THE GUY NEXT DOOR'

Kids take their heroes where they find them. When a boy growing up in the ghetto sees a pimp, he sees a big, beautiful, block-long car. A girl sees that hookers have fancy clothes. Numbers runners have money, pushers have cool. If they've never seen any better how can they know any better? That's why we've got to be there too. In the same neighborhood. On the same streets. At a Neighborhood Center, a kid can find everything from a cub scout pack to drug counseling . . . We figure the more a kid learns about himself and the rest of the world, the more heroes he'll have to choose from. And the better his choice will be.

232 Madison Avenue, NY 10016. National Federation of Settlements.

The other heroes on the block.

But who needs a punch in the face from a diamond-studded fist?

I have a friend in New York. Her name is Debbie. She is presently doing postdoctoral research at a hospital into the newly discovered connection between a lack of the chromosome that triggers puberty and adolescent female imbecility. She is the only child of a rich family. Her father made his fortune by marketing kosher pickles in jars with screw tops and selling out to a multi-national corporation at the right time. Debbie has offered to take us out for the day. She is going to pick us up at the Chrysler Building on 42nd Street. I am infatuated with the Chrysler Building, it has rapidly become one of my favourite buildings in the whole world. It is a wildly extravagant piece of art deco. The roof is a ziggurat, a set of shrinking silver steps, each decorated with a single semicircle (actually hubristic hubcaps), the whole coming to a cloud-piercing point. The interior is just as eccentric: marble floors, elevator doors inlaid in a variety of patterns, various examples of polished mahogany and exquisite marquetry. It all makes the more famous Empire State Building seem decidedly parvenu and rather vulgar. But even the Empire

State and those ridiculous winged American cars exude an exuberance and vitality that is infectious, that infuses the atmosphere of the city with something more than carbon monoxide. Good taste may caution you, but sometimes it's a pleasure to let yourself go, let yourself flow with the tide.

Some years ago, when I was still trying to get my first novel published, I presumptuously sent the first chapters to Jules Feiffer with a letter asking him if he would be so good as to illustrate it. He replied gently, several months later, from an address only a couple of blocks down on the street where we are now standing. 'It seems both foolish and arrogant to answer a letter so nice as yours so late,' he wrote, 'but I have fallen half a year behind on my entire life and I can't quite figure out when, or how to catch up.' New York is a giddy, restless place. It is the first city I have ever visited where I have had this precarious sensation of actually being able to fall off a moving thing known as life. And, as if to emphasize this civic momentum, as if to suggest that there is some great powerhouse beneath our feet, steam puffs up through each and every manhole cover.

Debbie rolls up in her stone-coloured Volvo. She shows us the Lower East Side where many of the shops still bear the name of Katz or Cohen, though most of the apartments are filled with Puerto Ricans. There are lots of derelict sites fenced off by barriers of diamond-shaped wire, with bright murals painted on the unoccupied walls, some representing hopeful scenes of reconciliation and redemption through joint effort, others bearing the clenched fist of revolution. The streets are covered with garbage. Not a hint of chicken fat, instead there is a faint odour in the air; reminiscent of teeth decaying, of calcium going off. The area seems drained of life, depressed, as if the Puerto Ricans are hiding in the shells abandoned by the Jews in their metamorphosis. It is very clear that these tenements with their rusty fire escapes are rotting. I'm glad to notice, however, that the building housing *The Jewish Daily Forward* still looks busy. 'If you think this area is bad,' says Debbie, 'you should see

Bedford-Stuyvesant.' Bedford-Stuyvesant is almost an unbeliev-
able myth; it is a place you do not visit under any circumstances;
a frightful Waste Land kind of place where innocents wander at
peril of their lives. Debbie tells a gruesome tale, of a foolish
friend raped and robbed, that sends shivers through us: New
Yorkers all have their own modern fairy stories which they
love to tell with grim intent. Bedford-Stuyvesant is a scabrous,
barbarous jungle of horrors; but in the man-made world it is a
mutation, an example of what a city might become; it is a
development, not a regression.

It is Saturday. Carefully synchronized bulbs beam out the time
on sides of buildings, flickety flick it's 11.06, then blankness
and on comes the weather report. It's still ninety out there. Today
the sky's the colour of a swimming pool, which momentarily
makes me want to turn the world upside down. The air-
conditioning in Debbie's car has packed up, so we're driving
north along Lexington Avenue with all the windows open. The
people on the streets are now nearly all blacks. Before we enter
Harlem proper we have to wind up the windows and make sure
that every door is locked from the inside. 'You hear of people
being dragged from their cars and beaten up in broad daylight,'
Debbie assures us. Harlem is hostile territory but negotiable, take
the correct precautions and you'll be OK; it does not have the
nightmarish associations of Bedford-Stuyvesant. The first house
we see in Harlem is painted bright red, rather jolly looking really.
Plenty of people walking around, all seeming to enjoy Saturday
morning at the shops. Girls in bum-contoured Levi's, braless
beneath bright T-shirts, stop at stalls selling wigs and try on
Angela Davis afros or fizzing blonde creations; men eye the girls,
whisper, nudge each other. There's the good smell of down-
home cooking outside a Southern Fried Chicken shop. And Al
Green is playing the Apollo tonight. Not a white face to be
seen. We pass terrace after terrace of elegant high houses, once
the height of fashion, each residence with its own flight of steps
leading to the front door. It seems that every step is filled with

people. The image of a vibrant community. But Debbie explains that everyone is outside because none of the houses has air-conditioning, and it gets too unbearably hot to stay indoors. On street corners the fire hydrants have been turned on, and thick jets of water arc into the air and tumble down in sparkling splashes onto giggling boys with thin shiny bodies and yellow underpants. I try to sneak a photograph through the windscreen but the children, on seeing the camera, cover their faces with their hands.

Down the side streets, where there is barely the width of three cars between the houses, the dilapidation is more obvious. Cracks in the sooty brickwork, broken windows. Homes decaying on their foundations, rotting away after decades of neglect. And in the road rusty wrecks of wheelless Buicks and Chevrolets. An overflow of cars is now blocking our way, and the street is too narrow for us to change direction. Stuck, we can sense the nearness of the lower depths. Slowly we edge toward the point where we can make the turn onto another main road and return to a recognizable facsimile of urban society. As we reach the end of our mean street I can see two white faces, but they are not welcome. Two cops have suddenly leapt from a squad car, the second door is still swinging shut. Some black kids are running about with sticks which they are holding like clubs, but from our position it is impossible to tell what they are doing. Coming down the road we can hear the hysterical hee-haw approach of more squad cars. The two cops start to move towards the gang, and I see that they have unbuttoned their holsters and that their hands are on the butts of their guns. And then suddenly everyone ducks behind the parked cars; it's a familiar choreography, the sort you see often on the news. Only this time we are in the middle of it, inside the television, as it were, and our locked doors and our rolled up windows seem like no protection at all. 'Let's get out of here!' I shout. Debbie pulls out into the main road and accelerates away. Behind us the screaming police cars execute dramatic stops. And we appreciate why it is best to stay inside your car in Harlem; because it does not take much to start an incident; a word misheard, a glance misinterpreted; and once that has happened there is no knowing how the event will end. Harlem, in a word, is unpredictable.

Black families picnic peacefully in the dusty strip of park beside the Harlem River. They sit on folding chairs beneath broad umbrellas beside their cars. Sandwiches, beer cans, and radios with long silver antennae stand in easy reach on makeshift tables. Other men take off their shirts and wash their newish cars. Kids throw footballs which skid across the ground, sending up wispy clouds of dirt. Sometimes mothers shout. It is a fine Saturday afternoon scene we're overlooking from the Expressway, a bucolic scene on the only available greenery. For the poorer blacks, the lower middle classes, this here is the country. But for us it's getting greener all the time, leafy Riverdale now, where psychiatrists live in the seclusion of rambling bungalows with private driveways. Latter day witchdoctors who commune with the spirits of the famous dead and bring comfort and tranquillity to Worried of New York City. Detached individuals who encourage the cohabitation of body and soul. Why even René Descartes would get no further than *cogito sum* in this uncertain place before having to consult a shrink. In fact most people would give their right arm to be able to make that tentative statement, 'I think I am'; they are still wrestling with a more basic question, viz., 'Who am I?' No conclusions nowadays, no *ergos*, just lacking egos and unsatisfied ids. The hero of this society is the Alexander Portnoy prototype, the Wandering Id. A refugee from the ghetto, having the freedom of the open city, but having found no satisfactory substitute for the abandoned tribal structure, the lost corporate identity.

We're travelling through quiet country villages with well-watered lawns and white clapperboard houses; where red fire trucks gleam inside spick and span fire houses and local post offices proudly fly the Stars and Stripes. The windows of the car are open again and along with the swish of the hoses we can hear robins singing. I ask Debbie to stop outside of one especially lovely wooden house, glowing in the afternoon sunshine, a flag on the pole waving in the breeze. Fran hands me my camera. Check the exposure. Frame the picture. Correct the focus. Click. One more for luck. Hey, what's this? An angry old man, an Eisenhower man, has emerged from the neighbouring house and is striding towards me across the sloping lawn. I can see the muscles working in those bony legs that protrude from his Bermuda shorts. He has freckles on his bald head, symptom of a sleepy retirement. 'Why are you photographing my daughter's property?' he demands. I reply in my best English accent. He is mollified. Some men believe that a camera can rob them of their souls, their materialist brothers have a suspicion that their properties (formerly houses) are somehow made less secure by being reproduced on Kodachrome.

At tacky Tarrytown we take time to see the home of Washington Irving. A dame dressed in the hooped skirts of the period is our guide. She obviously relishes being an anachronism. 'In those days people didn't have nearly so many problems as they do today,' she says standing beneath the purple flowers that bower the front door, 'it was the age of wisteria not of hysteria.'

Sunday's a good day for taking a walk. And here we are (hand in hand on this beautiful morning) strolling along Fifth Avenue. People in summer frocks or cotton shirts take turns in carrying baby, men in white coats stand beside metal boxes selling Cocacola, ice cream, and weenies, a woman holds a bunch of balloons. My camera dangles around my neck, constantly nudging me in the ribs. In passing a puffed-up porter from a swell apartment blocks says, 'Do you want to get a good picture?' We stop and he says, 'Well, I just seen Zsa Zsa Gabor take her dogs into the park, if you hurry you'll catch her.' Everyone is in Central Park today. A jazz band's playing beside the path, a honking saxophone, a clarinet going coochie coo; further on some boys in orange uniforms are practising baseball, while their contemporaries sit giggling contemptuously in the makeshift stands. The batter swings. Concentrate. Bam! The ball describes an arc. Thwack. A splutter of applause. The animals mooch in the zoo. Policemen in short-sleeved shirts patrol the pathways two by two. Dangerous-looking gangs of youths toss beer cans at the rocks that protrude from the earth and you don't criticize. Sexy girls in bits of denim or obviously naked 'neath caftans made in India lie prone on the gorgeous grass reading *Fear of Flying*. I buy Fran a strawberry ice-cream cone and upon discovering evidence of real strawberries munch half of it myself. 'Why didn't you buy one of your own?' says Fran. We trace the source of some bouncy organ music and come upon a great carousel going around and around with smart white horses cascading up and down, up and down. Envious, quarterless kids stand without watching the whirling bronco-busters. Haves and have nots? Have we happened upon a central symbol in the park? Does the horse (with all its booms and slumps) represent capitalism? Just imagine a carousel that no one willingly quits, so that there are more and more people jockeying for the same places. That's the new Social Darwinism; the triumph of the shittiest. But then the music stops. And with many howls protesting kids are yanked from the horses' backs by strong-armed mothers. We hear the smack of firm government.

Just look what's strewn all over the path; the contents of a pocket-book; photos of bearded boyfriend, dog, father, cut-out of mother, calling cards of TV producers and professors of physics, a library ticket, and a fountain pen. It doesn't take Sherlock Holmes to figure out that a lady's had her bag snatched, and it's not hard to find the item itself protruding from a pile of rubbish at the root of a tree. We collect all the bits and pieces together and replace them in the bag; afterwards we walk along on the lookout for a cop. And this absurd scenario starts in my mind, courtesy of Kafka. Girl: 'There he is! That's the bugger who mugged me!' Chorus: 'Stop, thief!' I'm caught red-handed and I can't prove that I didn't do it. Daft. I haven't done anything and I'm feeling guilty. Because innocence don't mean a thing to New York's *deux ex machina*. It's all random; effects without causes, crimes without motives; all a matter of luck. Takes us ages to find a cop. 'T'anks,' he says. 'My fingerprints are all over the bag,' I say helpfully, 'won't that hinder the hunt?'

'Listen,' says the cop, 'no one's that clever, this bag'll be put wid all the rest and if the owner comes to claim it, well, that's fine.'

He's right, it's fine, the sun is shining and sleeping dogs are lying in the shade.

On Sunday mornings, too, you can see promenading Jewish mothers *shepping naches* the length of Fifth Avenue. 'Ay,' says one to another, 'just look where we are already, that's my Benny's surgery.' Sure enough on the door is a brass plate which reads 'Benjamin A. Gold MD'. And next door houses a joint practice or Professional Corporation shared between Ezra M. Greenspan MD, Martin J. Weiner MD, and Seymoor M. Cohen MD. Such good sons! And so it goes on, door after door, until you've collected enough names to fill an immigrant ship. Then you see the name Guggenheim in gold letters on a big white building that looks rather like it's been screwed into a hole in the ground. Inside the gallery paintings circulate toward the roof, hanging alongside ramps that spiral upward, inviting you to toboggan down again on the last canvas. It's an airy, humorous, faintly mystical place that seems perfectly suitable for the present exhibition of Chagall's visionary paintings. There's also a dandy little restaurant in there that sells Orange Berry Spitzers. A grey-haired old lady, bespectacled and genteelly bedraggled, buttonholes Fran.

'Oh, those days at the Cap d'Antibes, when we were all young,' she says, 'everyone was there, you know. I used to sneak into the studio to watch Picasso painting; you know, he didn't like people to look at his work before it was finished. Once there was a woman with a baby-carriage, then when I saw it again he had painted over the figures and there was the sea instead. It's here now. Or is it the Museum of Modern Art? Lots of American girls used to bicycle down to see Picasso, you know, but his wife turned them away. I gave them tea.'

The lady sniffs and shuffles off in her grey mackintosh. We ask for our check and the waiter, who looks like an out-of-work actor, brings it on a saucer. We see that he has written 'Thank you, have a nice day' on the back. A pleasant gesture, we hope he has a nice day too, but I can't help thinking of Alex Portnoy's first encounter with 'good morning'.

> 'Good *morning*', he says, and now it occurs to me that the word 'morning', as he uses it, refers specifically to the hours between eight a.m. and twelve noon. I never thought of it that way before. He wants the hours between eight and twelve to be *good*, which is to say, enjoyable, pleasurable, beneficial! We are all of us wishing each other four hours of pleasure and accomplishment. Why, that's terrific! Hey, that's very nice! Good morning!

Have a nice day!

Before I left England I was told by the Creative Director that I must not represent Young & Rubicam (London), the well-respected advertising agency, in New York looking like a tramp. So this workaday Monday morning I don my corduroy suit, knot my tie (purchased by my mother in Harrods), and put on my Florsheim shoes. I pick up the folder which contains my work. The work that has been occupying me for the past few months: writing the copy for the United States Travel Service's new British advertising campaign. Yep, it's my job to sell America to the British, to promise a land across the Atlantic that's full of golden splendours, to fill boats and jets with hopeful holiday-makers. All right, I'm an Americanophile already, but this was a labour of love – get this for irony – while I was conjuring up bright images in Mornington Crescent my Fran was out there on an exchange programme teaching this twelvemonth in the suburbs of Chicago. Now here we are together in New York, to all appearances a businessman and his wife, expenses paid, thanks to Young & Rubicam in cooperation with the Department of Commerce.

I leave the Hotel R— and join the parade on Madison Avenue. Everyone looks very businesslike this morning; dapper fellas sneaking glances in Abercrombie & Fitch for the latest in conservative fashion, straight-laced ladies ever-ready to dot the i's and cross the t's. We all stop at the junctions when the red man flashes up, and wait while the traffic cop whistles and waves the rush of traffic onward. Whoosh! They gallop past in bouncing bunches, just like one of those cattle stampedes you see in Westerns. Then comes the green man and we're off again, jostling one another as we jog along. Unfortunately, it's turned out to be quite a slog to Young & Rubicam, and my disguise is beginning to cook me.

There are twenty-four floors in the Young & Rubicam building and each one, so far as I can deduce from the evidence I gather whilst the elevator doors open and close, is decorated in accordance with a different period of American history. I am like Schliemann seeing the cities of Troy, an archaeologist on a trip through the strata of Americana. I am shown at first hand the vertical progress of the American nation. I disembark eventually in the Colonial era. The black woman at the reception desk, however, won't have any of this white man's anachronistic crap, she's downright twentieth-century rude, and it's rather a relief. I'm sent down a sneaky snaking corridor to a conference room which contains a large round table bearing both the name of each visitor and also the flag of every nation where America is officially advertised. France, Canada, United Kingdom, Germany, Japan, Mexico. I sit in a chair opposite a place-tag marked 'Clive Sinclair London'. It turns out that all of the other delegates already know one another, being senior members of a multinational organization. Indeed, this present-day colonial system accounts for the fact that the men from Germany are Americans.

The Creative Director of the USTS campaign for the entire free world stands five foot five in his white leather shoes. His patriotic pants have blue and white stripes, and his jacket has red and white checks. His shirt, I notice, is decorated with strawberries. This puts me in mind of Iago, another persuasive man. He makes the 'opening remarks' referred to in the agenda in front of me. 'Now let's see what you've got,' he says sucking on the butt of an extinguished cigar. He expresses satisfaction with the work from most countries, but remains unsold on the Mexicans.

'I have some problems with your recommendations,' he says. 'I'm put off by the general approach which does not seem to be organic to any USTS proposition but rather self-consciously executional.'

The Mexicans say nothing.

'I doubt that your headlines would sufficiently involve readers to continue on to the copy,' he adds. 'Where is your benefit promise? To me this looks like an execution in search of an objective. Have you seriously decided what your selling message should be? Eh, Jesus?'

'We have carefully researched our target audience,' says Jesus (for that is the Christian name of the Mexican writer), 'and we think that AB Mexicans would get a kick out of the line "You be the tourist for a change".'

'OK, Jesus,' says the Creative Director. 'I recognize that these are harsh judgements but I would encourage you to consider them and reconsider your recommendations.'

In short, it's back to the drawing board for Jesus and his Art Director. The Creative Director's use of language fascinates me. I decide that it is based upon a profound awareness that the truth can hurt. He has taken the principle of the 'white lie' and structured an entire mode of expression around it, so that his speech contains one euphemism after another. He does this not simply to spare a colleague's feelings but mainly to avoid embarrassment for himself.

I am encouraged to make a few alterations to the British campaign before the final presentation to the actual client in the afternoon; the major one being to place 'America. The Unforgettable Holiday' as the endline of each advertisement. I meet the Art Director who has been assigned to help me. She's as tall as me, taller if you measure to the top of her afro haircut. The left lobe of her nose is pierced by a small gold ring. She is wearing a tight T-shirt with the words 'Go Fuck Yourself' across her tits. Her nipples make it look like a sign screwed to her chest. Her name is Afrikaa. However, she is extremely polite and competent, and everything gets done to everyone's satisfaction.

Demi avocado and shocking pink shrimps for lunch, plus dollops of cottage cheese posing as albino caviare. Afterwards I discover that all the toilets in Young & Rubicam have combination locks on the door, and that in order to relieve yourself you must remember the number 153.

The Advertising Manager from the United States Travel Service – our client – is an ambitious man. He is after one of the top jobs in the department, which is up for grabs because the previous incumbent was a Nixon appointee who somehow managed to get himself involved in the Watergate affair and was consequently put out to grass. He takes off his lightweight summer jacket, leans back in his chair, puts his feet on the edge of the table, and says, 'Right, what have you got to show me?'

'Well . . .' I say.

There are three of us at the table; M— from USTS, myself, and the Creative Director in his strawberry shirt. The room itself is enormous and without windows; all the light comes from the neon strips around the walls, just as the atmosphere comes ready-cooled from the air-conditioning unit. I pause because I notice that M— is staring, transfixed, at a bleeper which someone has left on the table. A bleeper is a thin onomatopoeically named instrument which Account Executives carry around with them in the event of someone wanting to reach them when they are out of their office. Actually, it looks exactly like Captain Kirk's communicator in *Star Trek*.

'Say,' says M——, 'what is that thing, it's not a tape-recorder is it? We're all kinda sensitive of the things at the moment.'

'Don't worry,' says the Creative Director, 'we're not into dirty tricks here, not yet at any rate.'

My presentation to M—— continues like this: What we have done is to divide America into six regions for the purposes of six advertisements. Each advertisement starts from a specific moment at a specified spot and works itself out from there. We have taken this approach because the United States is such a pseudo-mythical place that most people cannot automatically connect it with reality. For example, the Costa Brava suggests a single image, a combination of sun, sand, sea, and sex, whereas America blows the mind with a kaleidoscope of contrasting images. Result, confusion. We have sought a central image to represent each area, to act as a sort of focus. 'Finally, we want our readers to feel they have experienced America.'

The Creative Director nods. So I haven't done too badly, then. M—— puts a piece of pinkish Dentyne in his mouth, chews it over, then dispatches it into the wrapping paper which he squeezes and drops into an ashtray, after which he takes another Dentyne and repeats the performance. A chain gum chewer? A chain chewing gummer? 'Can I get a glass of water?' he asks. Sure. M—— then produces a bottle of kaolin and morphine mixture from his briefcase, shakes it vigorously, and tips two teaspoonfuls into the glass. 'I've got this problem with my stomach,' he explains. I notice that he has the figures 153 scribbled on his pad.

'Right,' says M——, having composed himself, 'my problem is that I don't see anything in the campaign about value, don't get me wrong, I don't just mean value for money, I mean all-round value, you know, like a valuable experience.' Ah, we explain that in fact the advertisements are all about the value of the experience, even though they do not say so in the exact words. But M— is a vain, neurotic, stubborn man; he is convinced that he knows everything there is to know about advertising and he wants to see the word 'value'. Many Americans, especially those connected with advertising, have an uncanny belief in the power of certain trigger words like 'value', 'genuine', and 'guarantee', like 'pure', 'natural', and 'free'. Indeed they flag an offer or an advertisement in the same unsubtle way that the words 'delicious', 'languorous', 'thrust', and 'ecstasy' signal a spot of pornography. But are they not now all somewhat devalued? Not according to M—. He believes, like Coleridge, in the willing suspension of disbelief.

Recently I was involved when Proctor & Gamble, a multi-national giant headquartered at Cincinnati, launched Crest toothpaste in Britain. The launch year was known as Year One, thus dividing time into BC and AC. I wanted to get Alistair Cooke to do the first commercials on the theme 'The toothpaste that began a revolution in American dental hygiene,' but this approach was thought to be too intellectual, besides which it offended against the official P&G credo based upon the theory of mass conversion by example. The typical P&G commercial consists of a dialogue between two women, one of whom believes in a P&G product, cleverly constructed so that in the course of sixty seconds the former converts the latter (the telepathetic representation of all the unenlightened women who are watching and thus also converted) to Crest or Fairy Liquid. Accused of exploiting housewives in their commercials, P&G men reply that, on the contrary, their products have liberated women from unending chores at the kitchen sink. What advertising demands is a quick mind and a straight face. I may have the former (despite P&G's branding of me as an intellectual), but I plainly do not possess the latter. I have been described in a secret file kept on me by one of the headhunters in the business as 'looking like a dirty phone call'.

'*There! There she is! Now go back to the agency and write something for* her!'

There's this *New Yorker* cartoon set in a supermarket. A dopey-looking dame is picking up a pack of washing powder, watched by a copywriter and his Creative Director. The Creative Director says, 'There! There she is! Now go back to the agency and write something for *her!*' I do not aspire to that degree of self-effacement, I cannot even cope properly with the suppression of individuality that copywriting demands. I remain a barmitzvah'd non-believer.

In the end we agree upon a compromise with M—. We add this sentence to the box where we have placed all the prices in the layout, the cost-box: 'Compared to other holidays and compared to what you get for your money an American holiday is just about the best value around.' 'Well, it looks like we've got ourselves an advertising campaign', says M—, stretching. I have, in a manner of speaking, sold America. I have earned my money.

Fran also has a friend in New York. Sal. A girl who works with the Quaker Mission at the United Nations. We walk over to see her in the late afternoon, passing St Patrick's gothic Cathedral just at the moment when a troupe of girls in pure white graduation gowns and matching mortarboards emerge from the gloom and walk purposefully out into the barbaric city, looking like a band of angels on a mission to convert the fallen, or maybe they are the dazzling white Daz girls from Proctor & Gamble worth $10 if you're carrying the right detergent. Either way they are quickly swallowed by the crowds who are hurrying now to avoid the approaching downpour. It is raining heavily by the time we reach the United Nations Building. At the gates the flags of all the nations flutter like butterflies on spikes. An African delegate in a natty grey suit walks across the shining Plaza, undisturbed by security guards, sheltering under his multi-coloured umbrella, heading for the equivalent of the stage door. Across the road someone has set up a tent looking for all the world like a nomad outside the court of some fabulous potentate, except that he is holding up a banner which reads, 'Hunger Strike for Family Reunion Communist Roumania ignores Human Rights'. Down by the East River some members of the Jewish Defense League in yarmulkes and sweatshirts are squatting beside torn placards which say, 'No to the PLO'. What are these Jews defending? Israel? Is the homing instinct still that strong? Are they New Yorkers? Or exiles? The poet A. Leyeless (né Aaron Glanz), leader of the Yiddish Introspective Group, had not been in America many years before he sat down and rewrote 'By the Rivers of Babylon':

> By the rivers of New York I sat down,
> I forgot nothing and remembered nothing at all,
> And I did not weep.

'And still with vain design New Babels, had they wherewithall, would build,' guessed Milton. Well, the wherewithal arrived – the largest cheque in history was written by a Rockefeller to purchase the land, formerly a rundown area of slaughterhouses, for the United Nations – and the building got done. It was opened in 1952. Inside there's this bluish panel of stained glass designed by Chagall. The Metropolitan Opera House at the Lincoln Arts Center also has three giant murals by the émigré-

Russian master. It seems that every large public building must have its Chagall or Chagall–equivalent, as if to illustrate that even the most austere-looking building does have a soul; a very Cartesian approach to architecture.

Sal escorts us to the General Assembly, a theatrical place. Beside every seat is a set of headphones to enable each delegate to receive a simultaneous translation – in the official UN language of his or her choice – of all the superfluous and mellifluous speeches that are declaimed during melodramatic sessions. Behind the scenes, I'm told, much good is achieved, but in this vast stage-struck hall (with its circular skylight four feet in diameter designed to admit a single shaft of sunlight onto the Assembly floor) you can't but recall that cautionary tale of the Tower of Babel, and you wonder if the advances made possible by modern technology are sufficient to ward off the ancient curse of knotted tongues.

There's a Quaker House in a group of brownstones called Turtle Gardens just a few blocks distant. A remarkably elegant set of buildings these, laced together with wrought-iron fences, and concealing in their centre a sweet communal garden. In it there is a startling absence of city sounds. The evening sun is shining on lush foliage while sparkling droplets trickle down their emerald veins and plop with a splat onto the crazy paving. Sal's mother is sitting out in a deck-chair watching a giggling birthday-suited granddaughter polish off a Red Delicious apple. Classical statuary glimmers palely in overgrowing recesses, and a grotesque gargoyle grimaces in the leafy shadow of a lime tree. Katharine Hepburn lives in the house directly opposite, we are told, but the curtains are drawn. A movie star's dark retreat.

Sal's burly black-haired husband returns from his afternoon stint at a downtown bar. Oversensitive, his Italian ancestry obvious. He cannot find a job in publishing in New York, so in the meantime he is a barman, and because Sal is so involved in what she does he compensates by being aggressively barman-like; he stays out drinking most nights with the swinging set he has met, coming home at three or four with a hurtful absence of excuses. 'The other day I suddenly wondered what his attitude to wife-swapping would be,' says Sal to Fran, 'and I wasn't sure that he would be against it.' We've just come through a difficult year apart with affections intact, so we've earned the role of understanding duo, but who knows if one day it will be one of us in turn confiding in a seemingly secure friend.

Night-time's the right time in New York. Be bop de boop. A band is playing Dixieland at a place called Michael's Pub. An amateur group made up of doctors, lawyers, and professional people plus Woody Allen on clarinet or liquorice stick. Woody Allen, ubiquitous urbanite, musician, movie director, playwright, writer, actor, philosopher, joker; Renaissance man of American culture. Sitting puff-cheeked on the dais, serious-faced, concentrating hard on converting valuable breath into gleeful music; dressed in Levi's and a green combat jacket, he's got black-rimmed glasses on a bigish nose and lanky red hair with a yarmulke-sized bald spot on his pate. Instantly recognizable as a hero of New York City, some mother's *bubeleh* who's made it in Babylon, loved by every diner in surprisingly smart Michael's Pub. When the set's over he wanders by himself among the crowded tables to the reflective facsimile of a Victorian bar, accepting en route all the accolades that come his way from show-biz acolytes. A Daniel in the lion's den. But also a *shlemiel*; Shane of the *shtetl*.

Bo bop de babylon.

America's getting on for two hundred years old. That means, really, that it is only now reaching its Middle Ages. Imagine, within this growing nation, a city state able to indulge its wildest dreams and most hubristic ambitions, and you've got the genesis and genius of New York. A modern medieval city full of golden palaces and silver towers, full also of the nightmarish horrors that creep through the dark side of the American dream. A city whose inhabitants are undergoing a trauma just as tumultuous and momentous as that which accompanied the final unlinking of the Great Chain of Being. Now all certainties are as extinct as dinosaurs and vertigo is rife amongst the people who constructed the skyscrapers. There is naturally superstition, fear and danger, not to mention the oft remarked tendency to chase hollow heroes and worship false gods. But there is also a willingness to experiment, to risk, to analyse everything, to laugh a lot. Above all, there's this tremendous excitement. Writing the Preface to Volume Two of *Democracy in America* (*circa* 1840) Alexis de Tocqueville had a similar thing to say: 'The links which formerly bound men together have been destroyed or altered, and new links have been formed. Changes in the pattern of civil society have been as great as those in the world of politics.' I've always believed that a stay in New York is an essential education for twentieth-century man. I still think I'm right.

We leave New York by train from Pennsylvania Station, going at a lickety click through the grey hinterlands of the city and the grimy yards of New Jersey out into the country toward the approaching night. Expense account run out, we're on our own now. We curl up in our coach seats and try to let the rhythm of the wheels lull us to sleep. Nothing doing. Round about Pittsburg way at two in the morning I reach out for Fran and my sleepless fingers begin to search for the source of the warmth at the delta of her thighs when a hand suddenly drops onto my shoulder like a night-hawk and the conductor says, 'Take it easy, mister, you're on a train here.' And so I sit restless in my rocking chair as the train surges through the chaste night heading for the interior.

# SOURCES

•••

Cabbage Face, *The Independent Magazine*, 5 August 1995.

First Love (originally Not a Cup for a Hendon Boy), *The Independent*, 16 June 1994.

In Praise of Optimism (originally Not Such a Naive Painter), *Jewish Chronicle*, 13 August 1993.

'I Feel Good', *Jewish Chronicle*, 5 August 1994.

16 July 1966, contribution to privately printed book in memory of Lynn Luria-Sukenick.

The *Nouveau Anglais*, *Neue Zürcher Zeitung-Folio*, March 1997.

A Soap Opera From Hell, *Granta*, January 1998.

My Life as a Pig, *The Independent Magazine*, 7 October 1995.

A Man of a Different Kidney, *The Independent Magazine*, 25 November 1995.

Kidneys in the Mind, first delivered as a lecture at the British Library, 28 May 1996, subsequently printed as British Library pamphlet, October 1996.

Where's the Beef?, *The Independent Magazine*, 8 June 1996.

The Truth is out There, *The Independent Magazine*, 15 June 1996.

The Spirit is Willing, *The Independent Magazine*, 22 June 1996.

The Son also Rises, *The Independent Magazine*, 29 June 1996.

Who Laughs Last, *The Independent Magazine*, 7 December 1996.

Good Grief, *The Independent Magazine*, 14 December 1996.

My Back Pages, *The Independent Magazine*, 21 December 1996.

Just My Luck, *The Independent Magazine*, 28 December 1996.

Introduction to *Enemies: A Love Story*, Penguin, 1996.

Bashevis the First, *Times Literary Supplement*, 30 April 1993.

Filling the Empty Coat, *Modern British Masters*, Volume X, Bernard Jacobson Ltd, 1994. An abbreviated version appeared in *Modern Painters*, Summer 1994.

Eating of the Apple, *Times Literary Supplement*, 26 February 1992.

The Naked Eye: Franz Kafka and Yosl Bergner, *Modern Painters*, Spring 1993.

Below the Morphine Line, *Times Literary Supplement*, 21 April 1989.

The El-Al Prawn, *Jewish Quarterly*, Autumn 1997.

All the Way to Hebron (originally To Hebron and Back), *Scotland on Sunday*, 2 March 1997.

$E = MC^2$ (originally A Postcard from the Levant), *The Independent*, 26 August 1996.

Bulgarian Optimists (originally Bulgarian Notes), *Times Literary Supplement*, 14 December 1990.

An Imperfect Destiny (originally Self-righteousness and the Serbs), *Times Literary Supplement*, 22 November 1991.

Sweet Water and Bitter Water, *The Edinburgh Star*, June 1989.

Babylon Visited, *The New Review*, October 1976.